This book is a revised and expanded version of *Ingmar Bergman: Four Decades in the Theater*, published by the same authors more than ten years ago. The developments that have occurred in the interim, clustered around Bergman's triumphant return to the Royal Dramatic Theatre in Stockholm after years of self-imposed exile, have profoundly altered the course of this extraordinary career. Still the only book of its kind in English, this amply illustrated study uses detailed and comprehensive analyses of a range of Bergman's productions to chart the full scope and depth of his achievement in the theater, from an early *Macbeth* in 1944 to his widely acclaimed reinterpretation of Ibsen's *Peer Gynt* in 1991.

Ingmar Bergman has held a place among the most innovative and prolific stage directors in Europe for nearly half a century. After his brilliant career as a film maker concluded with the Academy Award-winning *Fanny and Alexander* (1982), Bergman's search for new and exciting ways of creating theater has gone on with renewed energy. Especially in recent years, his touring Swedish productions of *Hamlet, Miss Julie, A Doll's House, Long Day's Journey into Night,* and other classics have reached a new audience of truly worldwide proportions, extending from London and New York to Moscow and Tokyo. Yet, for Bergman, there are never final solutions. Each new experiment seems to engender the next, in an ongoing process of creative inquiry that finds its fullest and most satisfying expression in his theater work.

The book will be of interest to scholars and students of theater history as well as to practitioners and the general reader.

Ingmar Bergman

Ingmar Bergman

A Life in the Theater

LISE-LONE MARKER   FREDERICK J. MARKER
University of Toronto

CAMBRIDGE
UNIVERSITY PRESS

Published by the Press Syndicate of the University of Cambridge
The Pitt Building, Trumpington Street, Cambridge CB2 1RP
40 West 20th Street, New York, NY 10011–4211, USA
10 Stamford Road, Oakleigh, Victoria 3166, Australia

First published by Cambridge University Press as *Ingmar Bergman:
four decades in the theater* in 1982

Second edition first published 1992

Printed in Great Britain at the University Press, Cambridge

A catalogue record for this book is available from the British Library

Library of Congress cataloguing in publication data

Marker, Lise-Lone
Ingmar Bergman, a life in the theater / Lise-Lone Marker,
Frederick J. Marker.
  p.   cm. – (Directors in perspective)
Rev. ed. of: Ingmar Bergman, four decades in the theater. 1982.
Includes bibliographical references and index.
ISBN 0-521-42082-2 (hardback). – ISBN 0-521-42121-7 (pbk.)
1. Bergman, Ingmar, 1918– . 2. Theater – Production and
direction.   I. Marker, Frederick J.   II. Marker, Lise-Lone
Ingmar Bergman, four decades in the theater.   III. Title.
IV. Series.
PN2778.B4M3   1992
792'.0233'092–dc20   91-46950   CIP

ISBN 0 521 42082 2 hardback
ISBN 0 521 42121 7 paperback

GE

Contents

Illustrations

FIGURES

Other photographs of Ingmar Bergman in the text are by
Wilfried Hösl (pp. 8, 13, 22) and by Bengt Wanselius
(pp. 11, 18, 20).

Preface

The long-awaited opening last year of Ingmar Bergman's chamber production of Ibsen's *Peer Gynt* marked the eighty-third stage production of this director's professional career. Later in 1991, a revival of Strindberg's *Miss Julie* and an operatic adaptation of Euripides' *The Bacchae* for the Royal Opera in Stockholm brought the swelling total to eighty-five. "Isn't it strange," the aging but tireless master has been heard to say, "that knowing that any play could be my last production only makes it more fun to work on?"

When an earlier version of this book was first published, some eleven years and fifteen productions ago, it was certainly not clear to us just how quickly the prolific subject of our study would succeed in rendering it outdated. Developments that have occurred in the meantime, clustered around Bergman's return to his native Sweden in 1985, have profoundly affected his artistic style and outlook. Hence, this revised and expanded edition is, in many ways, a different book and, in our opinion, a better and more balanced one. Considerable attention is devoted here to Bergman's more recent endeavors, for the simple reason that both his German productions of the early 1980s and the subsequent series of works he has directed at the Royal Dramatic Theatre must indisputably be ranked among his most important accomplishments. Fresh reinterpretations of such recurrent favorites of his as *A Dream Play*, *Dom Juan*, and *Peer Gynt* have, each in a quite different way, altered accepted views of these classics in performance. In addition, however, he has explored a broad stretch of new territory in later years, ranging from plays by Shakespeare, Ibsen, and Strindberg to works by several twentieth-century dramatists, including Per Olov Enquist, Eugene O'Neill, Yukio Mishima, and Bergman himself.

An ample, annotated chronology at the back of the book is intended to provide the interested reader with a sufficiently detailed synopsis of Bergman's astonishingly productive career as stage director, film maker, playwright, and more. In the book itself, meanwhile, we have adopted an approach that is neither biographical nor strictly chronological. Rather than attempting a comprehensive and correspondingly less detailed account of Bergman's entire oeuvre as a theater director, we have maintained a focus on major productions of the works of certain key playwrights who have continued to hold a central place in his theater poetics. These practical production analyses are intended to represent different aspects of his directorial syntax and interpretative approach. The perceptive reader will quickly begin to discern in them recurrent devices, compositional patterns, and interpretative choices that together add up to something like a Bergman "style." Ultimately, however, he is as fervently convinced as Max Reinhardt was that there is no single directorial style or method valid for all plays, that each play faces the director with a new and distinct problem of translation into the language of the living theater.

Max von Sydow credits his friend and sometime director with "an amazing ability to simplify complicated plays and complicated pieces of action in plays and make them crystal clear" – and it is, above all, this ability to achieve emotional clarity that explains Bergman's power to make a play from the past live in our time. The interpretative vision he brings to the particular work before him is at once deeply personal and keenly analytical, wholly responsive to the play's past and yet fully in touch with the contemporary world of the audience he seeks to engage. Impatient with what he calls the "trumpery" of pedantic "word fidelity," his faithfulness to a performance text is an intense loyalty to the inner spirit he discovers in it and to the artistic consciousness he perceives behind it. More recently, in such radically antitraditionalist productions of the past ten years as *Hamlet*, *Dom Juan*, or *John Gabriel Borkman*, one discerns an even stronger sense of his personal identification with play and protagonist, coupled with a more acutely critical attitude toward accepted assumptions about them.

The three playwrights at the center of this study – August Strindberg, Molière, and Henrik Ibsen – represent Bergman's own preferences as fairly as they do our own. His relationship to Strindberg has remained one of the most essential features of his artistic physiognomy. His cycle of Strindberg productions – particularly of *A Dream Play*, *The Ghost Sonata*, and *To Damascus* – has continued to strengthen the lasting bond between these two kindred spirits. Bergman's successive re-interpretations of Ibsen's plays are already recognized as milestones in the performance history of that playwright's work in this century. Finally, Bergman is in a very basic sense a classical director – someone with a true gift for assimilating the reality of past styles and traditions in staging a classical play. As a result, perhaps no director outside of France has had more success than he has in translating the essence and the inner spiritual reality of Molière's darkly comic vision to the contemporary stage.

Although this book is concerned primarily with the close critical analysis of completed productions and the conceptual interpretations underlying them, we hope that at least some sense of the intricate and methodical creative process that precedes the finished work will also emerge. Bergman's art is intimately bound up with an ability to establish a close and intensely creative personal contact with his actors. He has always been unwilling to discuss his rehearsal methods in either intellectual or mystical terms. "An immense amount goes on between the actors and me that cannot be analyzed," he says simply. "That is how it often is in relations with the actors. After all, I am one of them. I am the complementary part." The combination of creative sorcery and clinical clarity in a Bergman rehearsal is indeed fascinating to behold, and we are privileged to have been permitted to behold it on many different occasions over the years.

Although a study of contemporary theater practice is by no means less dependent upon the primary sources and objective documentation that are essential to all reliable theater research, there are important additional avenues of approach to a contemporary subject that are closed to the student of the more remote theatrical past. The most obvious and potentially most useful of these is firsthand observation – the recollection of certain rare and exciting moments in the theater that will, one senses, not soon be forgotten. Yet even the richest, most vivid of these received impressions is selective and thus potentially seductive. Hence, we have naturally tried in every instance to support personal recollection of particular Bergman produc-tions with as much documentary evidence as possible. In particular, we have made every effort to let contemporary newspaper critics speak frequently, in their own words, as descriptive (if not invariably reliable) seismographs registering the impact that a given theatrical moment had on its first audiences. (To simplify matters, where no date is given in the text, a review may be assumed to have appeared on the day following the date given for the opening.)

A second and very different kind of approach to a contemporary production is afforded by the possibility – at times only a hypothetical one – of direct consultation with the artists involved. On the whole, we have been very fortunate in this respect. We are greatly indebted to the actors who took time and trouble to talk with us about their work with Bergman. Uppermost in our minds in this regard are Bibi Andersson, Max von Sydow, and Erland Josephson, who gave their interviewers and audience a memorable morning of insights at the Nobel Symposium at Dramaten in 1988. Also, several of Bergman's assistant directors have generously permitted us access to their useful notes and work scripts, including Ulla Elmquist (Copenhagen), Johannes Kaetzler (Munich), and Annette Gassmann (Salzburg and Munich).

Above all, however, it is to Ingmar Bergman himself that we owe our deepest debt of gratitude, not only for treating our many requests and appeals for help with unfailing kindness but especially for stealing time from crowded schedules to sit down and talk with us so often about his theater life. He intensely dislikes the idea of looking over his shoulder at the theatrical past, be it his own or anyone else's. "The thing I like most about a theater performance is that it exists for a few evenings, perhaps a season. And then it's gone," he told us in one of our very first meetings. "I love the theater because it is only that single moment. Everything is there – and then it disappears." Unlike a film, the permanency of which causes him a curious kind of discomfort. Some of the reluctance has been overcome or set aside by mutual trust and friendship, and we have gone on talking together over the years – never, be it said, with the goal of "reconstructing the dinosaur with the amiable assistance of the Monster himself" (to borrow a wry phrase from *Pictures*, his candid new self-appraisal of his films).

Thus, although personal consultation has played a vital role in the preparation and shaping of this study, the book speaks with its own voice. Although some elements of personal history have been included where it seemed appropriate, it is intended as an analytical portrait of Bergman's theater work, not as a biography. The viewpoints expressed and the conclusions drawn here are entirely our own.

Like its predecessor, this book has relied heavily on the cooperation and active assistance of a wide range of institutions and individuals. The kindness and helpfulness we have encountered in this connection have been a source of lasting pleasure and encouragement to us. The roster of acknowledgements found in the earlier edition will not be repeated here, but our gratitude to these initial helpers remains entirely undiminished.

We owe special thanks to the theaters we have come to over the years for help, and whose librarians, press officers, and dramaturges were always so ready and willing to accommodate us: the Malmö City Theatre, the Danish Royal Theatre in Copenhagen, the Salzburg Festival, and, in particular, the Residenztheater in Munich and the Royal Dramatic Theatre in Stockholm. The latter is a special case altogether. Since Bergman's return to Sweden seven years ago, our attention has been concentrated principally on Dramaten and his productions there. Thanks to the cordial hospitality and capable help of such people as Ann-Christine Jernberg, Leif Östman, Dr. Tom J. A. Olsson, Sten Rodin, Nea Cleve, and their congenial colleagues at that wonderful theater, our working visits there have been a delight.

We are indebted to the major photographers represented here – Beata Bergström (Stockholm), Rigmor Mydtskov (Copenhagen), Eva Titus (Jean-Marie Bottequin studio, Munich), Wilfried Hösl (Munich), and Bengt Wanselius (Stockholm) – for their courtesy in allowing us to use their images. Their work, which goes far beyond publicity photography, forms a lasting documentary record of the scenes and settings in a given production. (Even here, though, some caution is needed, in that pictures taken at a photo rehearsal do not always correspond to the end result in a Bergman performance.)

Occasional use has been made here of edited excerpts from interviews and articles published previously by us in *Films and Filming, Maske und Kothurn, Modern Drama, Saturday Review, The New York Times,* and *Theater.* We acknowledge the courtesy of these publications, and we wish to mention our particular thanks to Dr. Joel Schechter, editor of *Theater*, for his loyal support and encouragement of our Bergman studies. Also on the editorial side, Professor Christopher Innes deserves our appreciation for his continued interest and constructive counsel. We are grateful to Sarah Stanton of Cambridge University Press for having suggested this book and to Victoria L. Cooper for seeing it through the press.

Most keenly felt of all is our gratitude to Ingmar Bergman and his wife Ingrid. Their forbearance has been this project's saving grace; their friendship is its best reward.

LISE-LONE MARKER
FREDERICK J. MARKER

Introduction: The magic triangle

Ingmar Bergman's long and productive career in the living theater still tends to be overshadowed, at least outside of Europe, by his fame as a film maker. For nearly half a century, however, Bergman has continued to hold a place among the most exciting and innovative stage directors active in the European theater. He has also been quick to point out that an understanding of this side of his creative activity is indispensable to a fully balanced assessment of his art. "There has always been a short distance between my work in the theater and my work in the film studio," he has reminded interviewers more than once. "Sometimes this has been an advantage and sometimes it has been a burden, but the distance has always been small."

From the outset, during his years of apprenticeship in the 1940s, the forceful and fiery young director's first professional productions at the city theaters in Hälsingborg and Gothenburg aroused the curiosity and then quickly won the respect of Sweden's foremost critics. Then, during the 1950s, his six luminous seasons at the Malmö City Theatre began to attract the same sort of wider international recognition that came during those years to such films as *Smiles of a Summer Night*, *The Seventh Seal*, and *Wild Strawberries*. And, indeed, by then Bergman had already forged a distinctive theatrical style of his own, achieved in close collaboration with the handpicked ensemble of performers he had begun to gather and train. The preeminent value of simplicity and suggestion had become his hallmark as a director. The basic and focal significance of the actor and the human face would continue to shape his conception of theater, film, and their interaction.

During the years that followed – filled with a succession of such memorable Bergman films as *Winter Light*, *The Silence*, *Persona*, and *Cries and Whispers* – his intense involvement in the living theater seldom waned. For three and a half onerous years in the mid-1960s, he even found time to serve with distinction as artistic director of the Royal Dramatic Theatre in

Stockholm. From the moment he began directing there in 1961, in fact, Sweden's national theater has remained Bergman's true spiritual home.

For a time, however, his lasting and fruitful relationship with Dramaten (as it is affectionately known to its friends and admirers the world over) was seriously jeopardized by his clash with a blundering Swedish tax bureaucracy. In 1976, police descended without warning or provocation on a Bergman rehearsal of Strindberg's *The Dance of Death*, and the director was taken off for questioning in connection with allegations that were later shown to be utterly groundless. No one who has read Bergman's account of the incident in *Laterna Magica* can be in doubt about the depth of his shock and anger. Shortly afterward, he left his native country and settled in Germany. During the eight years he spent at the respected Residenztheater in Munich, his artistic vision deepened and expanded. In all, he staged a total of eleven major new productions in German, including (even by his own grudging admission) some of the best work of his career. Among them, certain to be counted the most ambitious of all his achievements in the theater, was the mammoth Bergman Project – a simultaneous trilogic presentation of Ibsen's *A Doll's House*, Strindberg's *Miss Julie*, and his own adaptation of a familiar Bergman screenplay, *Scenes from a Marriage*. After four months of intensive preparation, often rehearsing six days a week and ten hours a day, he opened these three works on the same evening in 1981.

Even so prodigious a theatrical labor as this, however, is regarded differently by Bergman than film making, from which he retired in 1982 with the Academy Award-winning *Fanny and Alexander*. "I hope I will have the chance to work in the theater until they carry me out. Because that is a great joy to me," he told the authors at the time, in an interview for *Saturday Review*. "And besides, it's no strain. That is work for a lazybones." Three years later, the very morning after his successful production of Ibsen's *John Gabriel Borkman* opened in Munich, his self-imposed exile ended as abruptly as it had begun. His anger had cooled, his desire to direct again in his own language was keenly felt, and he went home to Sweden to live and work. Since then, his search for new and exciting ways of making theater has gone on without ceasing. Each new experiment has appeared to engender the next, in an ongoing process of creative inquiry that, for him, finds its fullest and most satisfying expression in the rehearsal experience itself, "learning to listen to the playwright's words and to his heart together with the actors."

Both in rehearsal and performance, the art of the theater, seen from Bergman's perspective, is always a collective art that can only arise out of intensely collaborative creative activity. This attitude predicates his familiar assertion that only three elements are ultimately necessary "for a theatrical production to function" – a text, actors, and an audience. Any discussion of his theater poetics must inevitably concern itself closely with the dynamic interplay of the three related components of this magic triangle: the conceptual design of his reinterpretations of particular texts; his (implied) philosophy of acting, characterized as it is by his strong conviction that it is the actor and the actor alone who must bring the text to life in the hearts of the audience; finally, and by no means least important, the deliberate strategies he has used to realign the audience's imaginative response, thereby forging an ever stronger bond between the performer and the spectator, the stage and the auditorium.

At the core of his experiments with this communicative bond is his preoccupation with the nature of theatrical illusion itself and the related process of the actor's "transformation" – in itself a magical (*i.e.*, suggestive and intuitive, rather than rational) process that takes place in the consciousness of the spectator and must accordingly always be calculated from the latter's point of view. Direct and unimpeded contact between the audience and the living actor is thus, for Bergman, the true basis of what we call illusion in the theater. The false reality of a scrupulously "lifelike" setting holds no place in his method. With increasing determination over the years, his economical, actor-oriented style has sought to eliminate everything that might potentially "detheatricalize" the actor by detracting from his presence, thereby dissipating his power to influence and ultimately control the audience's emotional engagement.

For, Bergman would argue, the actor does not and cannot transform himself; only the encounter with an audience permits that curious feat to be accomplished. The circus artist waiting to spring in "just for you who sit there and sense his presence," the watching character waiting (as often happens in a Bergman production) to step forward and play his part, the actors on the stage whose gestures and faces alone create the rhythm of the performance – each of these is a living signifier of a mutual pact that exists between actor and spectator. That pact acknowledges and, in turn, depends upon the spectator's willing participation in the event. The actor, with that "wonderful ability to suggest directly," is governed by the artistic obligation to guide the audience, to stimulate its emotional reactions, to activate its intuitive desire to engage itself in the theatrical experience – in a word, by the obligation to get across. Success in doing so is directly related to the vitality of the communicative bond between stage and auditorium. The process of transformation can only occur by mutual consent.

The basic key to the spectator's involvement in the mimetic experience lies, for Bergman, in his conviction that "the true theatrical creation must always remind the audience that it is watching a performance." He distrusts abstract theories about such matters, however, and a parable is often the closest he comes to an explanation. A favorite story of his (retold both in *Laterna Magica* and in *After the Rehearsal*) concerns his experience when, night after night at the age of twelve, he sat hidden in the flies at the Royal Dramatic Theatre, watching *A Dream Play* being performed:

It was the first time I became aware of the actor's magic. The Lawyer held a hairpin between thumb and forefinger. He bent it, straightened it, and broke it in pieces. There was no hairpin, *but I saw it.* The Officer stood behind the door in the set, waiting for his cue to enter. He was bending forward, gazing at his shoes, his hands behind his back. He cleared his throat quietly, just an ordinary person. Suddenly he opened the door and stepped into the stage light. He was changed and transformed: he *was* the Officer.

The one fundamental similarity between Bergman's work as a film maker and his work in the theater is, in his own opinion, the overriding necessity of arranging the actors, in relation to each other and in relation to the spectator (camera), in such a way that their persuasive charisma ("the magic of their faces and their movements") communicates itself as forcefully and unambiguously as possible. The "theater of circumstances," with its "busy" management of scenery, lighting, and sound effects that ultimately only serve to detheatricalize the presence of the living actor, has long since been put behind him. Instead, he has sought to restore the actor to his rightful place in the theatrical framework, in just relationship to the two other elements that, in Bergman's experience, are required to create that which we call theater – the words the actor speaks and the actively engaged audience he reaches out to encounter.

1   Talking about theater: a conversation with Ingmar Bergman

Despite his more recent excursions into autobiography and self-criticism (*Laterna Magica, Pictures*), Ingmar Bergman has remained as reluctant as ever to discuss his creative methods in explicitly theoretical terms – particularly, it seems, when it comes to theater. Over the years, many major interviews and public appearances have yielded their share of useful insights into his art as a film maker, but his long career in the theater (which cannot, he himself insists, be separated from his film work) has rarely been a subject of major interest on these occasions. In our own case, our later published interviews with Bergman have all tended to focus on details of interpretation in a new production, much more than on general principles and methods of work.

Hence, the conversation that follows (which is excerpted from two much longer interviews conducted in 1979 and early 1980) is still, to our knowledge, the only interview in English that concentrates in depth and detail on what might be called Bergman's implied philosophy of theater and the nature of theatrical communication. If what he says here seems at times to be echoed verbatim by Henrik Vogler, his introspective alter ego in *After the Rehearsal* (1984), it is hardly any wonder – for in that wry and sometimes very bitter film about the curiously ambiguous role of the director, "old" Vogler is allowed (for once) to express his creator's own views on the art of the stage with unusual frankness.

In these pages, however, Bergman speaks for himself, discoursing with wit and intelligence on a variety of concerns ranging from the nature of the actor's art to the relationship between stage and film in his own work, from the state of the contemporary German theater (in which he worked for eight years) to such key creative principles of his as rhythm, choreography, and suggestion. As he talks about his own productions and those of others, a great deal is revealed about his directorial vision and method – everything, perhaps,

6

except those closely guarded secrets ("a few small tricks") over which the master has always carefully and purposefully drawn a veil. "By all means, borrow my machines and duplicate what I am doing," he once remarked, some thirty years ago. "Take your time. Learn to be agile with your fingers, learn how, just at the right moment, to divert the attention of the audience with your spiel, learn speed, and the mysterious illumination! You will still not do what I am doing, you will still fail. You see, I perform magic. I conjure!"

TALKING ABOUT THEATER

LLM.   In writing about your long and richly productive career as a stage director, we're naturally very interested to know where you yourself would like to see the emphasis placed. Which performances are your own favorites? You have said before that you dislike looking back at any of your work from the past. But which stage productions do you feel are the ones you like best?

IB.   It's very difficult. I don't know. It has nothing to do with the result; it has to do only with the atmosphere – the time we had together when we worked on the play. The reason why I am much more a man of the theater than a man of the film is because theater is to me always . . . to work in the theater is a way of living. To make a picture is a heavy job, it really is. But to go to the theater in the morning, to go to the rehearsal room, to come together with the actors and sit down, and to work with them . . . learning to listen to the playwright's words and to his heart together with the actors . . . that is a way of living; that is the best of all. And if you are together with actors who share the same way of thinking, the same attitude toward their job, it's wonderful. I think I will make one or two or three more pictures – and then I will stop. But I hope I will have the chance to work with the theater until they carry me out. [Laughter.]

LLM.   I hope you don't mean that about your films.

IB.   Oh yes, oh yes, oh yes. That's very simple. Because film making is physically very, very heavy – it's a lousy job – physically. One day you feel very tired, you don't want to . . . and when you are tired physically, you need an enormous vitality every day to come through, to be on top.

Do you understand? You make about three minutes of the picture every day, and those three minutes must be on top, on the very top. You start at nine o'clock in the morning and then you work eight hours, very hard. And everything comes from you . . . it comes from me, everything, at every moment. And the whole crew depends on your feelings, on your most irrational reactions. And it's *very* difficult.

FJM.   Different from the theater in that respect?

IB.   At the theater, if you don't feel well, you don't feel well . . . and you can say to the actors: Today I don't feel well, let's go out for a walk in the park or go to the museum and see an exhibit or just sit down and have a chat. Or . . . today it was not so very good, but perhaps tomorrow or the day after tomorrow or next week it will be better. Film making is very neurotic – you're obsessed – your work is very neurotic; but the creative work of the theater, made together with the actors, is a very healthy way of creating.

FJM.   You often speak of the theater as a collective, in the sense of working together with the actors.

IB.   Yes, it's a wonderful way of coming together and being in contact with other people.

FJM.   As a director it must be difficult to reach that stage of

being able to be relaxed enough to take it that way. Do you know what I mean? Isn't the young director who is starting out much more tense . . .

IB. That's different. Of course. Every day, every morning while you are rehearsing, you wake up very, very early in a kind of tension, and the tension is always there; but you have to use it as a battery. You must not infect the actors, because if you infect them with your tension, they will be very unhappy. So you must simply tell the actors to sit down and then say to them: Children, let's relax; let's just take it easy. Let's listen to each other. Because acting is never – and that is a great misunderstanding – acting is never an *I*, it is always a *you*. Because the minute two actors forget themselves and take everything from the other one, then you have the great moments of performance. And that is the whole secret.

FJM. What I meant before about tension is also related to our earlier discussions of the director's script, which you always prepare and then put aside. You have often said that improvisation is dependent upon careful preparation. But what *is* the relationship between pre-preparation and then being able to put it all aside?

IB. You must be absolutely certain when you go to rehearsals. When you go to the first rehearsal, you must be absolutely sure; you must have prepared precisely and you must be absolutely sure – that *this* is what Strindberg has meant. And you must be happy with it. You must have made it your own experience – your own spiritual experience. And then you can relax in the material, you feel you are there. There are no longer any acts of violence, not against the text, not against the actors. Rehearsing in the theater has to do with contact, with listening, with tenderness, with love, with security. And then if, together with the actors, you can produce this atmosphere, it is a creative atmosphere – then it starts. It's a miracle. It starts. Yes, it is alive. Because I get things from the actors and I give things back to the actors.

FJM. Without worrying about what you had planned beforehand.

IB. Yes. But I have to prepare precisely for every little moment, in every little detail. I must know that *this* is what I want to do, and then I can improvise.

LLM.   You don't have the sounds of their voices in mind, then, before you go in?

IB.   Yes, sometimes. But not always. Sometimes very clearly . . . I have the actors in mind, always, when I prepare; I always have actors in mind. What can this actor do, and what can he not do? What are his limitations? What are his difficulties? What is his strength?

LLM.   Do you ever read lines for them?

IB.   No, never. Never. I can tell them the rhythm. We can talk about the rhythm of a line, but I never tell them how to play it. We can talk about the choreography and we can talk about the rhythm and the pauses, but I never tell them how to say it.

FJM.   Rhythm is very important to you, isn't it.

IB.   Rhythm is the most important. That is the most important of all. Also in film.

LLM.   Do you see a connection between film and theater in that respect?

IB.   No. Not very much. But rhythm is always the most important thing that exists. Because everything is rhythm. At every moment of our lives, without ever thinking about it, we live with different kinds of rhythm – breathing, the beating of the heart, the movement of our eyes, the cycle of day and night, of destruction and creation, everything in the world is rhythm. And therefore our artistic work must also be built on the fact that we work with it – we must listen our way forward to the specific rhythm of the play, to the specific rhythm of the text. And this is precisely the difficulty when you work so much with translations; if the translator has not captured the rhythm of the original – which happens very rarely – then we are caught in a hell, because you sense that you are working against the text, going against the play. It is very difficult.

LLM.   When you talk about rhythm, you don't mean merely speech rhythm and textual rhythm, do you. You mean visual rhythm as well.

IB.   Yes, everything. The entire arrangement of movements, the whole rhythm of the performance. This to me is essential. To go faster, to go slower, to stop, all those things.

LLM.   I think I understand what you mean. *The Misanthrope*, for instance, was a production you could talk about almost in

balletic terms. The movements were as clearly and precisely choreographed as they would be in a ballet.

IB. In Molière, you see, you must be very precise – at every moment, at all times you must be absolutely precise. And at the same time you must be very open, direct, vulgar, brutal, and sensitive. It has to be all of that. And you must forget about psychology; everything comes from the choreography, from the rhythm. Molière is almost impossible to translate, you know. When you translate Molière you have to be very free.

FJM. What do you mean when you say choreography?

IB. Choreography is movement, the moves – I don't know the word in English.

FJM. An ugly word: "blocking."

IB. The movements of the actors, going from a sofa, moving to that chair, coming back, stopping, turning the head toward the audience – all that is what I call the choreography.

LLM. It is much more than simple "blocking," though. You describe it almost as a ballet choreographer would; you talk not only about moving from one point on the stage to another, but also about gesturing, about the slightest turn of the head . . .

IB. Yes, everything.

LLM. You must literally demonstrate to your actors what you want, almost the way the choreographer of a ballet does. Do you do that?

IB. In a way, yes.

LLM. One is so struck by the precision of their gestures, their movements . . .

IB. Yes, I tell them . . .

LLM. . . . what you want.

IB. Yes. But sometimes the actor himself begins, and then I can say to him: Try to do it that way – and that may be better. It's a kind of collaboration. Very close. Very close, very erotic. It's very intimate. You are very close to actors when you work with them, at creative rehearsals.

LLM. Before you go in to rehearsals, do you know precisely, in visual terms, how the actor is to move, gesture, and so on?

IB. Yes, in a way. In a way. Especially the place where they are – the different positions of the actors. So I know exactly where they are. Where I have them. And – whether they have contact or no contact. Whether they look at each other or do not look at each other. That is all-important. The relationship [demonstrating] between an actor here and an actor there – how they relate to each other is extremely important. In Chekhov, it is the most important thing of all – to place all the actors in relationship to one another. To have them relate to one another – or not; and have them listen to each other – or not listen; and have them react – or not react. The whole secret of Chekhov is in the listening – in what the various characters hear, what they don't hear, what they pretend not to hear.

FJM.   Your concern with physical relations and pictorial composition would seem to make you an ideal ballet choreographer. Have you ever wanted to choreograph a ballet?

IB.   No, I can't dance a step, you know. I cannot take a step as a dancer.

FJM.   You did one ballet, didn't you – *Skymningslekar [Twilight Games]*?

IB.   *Skymningslekar* [laughs] – I didn't do it, I only wrote it. But I'm extremely fascinated by ballet. I have always been fascinated by it.

LLM.   I once sat in on some of George Balanchine's rehearsals

at Lincoln Center. He danced very little himself by then. You would naturally have someone beside you to assist and demonstrate, as he did.

IB. Yes. There must be some kind of intimate collaboration. But – I think there are people better able to do it than I am.

FJM. Speaking of attending rehearsals, your idea of holding open rehearsals for the public is a fascinating one.

IB. Yes. I like that very much. I – almost die – and the actors, too, almost die, but we have found it is very healthy. Because – slowly – the actors acquire an unneurotic relationship to the spectators, to the audience. And that is very, very good.

FJM. For whose sake is it done? For the sake of the actors?

IB. Oh yes, always for theirs.

FJM. Not for your sake?

IB. No.

LLM. Not so that you are able to judge . . .

IB. No. No, I know exactly. But I just want the actors . . . I also want the audience to come to us and see what we are doing. To see that there is no magic in our work, and that there is nevertheless a magic in it. That is very good for all of them, for the audience too.

FJM. Sometimes in costume, sometimes not.

IB. Yes. Most interesting for the audience, of course, is without costumes and without settings.

LLM. Do you ever conduct an open rehearsal as an ordinary rehearsal?

IB. No. I did with Woyzeck, but I don't think it is a good idea. Because if we do it as a rehearsal, with the audience there, then I play the director and the actors play the actors.

LLM. And the audience comes to watch you, no doubt.

IB. [Laugh.] Yes. So you see, that would be a sort of performance. I always refuse to allow people to watch our rehearsals when we are still in the rehearsal room. Once we are on the stage, it doesn't matter so very much, because we don't know that people are there looking at us – if a few people are there, it doesn't matter. But the moment we know at rehearsals, we start playing, we begin playing our parts. And that is not good.

LLM. Do you usually say something to the audience at the beginning of an open rehearsal?

IB.   Oh yes. I always bid the audience welcome, and I explain that they must help us, that now we must work together. A theater performance is to an exceptional extent a matter of give and take. It is in their hearts, in their imaginations that the performance must take place. Because there are only three things necessary for a performance to work: the play – the words – the actors, and the audience. Everything else is absolutely unimportant. But if you have those three elements, there will be a performance. Nothing else is needed.

LLM.   By that you mean settings, for example?

IB.   Theater, settings, directors, tickets, money, costumes, everything. Everything else is unimportant. It's wonderful to think about.

FJM.   But surely the director – I suppose, if you could go back to the nineteenth century or the eighteenth century, to another kind of actor entirely, you wouldn't need the director. The director as such wasn't there. But today there is no way one can eliminate – or wants to eliminate – the influence of the director. He has to be there, doesn't he?

IB.   No. I don't think so. If there are chamber orchestras playing without a conductor –

LLM.   That was, of course, Strindberg's idea. Strindberg thought the actors ought to be able to do it on their own.

IB.   Yes. Sometimes it is very good to have a director, but sometimes it is not necessary.

LLM.   But if there had been no direction of your *Hedda Gabler* or *The Wild Duck*, for instance, the actors setting out to do these plays would in all probability simply have followed Ibsen's stage directions, furnished a living room, placed the attic at the rear in *The Wild Duck*, and you would get . . .

IB.   No, that's something else entirely. For those plays you need a director. But if you play O'Neill's *Long Day's Journey into Night*, it isn't necessary; or if you play, shall I say, Albee's *Who's Afraid of Virginia Woolf?*; or if you play a piece by Marivaux, and the actors are *experienced* actors, there is no reason to have a director.

LLM.   But for Molière and Ibsen?

IB.   For them you must have a director, I think.

LLM.   Strindberg, too?

IB.   Yes.

FJM.   But if you perform *Who's Afraid* without a director, you won't get a Bergman production of *Who's Afraid*; you won't achieve the same rhythm and intensity.

IB.   No, if they are very good actors, they will find it, they will find a rhythm of their own. I am sure of that, I am convinced. It's not so difficult. You can read it – and it's all there. Everything works out quickly and easily, because there is no depth of dimension. It's no problem. There are lots of plays you can perform without a director. The actors soon start giving everything and holding nothing back. The last rehearsal weeks get a trifle boring, in fact.

LLM.   I remember something you said when you spoke to the Royal Theatre acting school back in 1958 or so: that there is a difference between directing younger actors – in an ensemble that you yourself have in a sense created – and handling older, more experienced actors, who must be dealt with in a somewhat different way. Do you still feel that is true?

IB.   Well, I have worked in this business – this profession – for about forty years; and I have had real difficulties with actors – *real* difficulties – three or four times. That's not very much. Because you always find some way to communicate with an actor. It's not difficult.

LLM.   They should surely be eager to communicate.

IB.   But you must understand: They stand there, they expose themselves, they are very vulnerable. You sit there and you are not vulnerable; you're always protected. But they stand there with their faces and bodies terribly exposed. And so you have to be careful, listen to them, take care of them, respect them. It is most important.

LLM.   To continue talking about your work with the actor, I wonder if you could say something about your concept of the so-called focal point of energy – the magnetic point where the actor is best located in a particular stage space?

IB.   Yes, of course, the magic point. It has nothing to do with the shape of the setting, only with the particular theater. It is there on every stage. You have to look for it, and you have to find it – the point where the actor is best and most effectively located. Approach and withdrawal effects are all created in relation to this point. That is the difficulty when you come to a new stage: You don't yet know where the magic point is located. The first time I experienced that, in a conscious way, was at the enormous theater In Malmö. You had to locate, very consciously, the point on the stage where the actors are strongest. And I remember it very well: It was a small rectangle, six meters by four meters, about two and a half meters from the front. After that, there was no problem.

FJM.   And then everything is choreographed in relation to that point?

IB.   Yes. At our Royal Dramatic Theatre in Stockhom – it's a wonderful house – you can be anywhere on the stage and it is magic all over. So close, so intimate.

FJM.   When you thrust the action forward on the stage, as you so often do, you like to use strong frontal lighting, don't you?

IB.   Oh yes, yes, I do.

FJM.   Because of the faces?

IB.   Yes, of course. It's – look now [pointing to sunlight striking the interviewer's face] you have it now. And then, you know, suddenly the actors are . . . The actors' relation to the stage is also a part of the rhythm of the performance, and if you change the angle at which the light strikes the stage, you achieve a completely new rhythm. For the eye. And it becomes a little bit of a shock, if you change the light like that.

FJM.   You've produced very interesting frescolike effects in *Hedda Gabler* that way. The impression created by that very strong, amber-colored front lighting is almost like a fresco or a frieze.

IB.   It's very strange, because it looks as though the actors are floating; they lift themselves off the floor.

LLM.   But they are lights that evoke a certain kind of *emotional* response in the spectator. As a spectator, you're not supposed to notice the changes very much, are you?

IB.   No, no, no, it's unconscious. For the spectator, of course, it has to be completely unconscious. I hate it when the spectator says: "Aha! *Beautiful!* – he changed the lights." [Laughter.]

FJM.   Because the lighting is not – horrible word – "symbolic," the sort of thing where suddenly a spotlight . . .

IB.   No. I hate that. I hate it when the director intrudes, when he reaches out and touches the spectator like this and says: "Look what I have done! See, how symbolic all this is!" Here

in the German theater, you know, when they play Kleist's *Prince of Homburg* – the whole stage is filled with potatoes [laughter], and you ask: "Why? Why is the stage filled with potatoes so that the actors have to walk around falling over potatoes the entire time?" "Yes, because you should know that the intention of the director is to make it clear that Prussia was an agrarian society, a farmers' country at that time." With that, you see, the director has mixed himself into the play, and he addresses himself not so much to the audience as to the critics. He has a conversation with the critics over the heads of the actors and the audience. That is very, very modern here in Germany today – that kind of neurotic conversation. They love it.

LLM. Why are the critics taken in by it?

IB. The critics love it, too. Theater tradition is so strong here, you see; every theatergoer has seen *Tartuffe* five times, *Faust* ten times, *The Prince of Homburg* six times. And so, as the Germans say, *man muss sich was einfallen lassen.* [Laughter.] You have to dream up something. And the critic sits there saying: "Aha! I saw this very thing in 1943 in Berlin or in Kassel or wherever" – they have 110 city theaters here, you know. It's incredible. But the vitality is enormous.

The Germans can have trouble with Ibsen or Molière – and they cannot play Strindberg; they don't understand him. They perform him without humor, very, very serious, very profound. Heavy. But they play the Russians beautifully. They do marvellous performances of Shakespeare; they have an enormous Shakespearean tradition. And, of course, they make their own classics seem so new and wonderful and fresh – not always, perhaps, but very often – at least the talented ones do. There is much to learn from the way they play their own classics . . .

LLM. As for yourself, though, you *have* been a renewer of the traditions of staging the classics, in the true sense. I am thinking now not only of Strindberg and Ibsen – but also of Molière, though perhaps less radically so in his case.

IB. No, not at all. My intention is *not* to be a renewer. I want only to present the plays and to make them live in the hearts of the audience. That is my only intention. I read the play, it lives in me. I infect the actors with my intentions, and they give me back many things in return. During a certain period

of creativity and of intimate relations, we develop a creation that is, I hope, fully alive. And the only reason why it has been made is in order to infect the spectator – so that it may be alive in his heart, in his mind. And that is everything.

LLM.   I was thinking of something so strikingly unexpected as your production of *The Wild Duck*, with the inspiration of placing the attic at the front instead of at the back. That is what I mean by renewal.

IB.   But it is very simple. To me, it's absolutely logical. Once you agree that the only important things are the words, the actors, and the audience, then it isn't the setting that matters. The actors must materialize, before the eyes of the audience, the magic of the attic. And they cannot do that at a distance; with their eyes, their way of walking and standing and moving, they create it in front of you. So you can see it. That is the magic of the theater.

LLM.   Perhaps, but few have recognized it so clearly.

IB.   But it's really very simple; it's completely logical. My experience has taught me the importance of simple suggestion in the theater. You are an actor and you take this terrible chair [demonstrating] and you put it up here on the table, and then you tell the audience: "My dear friends, you may think this chair looks terrible but you are mistaken. This is the most expensive and most beautiful diamond-encrusted gold chair ever created. It was made for a small Chinese empress six thousand years ago; she died sitting on it, and it was buried with her. Now it's here – and it is very, very fragile. But now take care of it, for I must leave you for a few moments." Then you come back as a scoundrel, and you begin to knock the chair around – and the entire audience will hate that scoundrel. They will become anxious because they have accepted the suggestion and have developed feelings about the chair. And *that* is theater.

FJM. And any chair, even a rehearsal chair, will do?

IB. Of course! It can be anything, everything, whatever you want. Shakespeare realized that. Shakespeare never tells you about anything, what is going on, how a scene looks; it is a street or a mountain or another part of the forest. But, suddenly, the actors would come on to his stage in the sunlight – because they always performed in broad daylight – carrying burning torches, and four oboes in the orchestra would play a small, small melody – and the whole audience knew at once that it was night. It can't be more fantastic than that!

LLM. Is that why in *A Dream Play*, for instance, you choose to eliminate the entire environment of the play?

IB. Of course, of course.

LLM. Again, that's what I mean by innovation in a positive sense – an absolutely effective way of making the audience relationship to Strindberg so much closer.

IB. But Strindberg himself realized it. He wrote about it to August Falck at the Intimate Theatre: "Couldn't we play *A Dream Play* with just a curtain?" And of course we can play it that way . . .

LLM. When I remember your Strindberg productions, I always think of the striking visual images in them. One remembers the emotional impression of the whole, of course – but above all those marvellous figure compositions. Do you feel that your work as a film maker and your work as a stage director overlap to some extent with that kind of thing?

IB. No, it is so different.

FJM. The question is a central one, though. And a very difficult one as well. In film interviews you have said that "there is a short distance between my work in the theatre and my work in the film studio" and that a "mutual relationship" exists between the two kinds of work. But exactly what sort of relationship?

IB.   Did you want to say something?

LLM.   I only wanted to ask whether you yourself feel that the question is worth discussing, or not.

IB.   Yes. Let us try. I do not think there are many connections; but let us try to find them. I have never discussed the problem in this way before, but let us try. For the moment, I can find only one connection. There are perhaps more, but I find only this one. When I work together with the actors in the studio, in front of the camera, I always place the actors in relation to the camera so that they feel they are at their best. They feel – not that they are beautiful, but that the magic of their faces and their movements will be registered by the camera. And they like that. They sense that, because I like them, I wish them to be as powerful and multidimensional as personalities and actors as possible. On the stage I do exactly the same thing. I position them, as we talked about, according to the principle of the magic point. I place them on the stage, in relation to each other and in relation to the audience, so that they feel they are effective – that their

charisma will work on the audience. And then they feel secure; they know they can do their best. Some actors, you know, have to fight against the settings, against the lighting, against the choreography, against the director – they have a need to fight. And that *can* be very good – with talented actors it can work marvellously – but they never feel secure.

And there you have one relationship. I must always function as a kind of radar, you see: I can tell whether an actor feels well, whether he feels secure, or whether he feels tense and unhappy. And I feel it faster than he feels it, I can tell before he says so, because my intuition is always at work and tells me at all times what is going on inside this man or this woman. That is, of course, an important connection between my film making and my work in the theater – the relation that must be established between camera and actors or stage and actors, seen in conjunction with the audience.

FJM.   What about technical things . . .

IB.   Don't you think this could be true?

FJM.   Yes definitely. [Laughter.]

IB.   I have never thought about it, but perhaps that is the way it is. I don't know.

FJM.   It's a very convincing point. But what about more technical relationships? When you choreograph on the stage, for instance, are the same or similar impulses at work as when you choreograph a film? In other words, your films are renowned, among many other things, for their astonishing use of closeup photography. Do you consciously or unconsciously try to incorporate that impulse toward the closeup into your theater work? Or, to take a different example, you have talked about the sense in which distance will tend to intensify whatever is horrible or terrifying; when Bertil Anderberg [as Raval] is smitten by the plague in *The Seventh Seal*, for instance, he lies screaming out in the forest, behind a woodpile, out of sight. What I'm asking is, does that kind of thinking about camera shots and spatial compositions find any specific equivalent in your theater work?

IB.   No, no, no.

FJM.   Not at all?

IB.   No. There are some tricks in common – but they are just details. A few small tricks. [Pause.] You know, there is a play by Sartre called *The Unburied Dead*; there is a schoolroom where a torture scene takes place before the eyes of the audience. The head of the theater in Gothenburg [Torsten Hammarén] staged it, and it was fantastic. But in this torture scene, the actor cried and screamed – and it looked just like an actor crying and screaming. A kind of *Grand Guignol*, not very impressive. Then one day he stopped to ask whether he could do it in some other way. So he piled up the chairs and desks for the school children in a straight line, and behind this mountain of tables and chairs the torturing was done. You didn't see it, you only saw some of the movements and heard the screams. And it was so terrifying that people couldn't take it. That is one of the secrets of our business – not to show everything.

FJM.   And in that, in the use of suggestion, film is like theater?

IB.   Yes. Yes, in that they are alike. Some years ago I made a film called *Persona*. There is a small scene in which the nurse tells the actress about a sexual experience she had had together with a girl friends of hers, with two boys. She tells her about it in detail, and the only thing we see, practically the entire time, is the face of Liv Ullmann [in the role of the actress, Elisabet Vogler], who eats the scene. She eats with her lips what she is being told – and it is a very erotic scene. If you had tried to re-create the scene with the two boys and the two girls, it would have been merely disgusting. Now, it's very erotic. It's strange, isn't it it.

LLM.   I would like to ask you about something else; in fact, I would like to ask you about two things. In many of your more recent theater productions, you seem to be very attracted to the idea of using a low platform stage set up on the stage itself. Does that go together with your concept of the magic point, the focal point of energy on the stage?

IB.   Yes, exactly. It's very – I like it very much because when the actor is standing outside the platform, he is private; the moment he takes a step toward the platform, he is an actor playing a part. He's someone else; it is a great magic. The platform is ancient. The platform is absolutely the archetypal theater, the very oldest form of the theater. You have a wagon or a platform or the steps of a church or some stones or an elevation of some sort on an altar – and the actor stands there waiting. Or a circus ring. And the actors stand there and then they climb up onto the wagon or the platform or whatever it is – and suddenly they are powerful, magical, mysterious, multidimensional. *And that is immensely fascinating.*

LLM. The one thing, apart from everything else, that stays in my mind from the performance of *Tartuffe* is the presence of Tartuffe's servant, that strange, heavy figure in black.

IB. Yes.

LLM. Often he just stands beside the platform watching; but what is he watching – all those mad people?

IB. Yes, exactly. It is very fascinating, very interesting . . .

FJM. The actor then becomes spectator.

IB. Exactly.

FJM. And a kind of bond is then established between the actor and the spectator in the auditorium.

IB. And that is truly magical.

LLM. Yes, it is. But is he, then, a sort of comment on these mad people in *Tartuffe*?

IB. Of course.

LLM. It's astonishing, because you never forget him – [laughter] even though he is a very minor figure.

IB. But he is there in Molière's text, he is talked about; it's just that Molière does not keep him on the stage throughout.

LLM. Basque, Célimène's servant in *The Misanthrope*, was so amusing, too; that was also a completely new idea, using him to link the scenes.

IB. But the Basque I had in Malmö [Lenn Hjortsberg] was the most brilliant Basque I have ever had, he really was. The Basque I had in Copenhagen was not that amusing; but my Basque in Malmö was so funny that people nearly split from laughing. He was amazing, unforgettable. – Yes, this Basque is a strange character; he is fantastic. In that incredible scene, the love scene between Alceste and Célimène, suddenly this fantastic figure of Basque turns up with his unbelievably complicated tricks and business.

FJM. In the Copenhagen production, you kept the actors who weren't involved in a particular scene in view, seated on chairs placed on the outskirts of the stage. They sat watching the action, casually awaiting their cues. You didn't do that in Malmö, did you?

IB.   No.

LLM.   How did the idea occur to you?

IB.   It occurred to me because, not so very long ago, it was actually the practice. During the 1940s it was still the custom that the actors at the Comédie Française did not go to their dressing rooms during the course of a performance, but sat on the stage behind the scene and read or knitted or just sat. It was a kind of tradition that they should do so; each and every one had his own chair, with his name on it. I find that an intensely fascinating idea, that the actors should be there the whole time. What is more, you can glimpse them there in the background, like shadows, as a presence.

LLM.   When they sat in the wings during your production of *The Misanthrope*, what did you tell them? Were they listening to what was happening on the stage, or . . .

IB.   It isn't necessary for them to listen. They have to sit down, they have to relax, and they are there. They are involved in the play.

LLM.   And in the atmosphere.

IB.   The entire time. They can't escape it. They cannot get out of it, because they have it in their bodies, in their nerves. I find it fantastic that you have them there on the stage; that seems so powerfully magical. Because theater is always magic, all the time.

LLM.   And the presence of these actor-spectators then reinforces the impression of theater within the theater?

IB.   Yes, of course. And besides, it's good for the actors not to go off to their dressing rooms and sit there drinking coffee.

LLM.   It helps to sustain concentration, you mean.

IB.   Yes. And that is enormously good for them.

LLM.   In Molière's own time, spectators were actually seated on the stage. Was that something that influenced your thinking about this idea?

IB.   The audience sat there on the stage, it is true, and Molière disapproved of that enormously. He was terribly angry about it, and that emerges continually in such works as *L'Impromptu de Versailles*. There you can really find his undivided hatred directed at that audience of nobles. And, after all, he had been subjected to some horrible experiences when he had written and acted in *Dom Garcie de Navarre*, his tragedy about jealousy. The story is told – even though it may not be confirmed as absolutely true – that one evening some noblemen seated on the stage forced him and black-mailed him to play that deeply serious role – the main role of the jealous protagonist – as comic. And he did so with an unbelievable sense of humiliation.

FJM. Your deep immersion in the Molière tradition goes back a great many years, doesn't it. Which productions did you see when you went to Paris for that famous first visit, back in the autumn of 1949?

IB. Everything.

FJM. And what do you remember?

IB. Everything.

LLM. Jouvet?

IB. Yes, yes, yes. I went to the theater every night. It was an unbelievable, completely overwhelming experience. It was my first experience. I had never been outside of Sweden before. Of course I had been to Berlin, in the summer of 1934, but that was only as a schoolboy.

When I was in Paris, the Comédie Française was doing productions both on the main stage, the old stage, and at the Odéon, and they were fantastic experiences. In particular I remember *The Misanthrope*, which was like a revelation to me.

LLM. Who played Alceste?

IB. Jean Meyer, I think it was, and I remember it as a totally astonishing production – staggering so far as hearing French was concerned because – brrrrt – they went through it just like that! It was one of those performances that seemed to – it was such a great revelation, a great personal experience to encounter the French theater tradition. One of the most incredible things of all was to see Feydeau on the stage of the Comédie Française – that was the most astonishing experience of all.

LLM. Haven't you ever thought of directing Feydeau yourself?

IB. Oh yes, many times, but first I must wait until I become old. [Laughter.]

LLM. Why?

IB. Because, you see, you need immense experience, you have to have enormous experience to direct Feydeau. I am not really very good as a farce director. Perhaps I'll get to be eventually, in due time. But I can't do it right yet. Maybe I can learn to do it eventually.

LLM.   But is that really true? What about the farcical elements that made your *Tartuffe* so entertaining, for instance?

IB.   Oh yes. But I lack the self-confidence. I don't really feel confident about farce yet. Unfortunately. Perhaps it will come in time. But I find it wonderful. And the thing I found most wonderful at that time was the amazing brutality of the French when they play farce. Their incredible brutality and power and tempo and then that black, savage humor that suddenly becomes absurd. – Well, then I saw Jouvet and Barrault, naturally. And, what is more, I also saw a thing called *L'Arlésienne [The Girl from Arles]*.

LLM.   It's from the story by Alphonse Daudet, isn't it?

IB.   Bizet wrote music for it. It was one of the strangest theater experiences of my life, both in the auditorium and during the intermission. We were at a matinee at the Odéon, and the part of the girl was played by one of the *sociétaires*, who must have been sixty – decked out in curls and dressed like a young girl and smartly made up and all, but very old. And the setting looked like it must have been a hundred years old at least. You've never seen the play or read it?

FJM.   No, never.

IB.   Well, it's unbelievably sentimental trash. A real old stinker, you see. The acting was astonishingly sloppy, and in the pit a forty-man orchestra sat and played those splendid pieces by Bizet, that golden music. The thing dragged on and suddenly I heard a peculiar sound beside me and, looking aside, I discovered this French bureaucrat – a little fat, a little bald – and his entire family dissolved in tears. They were all crying like mad people. [Laughter.] And then I heard the same peculiar sound again, and, turning round in my seat, I saw that practically the entire audience was in the grips of a hysterical sobbing attack. And then to watch this sixty-year-old battle-ax, you know, just standing there at the footlights going through the part. Frightful old hag. Later, during the intermission, I walked around a little – I was alone and was at that time young and handsome – and strolled in the lobby and took a glass of wine or something of the sort; when suddenly one of the attendants rushes over and says: "Come here. Yes, you, come on. Hurry up." So off we went, walked backstage and through an enormous corridor, until we came to a door. Here was a whole queue of handsome young men, and so I took my place in the queue. Then one went in and, after two minutes, out he came again, and then the next went in and, after two minutes, he too was back. Then came my turn; I went in and there, stretched out on a divan in some sort of outlandish dressing gown, was our battle-ax, made up like an Easter egg and holding a glass of champagne in her hand. The entire dressing room was filled with laurel wreaths and photographs. And then she grabs my program and scribbles her name and hands it back to me and the attendant ushers me right back out again. [Laughter.] That was their job, you see, to keep her in a good mood, and so the attendants had to go out and round up whatever young men might serve the purpose.

It is really marvellous how much the French love their old actors. So this old diva had to be treated as she had always been. And if young men were expected to be there, as they had been all her life, then young men would be there, waiting for her autograph. Isn't it charming? For *that*, too, is theater. I love it – as incredibly confusing as the experience was, it was at the same time truly marvellous.

[Four months later, our conversation in Munich resumed:]

FJM. Ultimately, the most fascinating problem of all remains the whole question of your method in working with actors. When asked in the past which method of directing actors you prefer, you have invariably replied: "my own." The heavily psychological motivation of much American acting is, for instance, obviously alien to your style. You have created your own personal method – totally independent of any acting-school conventions.

IB. Yes, yes, of course it is. Because I have never acted – or rather I have acted very, very little. But when I did act, it was a very good experience for me, because it taught me how vulnerable the actor is and how extremely dependent he is on someone who exists outside himself, just as the ballet dancer has the mirror and the musician has his tape recorder. Someone who watches him very objectively but very sympathetically.

LLM.   You feel very strongly opposed to Stanislavski and his method, for example, don't you?

IB.   I don't care for Stanislavski. Stanislavski was very good for the Russian theater, but I think he has been completely misunderstood by Lee Strasberg and others . . .

FJM.   In the excessive psychological identification of the actor with his role, you mean?

IB.   Yes. Some sort of – some sort of masturbation. Now I must say I have nothing against masturbation, but when one comes upon it in the theater, when they all sit there together masturbating their souls, I find it . . .

LLM.   Self-indulgent?

IB.   Yes, exactly. No, I must say I have no method at all.

LLM.   But if you were to advise a young actor, what would you say to him? What kind of training would you tell him to get? Or wouldn't you tell him to get any training?

IB.   No. When we work together – when I work with young actors – or with any sort of actor – very slowly we try to discover the meaning of the play, what we are going to think at this particular moment, what we are going to feel at that particular moment. Very precisely. And the movement must correspond precisely to the emotions and the rhythm of these moments. Everything in life is rhythm, and when we create art we must also discover the rhythm of what we are attempting to do. This must be the basis then: First of all the meaning of the play; then absolutely to know at every moment, at every second, what to think, what to feel – the movements, the tune, the key, the rhythm.

LLM.   The terms you employ to describe it suggest that it would be almost impossible for you to work with an actor who was unmusical.

IB.   Music has all my life been just as vital as food and drink. One of the important basic inspirations, perhaps even the most important. Music is a great source of strength. And most actors *are* musical. Sometimes they may not know it, and then you have to exercise their ability. For instance, the German actors are generally so used to playing their parts on their own, in isolation, that they aren't very interested in listening to their fellow actors. They don't know how to listen. Of course they listen, but they don't know *how* to listen. When you are acting a part, you are not an I, you are always a you. You must concentrate not on yourself but always on your fellow actors. And you must do so all the time, even when you are not on the stage. The actors must not drift off to the canteen; they must remain there on the stage. Usually I tell the actors: Stay on the stage; and I try to make the setting so simple that no stagehands or electricians or others are needed. Because whenever they take away a setting, they always take something more with them. So I try to keep them out of it, to find a solution that is so simple that we won't need any stagehands.

LLM.   What do you tell your actors concerning the audience? Are they aware of the audience, or are they meant to be totally unaware of its presence during the performance? Or does it have to do with the particular play?

IB.   I believe that every actor, even if it may seem that he is not aware, has to be one hundred percent aware of his audience, at every moment. He must never forget the audience for a moment, because if he does he retreats into some sort of private solitude. And then it's all over, you know, then it becomes completely uninteresting. So we always try, in all our work, to find our way to the audience – to discover how it will react to this thing or that.

LLM.   Then if the actors are aware at all times of the presence of an audience, do they adjust themselves to its reactions during the course of the performance – or don't you think that matters? Do they in fact control the audience's reactions?

IB.   Yes, I think they do. In the beginning, the first time somebody is sitting there, their nerves begin to work. But slowly they learn to rule – both their own nerves and the audience. The actor must make sure at all times that the audience is never allowed to become passive, but remains active.

FJM.   Viewed from the audience's side, though, the effect created by a technique such as the continued visible presence of the actors on stage is very decisive.

IB.   Oh yes.

FJM.   In other words, you say that you do this for the sake of the actors, as a means of maintaining their involvement. Seen from the audience's point of view, however, it then creates a very consciously theatricalized experience.

LLM. Do you regard this device – keeping your actors seated on stage throughout a performance – as something that focuses audience attention more sharply on the stage, or do you feel that, on the contrary, it serves to distance the audience – that it reminds the audience that it is watching a performance?
[Long pause]

IB. The real theater always reminds – the real theatrical creation always must remind the audience that it is watching a performance. I believe that if you try to depart from that rule, you will very soon collapse. Because the function of the spectator – if we talk about an ideal spectator watching the ideal performance – is that he continually undergoes changes of mind, changes in his concentration. From being completely involved at one instant, he is in the very next instant aware of being in the theater. The next second he is involved again, completely involved; then after three seconds he is back again in the theater. And that is a part – and a very, very important part – of his being a participant in the ritual. – Because that word *verfremdung* [alienation] is a complete misunderstanding. The spectator is always involved and he is always outside, at one and the same time.

LLM. Theater is very different from film in that respect, isn't it?

IB. Oh yes. In film, you see, the spectator is hypnotized – because he is also in the position of someone who is being hypnotized. As you know, when you are being hypnotized the mesmerist very often uses a small lamp, a spot of light, and says: "Follow this with your eyes." [Demonstrating.] Then he moves the spot of light up there, on the ceiling – and you look at it, he says, and you concentrate on that. With film it is exactly the same. You sit comfortably, I hope, with light in front of you, in the dark, very silent, very far from other people.

LLM. We saw your *Magic Flute* again recently and I was just wondering whether you consider that filmed theater or theatricalized film? For example, I'm thinking of the way in which you stress certain themes by letting the spectator read the text of what is being sung. Which is a wonderful device, to be sure. But is the intended effect something in between theater and film?

IB. It's not a film – it was made as a television play, and that's different. The spectator's perception of a TV play is completely different from his perception of a motion picture. The spectator is placed in three completely different situations, sitting in the theater, sitting at home watching a TV play, or sitting in a movie theater. They represent three entirely different ways of perceiving something. And you must always bear that fact in mind – the situation of the spectator and his particular manner of perceiving. In all the years I've been working at this, I have never stopped being fascinated by the kind of interaction that takes place between actor and spectator.

2　First seasons

By the time Ingmar Bergman embarked on his professional theater career, at the age of twenty-six, as the artistic director of the Hälsingborg City Theatre in southern Sweden, he had already established a solid reputation for himself as a director and, to a lesser degree, even as a playwright. Half a dozen years before being called to Hälsingborg in 1944, he had already begun to attract critical attention with his imaginative amateur productions of Strindberg, Lagerkvist, Shakespeare, and others at Mäster Olofsgården, a religious settlement house located in the old part of Stockholm. By the early 1940s, his abilities had been strikingly and conclusively demonstrated in his student-theater productions, in his organization of an experimental children's theater in Medborgarhuset (the Civic Center), and in several successful productions that he directed for the enterprising Swedish Playwrights Studio, a professional group formed to foster new Swedish drama. "If you want to see something truly interesting right now and need to have your faith restored in the fact that Thalia still lives, it is clearly to the Student Theatre you must go," Nils Beyer proclaimed in *Morgon–Tidningen* early in 1943. "The credit is due, above all, to the principal director of this small academic amateur theater – one of the most remarkable young directing talents we have in this country at the moment – Ingmar Bergman."[1] No promising young artist could have wished for a clearer mandate.

Much earlier, during those otherwise so traumatic adolescent years of remorseless psychological warfare in his father's rectory at Uppsala (a period that Bergman has looked back on as "a life and death struggle: either the parents were broken or the child was broken"[2]), the embryonic director had practiced and perfected his craft through the traditional medium of toy theaters – in this instance, sophisticated scale models that were eventually equipped "with lighting boards, turntables, elevator stages, and everything conceivable: big, solid affairs that filled my whole room so that no one could get in."[3] The young

34

enthusiast drew upon "all of world drama" for his solitary productions: "I staged *Lucky Per's Journey* and *Master Olof* – I performed a great deal of Strindberg in my theater, and even did Maeterlinck's *The Blue Bird*. Above all, though, I wanted spectacular shows that required a lot of work with stage machinery and lighting effects," he recalls in another interview.[4] As he began to see more and more live theater and opera in the Stockholm of the 1930s, his miniature stages grew in direct response to the influence exerted on him by the productions of Sweden's two foremost directors of the period, Olof Molander and Alf Sjöberg.

The Hälsingborg engagement meant that Bergman could begin to try out the ideas and methods he had acquired in a professional theater of his own – albeit a modest one, venerable in its traditions (it had been established in 1921) but possessing distinctly limited technical and financial resources. When he became the fourth artistic director of the Hälsingborg City Theatre in the autumn of 1944 – during the same period that his first original screenplay, *Hets [Torment]*, was released under Alf Sjöberg's direction – his principal mission was literally a rescue action. The institution's state subsidy had just been withdrawn and morale was low, but the town of some eighty thousand inhabitants had made up its mind not to let its theater die. Bergman and his young company set out to infuse new life into the staid municipal playhouse by making it a meaningful, even controversial forum in the community. "The town's unquiet corner" was the spirited phrase adopted by the young manager in one of his frequent program declarations.

During two vigorous seasons at Hälsingborg, Bergman directed an astonishing total of nine productions himself. All but three were works by modern Swedish dramatists (including Hjalmar Bergman, Olle Hedberg, Björn-Erik Höijer, and Brita von Horn) – a fact that in itself reflects a commitment to native Swedish writing that has remained characteristic of his work in the theater. (On the other hand, one should perhaps emphasize at the very outset Bergman's outspokenly pragmatic attitude toward the whole question of the choice of repertory: "I have never had a program in my selection of plays, rather I have directed whatever I have had a desire to direct or have been invited to direct or have felt obligated to direct. I have never adhered to any rigid principle."⁵) Probably the single most interesting production to emerge out of these first formative seasons, however, was the pictorially expressive and politically engaged version of *Macbeth*, which he presented as his third bill in November 1944. His earlier amateur production of the play at Mäster Olofsgården had attracted widespread interest when it coincided with the German invasion of Denmark and Norway in April 1940. Now, the time was the last autumn of the war, and Bergman once again saw in the figure of Macbeth the embodiment of Nazi totalitarianism – the personification of those fascist qualities that also color the character of Caligula, the Latin teacher, in *Torment*, and that he had seen infect the attitudes of his family and his teachers in Uppsala. The young director – if one is right in seeing his hand in the unsigned program note for the production – viewed Shakespeare's play as "an anti-Nazi drama, a ferocious confrontation with a murderer and a war criminal. Remorselessly and with psychoanalytical logic, the mighty dictator is torn apart. With an increasing, incomprehensible power his crimes multiply, one giving birth to the next, until at last they annihilate him."

Technical resources at Hälsingborg were minimal ("some foots and twelve spotlights and four floodlights for the backdrop"), but with them Bergman and his designer, Gunnar Lindblad, created for the play a simple but effective visual framework that depended chiefly on a ramp of stairs, scattered suggestions of scenery, projected silhouettes, and a threateningly red or black sky in the background. This *Macbeth* was no elaborate historical saga of bloodshed and ambition played out against a background of brooding granite castles and wind-whipped stretches of heath, but rather a concise, modernized indictment of the "curse of usurped power, the overwhelming force of evil" that the young director saw as its real subject. Interestingly enough, even at this early point one critic applied the term "chamber play" – a designation that has since become virtually a critical cliché in discussions both of Bergman's films and of his stage productions – to his simplified approach. ("It was plenty aestheticized with the resources we had, but without the possibilities to aestheticize," Bergman himself has remarked with typical frankness. "Sometimes it worked, but more frequently it didn't work at all.")

It is worth pausing over a few of the more startling textual modifications introduced in this production, particularly because of the piquant foretaste of Bergman's mature style that they provide. The witches – Macbeth's "secret, black, and midnight hags" – become a more concrete and more persistent influence. The heath on which they first appear was now evidently a battlefield where the bereaved wives of the fallen gathered; the most talkative of the weird sisters was translated into a fortune-teller figure who reappeared at intervals throughout. Herbert Grevenius, among the first major critics to make the pilgrimage from Stockholm to review the activities at Bergman's "unquiet corner," painted a vivid verbal picture in *Stockholms–Tidningen* of a subsequent pantomimic interpolation:

The witches have obsessed Macbeth's mind, and as he writhes on his bed beside his wife in a gaping black chamber with quivering fever-shadows on the walls and an immense crucifix glimpsed in the haze of the background, the fortune-teller and her sisters from the battlefield

The opening scene of *Macbeth*, Hälsingborg, 1944. Setting by Gunnar Lindblad.

appear in a ragged group at the foot of the bed, and the room is filled with the sound of disembodied voices. This is poetry on a level with the poem.

During Lady Macbeth's illness, Grevenius continues:

Macbeth carouses with endlessly laughing girls and sinister men, hushed for a moment by the physician in his black cape who glides like a shadow down a winding stairway. Then he shouts and the motley crowd rouses itself again in a drunken and possessed gavotte, which becomes doubly grotesque as they dance out of the darkness of the room past a blood-red spotlight.

Sune Ericson's performance in the title role added its full share to the grotesque and macabre atmosphere of the final acts. His "Life's but a walking shadow" speech (V.v) was delivered, for example, not in reaction to the cry that proclaims Lady Macbeth's death, but seated and cradling the corpse of his dead wife in his arms. Even these few glimpses from this production – the orgy with the laughing girls, the drunken danse macabre, Macbeth spiritually impaled between the crucifix and the witches – indicate clearly enough the propensity for simplified but boldly suggestive visual concepts and emphatic figure compositions that we have come to identify with Bergman's style.[6]

His third attempt at *Macbeth* represented a contrast to the modest Hälsingborg performance in almost every respect. By the autumn of 1946 Bergman had been hired as resident director at the larger and more important Gothenburg City Theatre, where he remained for a three-season engagement that taught him to master one of the most technically advanced stage facilities in Europe. His controversial revival of *Macbeth* at Gothenburg, which opened on the main stage on March 12, 1948, was a picturesque visual spectacle that seemed to many critics, however, to overwhelm both Shakespeare and the actors with what one of them called its "numerous periphrastic flourishes around the heart of the drama . . . The sensations keep our attention alive, but they distract our gaze from the faces of the actors, which ought to be the true focus of our attention" (*Göteborgs Handels – och Sjöfartstidning*). It is a point that the mature Bergman would not lose sight of again in his later work. At this juncture in his career, however, a critic like Karl Ragnar Gierow was inclined to observe that he had:

A good grasp of and eye for the external things: corpses hang from ropes above the stage almost all the time; the witches, far from being half-real presences conjured up out of terror, take part in the celebrations for King Duncan and stretch forth their highly corporeal legs and arms at every opportunity from start to finish. Drums are banged, trumpets blare, gongs are sounded. Processions and magnificent stage pictures are provided as frequently as occasion allows. But the rhythm of the play tends to be obscured by the theatrical coups (*Svenska Dagbladet*).

One major aspect of the problem was obviously the stage setting itself. "The scenes emerge with unprecedented wildness and energy in their composition," Grevenius declared, but even he was obliged to add that "eventually the ceaseless raising and lowering of stage machinery and the whole weight of the scenic apparatus served to dissipate the ability to listen with real attentiveness." The enforced simplicity of the

Multiple-level setting for *Macbeth*, designed by Carl-Johan Ström. Gothenburg, 1948.

Hälsingborg set was now replaced by a massive Wagnerian apparatus that included an elaborate playing area on two levels, connected by a perilously steep spiral staircase. It could incorporate at various times a two-story drawbridge capable of being raised and lowered; a hall in reddish purple tones for the banquet scene and Banquo's apparition; and even a small, stylized arcade for two interpolated dance sequences, "which established the mood of dour Scotland and of the lighter, more airy Renaissance festivities of the English court" (*Göteborgs–Posten*). Carl-Johan Ström, who designed the majority of Bergman's productions in Gothenburg, found full scope for his customary technique of placing dark, neutral foreground silhouettes against a contrastingly bright, vivid background.[7] In this case Ström framed his stage between the dark outline of a brooding watchtower and the winding stairs on one side and the silhouette of an ancient, towering oak tree on the other. Bergman being Bergman, he lost no opportunity to exploit the visual potentialities of Ström's gargantuan tree. Carcasses of roasted oxen were suspended from it during the fateful banquet; sinister silhouettes of hanged men dangled ("like overripe fruit") from its branches during the more diabolical scenes; and the omnipresent witches – the leader of whom by now had become a whore in a tight, red dress, wearing a mask copied from Lady Macbeth's face – climbed decoratively among its limbs.

Bergman has always been ready to utilize the plastic and visually expressive aspects of the physical theater to their fullest extent, but the more flamboyant experiments of his Gothenburg period eventually taught him to mistrust effects that are not organically integrated or motivated. "Superimposed trappings always hang loosely and rattle," he remarks drily. "One hears and sees from them that they hang on the outside and are dead, no matter how unusual or tasteful they may otherwise be. I've done a lot of that kind of thing, too." In terms of the use of stage space, for example, a revealing contrast exists between this early *Macbeth* and subsequent productions of *Twelfth Night* staged at Dramaten in 1975 and 1979. In these later productions, designed by Gunilla Palmstierna-Weiss, the entire play was acted on a simple, rough-hewn platform erected in the shadow of an encircling Tudor framework of beams and gables – suggestive of an

Elizabethan playhouse, perhaps also of a Tudor hall, maybe even an innyard. Across the back ran a musicians' gallery, from which six costumed players accompanied the action. Held to a bare minimum, the furnishings on the small platform – chairs, a pair of screens, a bench – were carried on and off by costumed stagehands. The characters – including even Sebastian, the twin brother whose presence alone is needed to resolve the comic confusion in *Twelfth Night* – sometimes stood awaiting their entrances in full view of the audience. At the back of this miniature stage, a picturesquely stylized painted hanging was used to announce the location – the utopian realm of Illyria. Nothing more was required to evoke the intrinsic sense of theatricality, of a game of illusion and make-believe that infused Bergman's conception of Shake-

Unit setting for *Twelfth Night*, designed by Gunilla Palmstierna-Weiss. Dramaten, 1975.

speare's comedy. At the height of his apprenticeship some thirty years earlier, however, the young director was still taken up with the idea – not an unusual one for 1946 – of a much more ponderous version of an "Elizabethan" stage, shaped (as he proclaimed in an interview in *Ny Tid*) "entirely in the style of the theaters of Shakespeare's time, that is, with an inner space that can be closed off by doors."

Bergman has also alluded in later interviews to another difficulty that obviously compounded any confusion caused by the top-heavy physical staging of his Gothenburg *Macbeth*. He and Anders Ek, who played Macbeth, appear to have held diametrically opposing views about the nature of the central character and his conflict. "Anders saw it such that the murderer is driven to his crimes, yet nevertheless retains his innocence," Bergman has explained. "I had staged a work at the center of which stands a character who is, little by little, morally broken; Anders created an individual who is unyieldingly innocent, who remains pure from start to finish."[8] For Bergman at this stage of his development, Macbeth embodied the presence in human nature of what he calls a "virulent evil." For Ek, on the other hand, the character remained a victim of the feudal society that has corrupted him. This highly analytical actor's script describes Macbeth as "unstable, naive, excitable, impressionable, an easily inspired poet with profound sensitivity and enormous imaginative power."[9] Needless to say, such an obvious conflict of interpretation was bound to leave its mark on the overall conceptual unity of the production.

This conflict points up, in turn, another of the lessons that Bergman had begun to learn in "the strict school" at Gothenburg, where Torsten Hammarén and a skilled ensemble of strong actors "demanded of me that I account for what I did – why are you doing it? Why have you imagined it that way?"[10] For the first time in his young career, he found himself obliged to adopt "a certain intellectual consciousness" in relation to the playwright and his work. For a man whose gifts as a director of actors are legendary and perhaps unequaled, he is surprisingly candid about the slow and painful process by which he arrived at one of his cardinal rules as a director – that "compulsion won't work" in dealing with an actor:

When you start out as a director – at least when I started out – you're terribly afraid. If you are afraid and insecure, then you must not say you're afraid and insecure and you adopt the opposite attitude – you become decisive, you insist, become ruthless . . . Now I am completely open. The other way was such a strain, so terribly exhausting. But you young people have a different climate and a different point of departure. And you mustn't forget either that fashion changes. I was born and grew up in the age of the big guns, and naturally I wanted – even though I was only a little peashooter – to be a big gun too, to behave like a big gun. And those manners are something you pick up damned quickly.[11]

Behind Bergman's practical education as a director looms the ambivalent figure of Torsten Hammarén, the indomitable manager of the Gothenburg City Theatre to whom a revealing chapter in Bergman's highly impressionistic autobiography, *Laterna Magica*, is devoted. The first secret learned from his new master, Bergman recalls, was the value of clarity and simplicity in preparing a production: "Staging must be clear and directed. Fuzziness in emotions and intentions must be eliminated. Signals from actors to recipients must be simple and lucid." Hammarén's method quickly persuaded him that "voluntary cooperation between the parties concerned" is the only means of achieving a finished result that will continue to hold up before an audience. "If the director forces an actor, he can get his own way during rehearsals," he writes, but "after five performances, a 'tamed' production has fallen apart." More than anything else, however, Hammarén's example taught Bergman the true significance of calm and methodical preparation as the indispensable basis for fruitful improvisation in the theater. "Now I make my preparations down to the very last detail, forcing myself to sketch every single scene," he continues in his autobiographical tribute to his acknowledged mentor. "When I go into rehearsal, every moment of my performance must be ready. My instructions are clear, useful, and preferably stimulating. Only someone who is well prepared has the opportunity to improvise."[12]

Some of Hammarén's other practical, straightforward principles of theater management also left a deep and lasting impression on his most famous disciple – so much so that they formed the basis for the laconic statement that Bergman himself chose to issue when he succeeded Karl Ragnar Gierow in the onerous post of managing director of the Royal Dramatic Theatre in Stockholm in 1964. This terse but revealing document, printed at the front of Dramaten's first program for the

1964–5 season, takes the form of "Three Questions" posed by the new manager to his old teacher. The first concerned choice of repertory, and the answer came back crisply: "I can play only those plays that I myself like – and want to see. Anything else is hypocrisy." The second lesson dealt with the hiring of actors, and here the reply was even terser: "There are two kinds of actors – those who should walk on, and those who should walk out." The third and final question asked for the most essential characteristic of a theater manager, and Hammarén answered: "Trust. In your co-workers, in your audience. And perhaps even, to a certain degree in spite of everything, in the press."

As a director, Bergman has been strongly attracted to the idea of returning to certain plays, almost in the way a conductor returns to a symphony many, many times during the course of his career. "I have plays that follow me, that pursue me through the years, and my view of these changes," he says. "I discover new attitudes toward the text, and create new performances." Prominent among these recurrent favorites have been such works as Strindberg's *A Dream Play*, Ibsen's *Hedda Gabler*, Molière's *Dom Juan*, and Hjalmar Bergman's bittersweet fantasy, *The Legend*, each of which he has directed at least three times. In general, one finds that Molière, Ibsen, and, above all, Strindberg have remained the three classical dramatists in whose writing Bergman has found special inspiration, and in whose service he has come to forge a new theatrical style. Shakespeare, on the other hand, has been a rather different matter. Until his two successful productions of *Twelfth Night* in the 1970s, in fact, *Macbeth* had been his sole Shakespearean venture – a circumstance that appears to have been directly related to his high regard for Alf Sjöberg's epoch-making Shakespearean revivals at Dramaten in the 1950s and 1960s. ("In the theater he was my superior, a fact I accepted without bitterness," he writes in *Laterna Magica*. "To me his interpretations of Shakespeare covered everything. I had nothing else to add; he knew more than I did, had looked deeper and had given form to what he saw there."[13]) However, inspired by his reading of Georg Brandes on Shakespeare, Bergman returned to this dramatist in the 1980s with renewed interest and a decisively new attitude. Ultimately, as we shall come to see, his boldly conceived theatrical deconstructions of

King Lear (1984) and *Hamlet* (1986) bear scant resemblance to the essentially traditionalist approach adopted in his earlier Shakespearean productions. The foundations for the impressive program of classical revivals on which Bergman's reputation as a theater director rests was laid very slowly, however. For a long time, as he admits, "all theater was to me simply suggestions, atmosphere, situations. But the fact that a stage play had an intellectual intention – I arrived at that much later. And the fact that I myself might have an intellectual intention with a stage production – that came later still."[14] In Gothenburg, where *Macbeth* was really the only classical text that he had an opportunity to direct, the majority of his other productions (three on the main stage, six in the theater's intimate studio) reflected the popular repertory and tastes of postwar Scandinavia – specifically, French existentialist plays (Camus, Anouilh), recent American drama (Tennessee Williams), and a sampling of contemporary Swedish works (including another Björn-Erik Höijer premiere and two of Bergman's own so-called morality plays, a bitter allegory about death-in-life called *Dagen slutar tidigt* [*Early Ends the Day*] and a more personal piece about a young writer's marital and metaphysical problems, entitled *Mig till skräck* [*To My Terror*][15]).

In retrospect, one of the most exciting of his early achievements was Albert Camus' existential drama *Caligula*, the production which marked Bergman's debut as director on the demanding Gothenburg stage (November 29, 1946). In this instance, an almost perfect coordination was attained between Carl-Johan Ström's imaginative, carefully controlled stage design for an imperial Roman palace and the grotesque, surreal, at times even acrobatic conception of Camus' somewhat cerebral play that the young director presented to the startled burghers of Gothenburg. "A genuine *angst* is always there behind his commitment to form," observed Grevenius in *Stockholms–Tidningen*, "and this has induced even so placid a temperament as designer Carl-Johan Ström to work up a palace room which, with its leaning red columns, its huge Egyptian portals, and its masks grinning in the darkness, draws, so to speak, a magic circle of barrenness and death around the drama's central character." Seen from various angles on the turntable stage and dominated by an obligatory Ström sil-

Scene from Camus' *Calugila*, with *right*, Anders Ek in the title role. Gothenburg, 1946.

houette of a quadrangular roof pattern projected against a bright horizon, this expressive vision of Caligula's palace (also called by one critic "a cross between a modern hatbox and an Aztec temple"!) won high praise from Elis Andersson in a perceptive review in *Göteborgs–Posten* for its spaciousness, perspective depth, and brilliant colors. "The setting facilitates entrances and groupings; with its stairways and its multiple divided planes it affords the ideal conditions for accentuating the action," he declared. Individual critics might complain about the use of "movement for its own sake" in Bergman's dynamic and explosive choreography or (even more absurdly) about his disregard of historical accuracy, but most agreed with Andersson's view that, in this case, "it is well worth the risk that the pictures themselves can sometimes take the wind out of what is being said."

Often enough, Bergman's "pictures" – the bold visual accents with which he punctuated his production – did just that. In the first act, Caligula (who earlier has told his friend and aide Helicon of his desire for "the impossible" – "the moon, or happiness, or eternal life") summoned his staff by hammering on an immense gong "suspended like a glowing full moon against the night sky" in a vivid moment that seemed, to critic Ebbe Linde (in *Ny Tid*) "a brilliant impulse both in symbolic and in visually functional terms." Gigantic, glowering masks hung in corners and between the pillars of Ström's constructivist set, and, as they caught the light from various angles, they made their own silently mocking comment on the vision Caligula reads in his mirror of "an end of memories, no more masks."

The violent second-act banquet at which Caligula displays such wanton cruelty toward his enemies became, in Bergman's hands, a surrealistic "orgy of loathsomeness" that reached a crescendo in an "equilibristic" murder scene. Acrobatics played a large part in the production as a whole, particularly in the physically and psychologically intense performance of Anders Ek as Camus' obsessed protagonist. "He dances and crawls, he makes fantastic leaps, he strikes the most unusual plastic poses, he is – with the exception of a few quiet moments – a whirlwind of unrest throughout the performance," Elis Andersson noted. "In fact he fulfills all the physical demands of the role in a manner that should leave even an adherent of Meyerhold's biomechanics satisfied." *Expressen* too, described Ek's characterization as "an unbroken series of virtuoso acrobatic numbers, but acrobatic numbers that were transformed into dazzling metamorphic art, even in the facial expressions." The chiseled countenance of this Caligula was not that of "the beautiful and familiar marble bust, but of an inwardly consumed individual with sleepless eyes and tense facial features," remarked another observer. (Surely no one who has ever seen Ek's face as Frost, the tormented circus clown in Bergman's film *The Naked Night*, will ever forget its supple expressiveness.)

Caligula's desperate pursuit of some point of logical certainty in an illogical universe took its most radically grotesque turn in Bergman's third act, when Ek appeared as a nightmarishly distorted Venus – wearing a flame-red fright wig, false hips, and enormous breasts. "Venus strikes a highly unflattering acrobatic pose atop a pillar, and turns toward the audience that part of the body on which one usually sits," reported the critic for *Aftonbladet* with propriety. "Around the pillar of Venus storms the clown-show of life, with harlots, dancing skeletons, and all the curiosities that could ever be imagined on life's fairgrounds." In general, the Caligula conceived by Bergman and Ek – for, unlike their *Macbeth*, there was no hint here of any discrepancy between the director's concept and the actor's performance – was a warped, sardonic *Stürmer* of immense physical powers who thumbs his nose at a meaningless world (or, to be more exact, thrusts his backside in its face). In his malice and violence, however, one ultimately detected little of that terrifying methodical "logic" that drives Camus' complex protagonist – his determination, as Sartre puts it, to "choose to be the man to persuade other men of the world's absurdity."[16]

AMERICAN REALISM

No doubt for a variety of reasons, *Caligula* has remained Bergman's only encounter as a director with the philosophical nihilism of French absurdist drama – although he had been preparing to make a film of Camus' novel *The Fall* shortly before the French writer's death in 1960, and had been in lengthy correspondence with him. (The two popular plays by Jean Anouilh that he directed in Gothenburg, *La Sauvage* and the delightful *Le Bal des voleurs*, can hardly be said to fall into the absurdist category.) In terms of the sharp distinction that Sartre draws, in his essay "Forgers of Myths," between a psychologically preoccupied "theater of characters" and the existential "theater of situation and choice" represented by his own work and that of Anouilh (specifically his *Antigone*), one is inclined to suggest that the young Bergman was constitutionally much more attuned to works in the first of these two classifications. Perhaps for this reason, the more concrete, psychologically grounded emotionality of modern American drama held a much stronger attraction for him – for a period, at least – and found provocative, at times even explosive articulation in the increasingly more direct, uncluttered, actor-oriented style that he gradually developed. Tennessee Williams was in high favor throughout Scandinavia during the years around 1950, and Bergman staged three of his plays in that period – *A Streetcar Named Desire* (1949), a radically altered version of *The Rose Tattoo* (1951), and *Cat on a Hot Tin Roof* (1956). During the 1960s, Bergman's interest shifted briefly to the plays of Edward Albee, and he presented probing and erotically intense interpretations of both *Who's Afraid of Virginia Woolf?* (1963) and a partially rewritten and demystified version of *Tiny Alice* (1965) – the latter so sexually explicit that, one critic observed, "hardly ever have we come closer to seeing the sexual act performed on stage" than in an interpolated copulation scene between Alice and the Lawyer.

Although Bergman's production of *Streetcar*, with which he concluded his three-season contract at Gothenburg in 1949, was naturally considerably tamer in this regard – the 1940s were not the 1960s, after all, even in Scandinavia! – it represented a critical sensation in almost every other way. The choice of the play itself was anything but unusual, of course – *Streetcar* seemed to be de rigueur for theaters throughout Scandinavia at that moment[17] – but the approach that he took to it was wholly personal and original. The result was a veritable theatrical paraphrase and intensification of the inner spirit of Williams' drama, "held together by a clarity and with a forcefully conceived totality of vision that actually made the play finer than it is in the text by itself."[18] The acrobatic Anders Ek was an appropriately athletic Stanley Kowalski; the superbly self-possessed and authoritative actress–director Karin Kavli was Bergman's Blanche Dubois. (Because he is nothing if not a genius in the art of casting actors, his choice of these two performers for other roles in the subsequent plays of his American series is worth noting in passing: Ek was later seen as Brother Julian in *Tiny Alice*; Kavli was both Serafina in *Rose Tattoo* and the formidable Martha in *Who's Afraid*.)

As a framework for the focal life-and-death struggle between Blanche and Stanley, Bergman created a highly concrete, pliable atmosphere of light, shadow, and sounds to intensify the mood of desperation that prevails in the play. "He has coordinated all these thousands of sounds that flow through the house and around it – the clatter from the street, the vendor's cry, music from the movie-house, the creaking and grinding from the train station, thunder, rain, and church bells, a mighty arsenal of sound effects – with the neon lights and the rather dilapidated interior to form a suggestive background for Blanche's fate," Elis Andersson recorded in *Göteborgs–Posten*. Both the passing of time and Blanche's vicissitudes of fortune were suggested by "a small symbolic apple tree that lives its life in Desire, from its flowering to the falling of its leaves." The chant of the blind Mexican flower vendor in scene nine was carried as an echo through the entire last movement of the play.

In turn, the director chose to delete most of the playwright's own very specific instructions for staging and stage effects. "He quite simply has no need for them," Andersson remarked, "given the way in which he has built up the house in Desire and the street and his utilization of the turntable stage." As this comment suggests, it was above all in its free, fluid use of the remarkably flexible stage space at Gothenburg that Bergman's version of *Streetcar* departed most radically from the familiar pattern so firmly established by Elia Kazan's direction and Jo Mielziner's design concept for the Broadway production of the play. Carl-Johan Ström, himself a disciple of the style represented by American designers like Mielziner and Boris Aronson, created in this instance a setting that, in a

A Streetcar Named Desire, the setting for 632 Elysian Fields. Gothenburg, 1949.

sense, transformed the tactile values that are suggested in Williams' stage directions – but were only indicated in Mielziner's painted street backdrop – into a three-dimensional environment.[19] Desire, for Bergman and Ström, was first of all a place. Blanche's entrance opened the play, as she seeks (*"with faintly hysterical humor"*) to explain to Eunice the directions she has received, and on Bergman's stage she found a very specific source for her hysteria in the bewildering street scene into which she was suddenly thrust. "To the left a large boarding house, to the right a place called Desire or the Pleasure Garden, conceived of here as a nonstop movie house," wrote Ebbe Linde in *Dagens Nyheter.* "People stream out past a black doorman in red uniform, sailors and girls; bicycles are mounted, a real automobile roars into the street and races out." In the midst of this raucous neighborhood scene, the shadowy precincts of 632 Elysian Fields swung slowly into view on the revolving stage; but even when the Kowalski apartment occupied the stage, the shape and the flashing lights of Desire, Bergman's surrealistic picture palace of dreams, continued to be visible in the background.

"It is always my intention to be exact, to be concrete," Bergman told John Simon in an interview (in a reply that referred to the final striking image of the Dance of Death in *The Seventh Seal,* but which applies with at least as much validity to his work in the theater). "My intention is always to be very simple."[20] By "simplicity" Bergman, here and elsewhere, means "clarity," the absence of metaphysical topsyturvydom. Understood in this manner, his early production of *Streetcar* – with its battery of exact, specifically directed visual and aural effects (or "suggestions," as Bergman would call them, that together "create a dimension") – was "simple" and typical of one stage in his artistic development. Step by step, as the actor in Bergman's theater has gradually become his undivided focus of attention ("the actor is always the most suggestive of all, provided he has something to offer"), the concrete physical effects or "suggestions" in a production of this kind have been steadily and drastically reduced in number and in apparent randomness. This steadily increasing physical simplification was clearly in evidence in the subsequent productions of his American series, for example. In the production of *Who's Afraid* at Dramaten in 1963 (the European premiere of the play), one saw only an uncompromisingly bare gray room that consisted of a primitive wall-screen at the back and an absolute minimum of furnishings – an omnipresent bar wagon, a fringed, bourgeois sofa and armchairs – around which the scenes of Albee's dance of death were choreographed in acrobatic contortions. "His entire objective has been to enclose and transfix – in a milieu of rat-gray furniture and dishcloth-colored cretonne covers – a model marriage of hatred and humiliation, a relentless battle of the sexes," wrote Per Erik Wahlund in *Svenska Dagbladet*.[21] The physical presentation of *Tiny Alice*, which Bergman took on after the play's intended director fell ill, was starker yet – a stage enclosed by drapes, furnished only with two formal chairs and (for the scenes in Miss Alice's mansion) a stylized, man-sized model of a castle. Dimly visible on two luminous hanging globes that flanked the proscenium – and that find no origin whatever in Albee's stage directions – were a list of authors' names and an outline of the various branches of science (including both magic and ethics), scrawled in a schoolgirl's handwriting.

The bare, grey room designed by Georg Magnusson for Albee's *Who's Afraid of Virginia Woolf?* Dramaten, 1963.

The thrust of such extreme and suggestive simplification is certainly not toward abstraction, however, but toward greater concentration and emotional intensification – animated, in Bergman's own words, by a growing "need for clarity".

an awareness that a suggestion that aims at many targets reaches none of them. But a suggestion that is single and directed, that always strikes home. If you set up a series of suggestions like that beside one another, all of which are directed at the same target but each of which has a different coloring, you will get an immensely faceted spectrum. But if the suggestions go toward different targets, then you get no unity and merely become exhausted. It is on this theory that my productions build.[22]

Most would agree that, in this regard, the seasons in Gothenburg were crucial years (if perhaps not entirely contented ones) of experiment and growth for Bergman, during which the place of this discipline and formal clarity in his art was established – years during which "he coaxed from the great theatrical machine its secrets, tested the possibilities, and learned to control them."[23]

SAVAGE COMEDY

During the eleven months that elapsed between *Streetcar* and his next stage production – an unprecedented respite for a man like Bergman, who had been used to directing at least three or four productions a season – he found his first opportunity, at the age of thirty-one, to travel outside of Sweden and to experience modern European theater at first hand. In Paris in the autumn of 1949, he discovered Molière and the performance traditions of the Comédie Française ("an unbelievable, totally overwhelming experience," he calls it: "It was such a great revelation to encounter the French theater tradition"), and this discovery has, as we know, had a profound and lasting effect on his art. When he came back to the Gothenburg City Theatre to stage a guest production early the following year, however, it was not yet a Molière comedy but one of the most savage of the so-called *comedias bárbara* of Ramón María del Valle-Inclán that he presented.

In itself, the bold decision to produce Valle-Inclán's sprawling and complicated tragicomedy *Divine Words* (*Divinas palabras*, February 3, 1950) inevitably confronted the director with great formal and organizational difficulties – and yet, Grevenius declared in *Stockholms–Tidningen*.

it couldn't be done more simply. Already in *Caligula*, Ingmar Bergman succeeded in creating artistic mass effects with a small number of actors and sparse scenery. The austerity of that play almost automatically provided for such a solution. To find a simple and contained shape for a play as chaotic as Valle-Inclán's is considerably harder. But this clearly shows how it ought to be done.

Although not all the Swedish critics agreed with this assessment of Bergman's success in taming this wild and brutal epic of human depravity in the lower depths of rural Spain, the production is central to his development as a director in several respects. The monochromatic visual effects and arresting figure compositions that he created within Ström's stylized highway setting stood out with a clarity of definition that seems to predict some of the film maker's most memorable works of the 1950s:

The sun's red eye flames in a coal-black heaven. A procession of glittering torches moves brilliantly across the night sky. Frequently, entire scenes are built up as long frescoes of figures set against black space. The small, white rustic church around which the events are occasionally drawn together glows against a sky of thunder (*Göteborgs–Posten*).

Valle-Inclán's concept of *esperpento* – a truthful vision arrived at by systematic deformation, achieved by "the mathematics of a concave mirror" – found concrete scenic realization in the steady rhythmic progression of harsh black-and-white (or, more exactly, black-and-red) constrasts created by Bergman. The play's strange collection of vagabonds, bandits, and beggars (exhibiting in the production a "resplendent, gypsylike wretchedness, with much naked flesh and much undisguised shamelessness") was juxtaposed with a particularly vivid, Bergmanesque counterimage – pious pilgrims hurrying along the highway past this valley of sin, displaying their crucifixes, icons, and stigmatized hands. Not surprisingly, perhaps, the director himself has apparently admitted that this production provided the direct inspiration for the grotesque procession of howling, twisting flagellants in *The Seventh Seal*.[24]

The character of Mari-Gaila, the adulterous wife of the village sexton and the chief focus of interest in *Divine Words*, represents a severe challenge to the abilities of any actress. In the play she is a callous, lascivious figure with few redeeming actions to her credit. Among much else, she derives profit (and sadistic pleasure) from exhibiting her dead sister-in-law's hideously deformed idiot child, a hydrocephalic dwarf, as a freak; she drives her humiliated husband to drink and even attempted incest because of her flagrantly licentious behavior; in the end an angry crowd discovers her copulating in an open field; they proceed to strip her and drag her naked atop a wagon to her husband's church. Only the sexton's intonation of some randomly chosen "divine words" of unintelligible Latin, as he leads his naked wife into the safety of the sanctuary, succeeds in dispersing the superstitious mob. (It is perhaps self-evident that this graphic sequence of humiliation and counterhumiliation strikes a chord that is fundamental not only to a specific motion picture like *The Naked Night*, but indeed to the entire corpus of Bergman's films.)

Karin Kavli's intense performance as Mari-Gaila directly anticipated her even more defiantly unrepentant and demonic

The stylized monochromatic setting designed by Carl-Johan Ström for Valle-Inclán's *Divine Words*, Bergman's last production in Gothenburg, 1950.

interpretation of Kersti in Bergman's first major Strindberg production, *The Crown-Bride*, less than three years later. As Mari, she developed swiftly from a blond, gentle, essentially naive peasant wife to a woman who, once seduced into evil ways, remained possessed by and exultant in her sensuality and carnality. Confronted by the mob in the field, "she tears off her own blouse and stands there in her red slip like a triumphant sinner and a witch," one observer declared. "A wonderfully directed scene acted with compelling ferocity."[25] (Those inclined to smile a little at the commotion caused by the degree of Kavli's "nakedness" in this scene should be reminded that the innocent bucolic nudity of Harriet Andersson in *Summer with Monika* [released in 1953] had caused that film to be banned in Nice and Los Angeles, to run a year in Montivideo, and to enjoy wide circulation in pirated underground prints. Had Bergman chosen the supremely erotic Andersson to play Mari-Gaila, Gothenburg might well have had a riot on its hands!) The stripping and elevation of the adulteress became, in Bergman's handling of this – otherwise precariously operatic – scene, a mystical, ritualistic act that exposed the true subject of Valle-Inclán's tragicomedy – the latent paganism and thinly cloaked moral hypocrisy of the Spanish populace:

When the adulteress trapped in debauchery is lifted up onto the hayrick by the furious and enthusiastic harvesters, the doubleness of their action suddenly becomes clear. Behind outraged moral feelings one detects the echo of an age-old fertility rite, mixed with fear and lust, as the half-naked sinner (completely naked in the original) becomes both human victim and divine symbol. And it is not until the biblical words are uttered in Latin that the church reasserts its power over the primeval demons and their awakening recedes. That this scene works must be called a triumph for the director (*Göteborgs Handels – och Sjöfartstidning*).

In his review of *Divine Words*, Herbert Grevenius, Bergman's staunchest critical supporter during the 1940s and a frequent collaborator on his early films, tried to formulate a broader judgment that, in retrospect, supplies an apt and prophetic summary of the outcome of these first formative seasons in the director's long career:

It is usual to call Ingmar Bergman possessed. That has become the cliché. If by it one is trying to describe his artistic passion, then it must be accepted – provided we do not forget that it is a passion for truth and not an aesthetic passion for beauty. But the time has come to take notice of the control, the method, a search for form that is, for once in a Swedish director, . . . more Gallic than Germanic (*Stockholms–Tidningen*).

It is, Bergman himself declares, "only through experience, through my mistakes and to a certain degree through my successes, through an increased self-confidence, that I have little by little taught myself artistic selectivity."[26] Out of his score of early productions at Hälsingborg and at Hammarén's stricter school in Gothenburg, however, the "demon director" quietly and methodically extracted the most important lessons of all – the ability to use and to control the technical resources of the theater, the preeminent value of simplicity and suggestion, the basic and focal significance of the actor in the scheme of things, the need for that painstaking preparation without which improvisation becomes mere amateurish self-indulgence.

Two more seasons were to elapse – seasons of bitter frustration during which the Swedish film industry was shut down, and Bergman supported himself by making one-minute advertising films for Sunlight and by directing a few unremarkable stage productions in Stockholm and Norrköping – before he transformed the newly built 1700-seat Malmö City Theatre into one of the most vigorous and innovative theater centers in Europe during the mid-1950s. But by that time, of course, Bergman had already become Bergman. He had by then begun to gather around him a group of such "favorite" actors as Anders Ek and Gertrud Fridh, and his six-year stay at Malmö as director and artistic adviser enabled him to build and train a veritable Bergman ensemble of performing artists – Bibi Andersson, Harriet Andersson, Ingrid Thulin, Gunnel Lindblom, Naima Wifstrand, Max von Sydow, and others – who were to appear with regularity both in his stage productions and in his major films. He had taught himself to master the considerable complexities of the theater machine at Gothenburg, but the Malmö engagement represented a challenge of quite another magnitude. The vast open stage at Malmö had been completed in 1944 in response to Per Lindberg's call for a flexible, classless "folk theater," but the result had been a curious hybrid. "The project manifested an insoluble collision between Per Lindberg's monumental people's theater, with an arena stage and democratic seating, and Knut

Ström's dream of visual theater, created for scenographic visions in the spirit of Meyerhold and Reinhardt," Bergman remarks in *Laterna Magica*.[27] It took all his skill and determination to prove that the gargantuan complex that had resulted from this clash of ideas could indeed be used for normal dramatic productions. In turn, the special demands of this space exerted a profound influence on the maturation of the aims and methods of his scenic art.

Most significant of all, however, was the change in Bergman's repertory that clearly heralded a new and more important phase of his directing career. During the Malmö years of excitement and experiment between 1952 and 1958, he began for the first time to devote himself in earnest to that impressive succession of classical revivals – of Strindberg, Hjalmar Bergman, Ibsen, Goethe, and, in particular, Molière – that has since grown to form the keystone of his contribution to the modern theater. It is, above, all, in his numerous productions of Strindberg, Ibsen, and Molière during the past four decades that we find a unique and stimulating synthesis of tradition and innovation at work. It is a synthesis that arises out of that functioning of a historical sense which, as T.S. Eliot once put it, "involves a perception not only of the pastness of the past, but of its presence."

3 The Strindberg cycle

It has long been a critical commonplace to observe that Ingmar Bergman and August Strindberg are, in many complicated ways, kindred spirits. "I have been reading him since I was twelve or thirteen," Bergman has told more than one interviewer. "Strindberg has generally been my companion throughout life, alternately repelling and attracting me" – not, he adds, because of shared attitudes or temperamental affinity, but "simply because he expressed certain things in the same way that I experienced them but could not myself describe them."[1] It is, then, the Strindbergian *manner* of expression and perception – his forging and rearranging of crystallized images of a fleeting, fugitive reality – that has been the real source of attraction and inspiration for this director, both in the theater and on the screen. Critics have frequently suggested more or less convincing thematic parallels between certain of Bergman's films and certain of Strindberg's plays – *Persona* and *The Stronger*, *A Passion* and *The Ghost Sonata*, *Wild Strawberries* and *A Dream Play*, *Through a Glass Darkly* and *Easter*, to mention four examples picked at random.[2] But, although Bergman himself has readily acknowledged the Strindberg resonances in, for instance, *Wild Strawberries*, few film critics have paid much attention to the remark that is intended to clarify the nature of such resonances: "There is naturally theater work going on alongside all the time. Much could be said about the mutual relationship between my work in the theater and my work in film."[3] It is precisely in the broader context of this "theater work" – specifically, the various and often quite dissimilar productions of the fifteen or more Strindberg plays that Bergman has directed over a forty-year period – that the stylistic, formal, and theatrical characteristics shared by these two artists can best be appreciated. Bergman's lifelong "Strindberg cycle" has included a broad range of performances for radio (*Playing with Fire, The Dutchman, Mother Love, Crimes and Crimes, Easter, The First Warning*), television (*Storm Weather, A Dream Play*), and the stage (*The Pelican, The Crown-Bride, The Ghost Sonata*,

59

Erik XIV, A Dream Play, To Damascus, Miss Julie). At the core of this impressive body of work are the seven Strindberg plays which this director and his ensemble have performed before a live theater audience.[4] Each approach has shown a keen sensitivity to the rhythm of Strindberg's prose-poetry, to the associational logic of his dramaturgy, and, above all, to that free mingling of dream and reality that characterizes this playwright's vision of the human condition.

EARLY STRINDBERG PRODUCTIONS

Even in the toy theaters of Bergman's youth, Strindberg productions had figured prominently. By the early 1940s he was directing highly regarded amateur productions of such difficult works as *Lucky Per's Journey* and *Swanwhite* at Mäster Olofsgården in Stockholm.[5] The first real notice of what was to come was served in 1945, however, when he directed a guest production of *The Pelican*, Opus Four of Strindberg's Chamber Plays, on the intimate studio stage of the Malmö City Theatre. The program for this production (November 25, 1945) contains a brief article by the director that provides an unusually direct and revealing personal comment (unusual for Bergman, at least) on Olof Molander's approach – and hence, by implication, his own preferred approached as well – to the staging of Strindberg:

At first, Strindberg's inferno dramas put the strangest visions into the heads of Europe's directors, who felt they were out after Freudian deep-sea fish and began to throw themselves into levels, projections, and other devices for all they were worth. It was director's theater, display theater, but it wasn't Strindberg. Molander has made us see the magic in Strindberg's dramaturgy. We have begun to understand that the strange fascination of the stage itself and the Strindbergian dialogue are compatible. Molander gives us Strindberg without embellishments or directional visions, tunes in to the text, and leaves it at that. He makes us hear the poet's anxiety-driven fever pulse. It becomes a vision of toiling, weeping, evil-smitten humanity. We listen to a strange, muted chamber music. And the dream play emerges in all its grotesqueness, its terror, and its beauty . . . I want only to express my debt of gratitude to Molander.
    First it was *A Dream Play*. Night after night I stood in the wings and sobbed and never really knew why. After that came *To Damascus, Saga of the Folkungs*, and *The Ghost Sonata*. It is the sort of thing you never forget and never leave behind, especially if you happen to be a director and least of all if, as one, you are directing a Strindberg drama.

At the core of this warm *hommage* is the unmistakable consciousness of being part of a tradition – a consciousness that is one of the most characteristic features of Bergman's artistic physiognomy, both as a film maker and as a stage director. "I don't think that somebody just becomes a director, you know. We are like stones in a building, all of us," he has said repeatedly. "We all depend on the people coming before; I am just a part of this."[6] In the case of Strindberg, as Bergman quite rightly observes, it was Molander's impressive cycle of productions at Dramaten in the mid-1930s that ultimately succeeded in forging a fluid, responsive scenic form that was perfectly attuned to Strindberg's associational, mutational dramaturgy. "It was Max Reinhardt who discovered the unique scenic music of *The Ghost Sonata*, and Olof Molander who transposed that music into Swedish," one reviewer of Bergman's 1954 production of that play was prompted to remark.[7] The observation is as apt as it is concise. In Scandinavia, Reinhardt's touring productions of Strindberg had been seminal events that, in the words of the Swedish reformer Per Lindberg, "opened our eyes to the visionary, musical power in Strindberg's last dream plays." His boldly expressionistic *Ghost Sonata*, which came to Stockholm in 1917, made Hummel into a ghastly personification of evil and transformed the play itself into a grotesque and terrifying "nightmare of marionettes." Even the young Olof Molander found in his virtuoso interpretation of *The Pelican*, which played in Gothenburg and later in Stockholm in 1920, "a scenic masterpiece that is not even suggested by a reading of that chamber play."[8] One year later, his strange, starkly dematerialized Swedish-language production of *A Dream Play* at Dramaten contributed even more provocatively to an overall vision of a Strindberg in which, to borrow Siegfried Jacobsohn's words, "a shivering, desperate, shrieking humanity" struggles in an atmosphere "so distorted, so gloomy, so full of fantastic life and motion, that it might be Van Gogh's."[9]

On the same stage fourteen years later, in October 1935, the first of Molander's seven very different productions of *A Dream Play* – which Bergman singles out again and again as a "fundamental dramatic experience" in his own career – became a pivotal event in Scandinavian theater and culture. It was a turning point because it established a deliberate and, in the minds of many, a more authentic alternative to the Germanic Strindberg of Reinhardt and his followers. In direct contrast to the Reinhardt experiment, Molander's pioneering production reaffirmed a lucid undertone of resignation and consolation, a recognition of the humanity that so often seemed absent in the German *Schrei*-versions of Strindberg's plays. Both Molander's identification of the Dreamer, in all three of his voices, with Strindberg himself and the use of specific, recognizable projections of *fin de siècle* Stockholm to which he attached the action served to restore a relevance and a Swedishness to the work. Most important of all in terms of its influence on Bergman, perhaps, was the surrealism, or "fantastic realism" that this director applied to the staging of Strindberg. His style depended on a fluid progression of suggestive, dreamlike settings, each one composed only of fragmented bits of sharply etched reality (a table, a portion of a wall, the cloverleaf door) suspended in a void of darkened space and supplemented, in this instance, by the projected views of Strindberg's Stockholm – the old Dramaten with Jacob's Church in the background, the Horse Guard Palace, a corner of the old Royal Opera where the Officer waits a lifetime for his Victoria.

Not long after Bergman had published his program declaration apostrophizing this method and repudiating the empty European (read German) "director's theater" that it had replaced, Molander himself appeared in print to renounce, in notably similar terms, even his youthful flirtation with the Reinhardt formula for Strindberg:

The German, Reinhardt-inspired romantic expressionism, which during the years between the world wars came to characterize theater art in Germany, has always been alien to me. I also felt that *The Pelican* was a grotesque manifestation of this romantic expressionism, and was completely foreign to Strindberg's surrealistic dreamplay dramaturgy. It is certainly true that nightmares are often its subject, but the nightmares of everyday, of life as we live it, not a nightmare life in any higher sense, not caricature.[10]

Indirectly, this comment speaks to Bergman's production of *The Pelican* as well, which, although it was in no sense merely a Molander imitation, derived its power from his method – from the preservation of a cold, relentlessly concrete sense of reality in which the play's more mystical signs (the creaking of the rocking chair, the mysterious Maeterlinckian sounds outside, the final holocaust) could be resolutely anchored.

A severe, cheerless interior, designed by Martin Ahlbom, was steeped in the cold whiteness of its essential elements – the rocking chair, a tiled stove, a row of windows – and decorated with a sprawling potted palm and a crepe-hung portrait of the recently deceased father, which bore the unmistakable features of Strindberg himself. Within the stark confines of this domestic wasteland, Bergman worked to create a performance from which all extraneous "symbolic" overtones were expunged, and that concentrated instead on the central thematic action of the play – the unmasking, to which the Mother makes explicit reference at the end of the first scene, of Strindberg's blind and suffering self-deceivers. "As the play was now given, it depicted a series of awakenings on the part of those who had previously been sleepwalkers," the critic for *Dagens Nyheter* observed. "The Son, anxious from the outset to find reality, awakens when he reads the letter that his father left, with its revelations about the Mother. Gerda awakens when she reaches clarity – or certainty – about her husband's deception of her with the Mother. Even the Mother sees herself, at least in a glimpse, in her confrontation with Gerda. There is less oversized evil but deeper human insight in this interpretation. We see a dreamplay about bewildered and suffering humanity." At the heart of Bergman's interpretation was an intelligent, Oswald-like portrayal of the Son by Anders Ek, "a frightening portrait of an individual stricken to the heart and sick to the very marrow. The bent knees and head held at an angle, the stammering speech and discreetly suggested imbalance – all of this gave us in a nutshell the tragedy of someone doomed from the outset" (*Morgon–Tidningen*). The critics were by no means uniformly favorable toward the production, however, and this particular comment on Anders Ek's performance might well suggest a reason why some, Herbert Grevenius among them, argued that suspense was lost because "the characters never do walk in their sleep: they are already awake, and hence the play is robbed of the tension that lies in the fact that they are injected, one dose at a time, with truth and with black perspicacity" (*Stockholms–Tidningen*).

As could be expected, the climactic fire scene in which this drama of suffering and purgation culminates ("a domestic

Götterdämmerung," Evert Sprinchorn has called it, which "announces the bankruptcy of the family as an institution and the end of bourgeois drama"[11]) presented the director with his severest challenge and called forth some of his most interesting and most controversial antinaturalistic moves. No sounds of burning wood or puffs of smoke accompanied this inferno – much to the regret of a few literal-minded reviewers who admitted that they would have liked "a more violent crescendo accompanied by crackling sound effects." (After all, even Molander had nearly caused a panic when, during his first production of the play in 1921, clouds of smoke had billowed out into the auditorium!) Instead, Bergman suggested the fire by the simplest possible means, with a flickering red glow that played over the background. Also eliminated in his simplified scheme of things was the perilously melodramatic moment when Strindberg's demonic vampire–mother leaps through a balcony door to escape the flames; here, she was seen instead collapsing in the doorway to the dining room – ironically, the place of nourishment from which she had just been barred by the rebellious Gerda and her husband. Perhaps Bergman's most expressive visual comment was the image with which he chose to clarify the Son's closing summer-poem of serenity and peace. At the moment of death, the "fire" was extinguished and a translucent white curtain was lowered behind the door and windows in the background, with the result that the room stood bathed in light as brother and sister sank to the floor together. "'Now summer vacation is beginning,' was their last reply, and they were engulfed in the light of liberation," wrote Ragnar Josephson in *Svenska Dagbladet*. "It was very beautiful." One might well be inclined to suppose that the director had not forgotten the tone and the luminous atmosphere of that famous speech when he came to create his own cycle of "summer" films a few years later.

The *Crown-Bride*, Bergman's first major Strindberg production and also the work with which he made a sensational directing debut on the immense main stage at Malmö in 1952, has often been called a national-romantic folk drama – the playwright himself regarded it as the most Swedish of his plays. It has also been viewed by critics as an example of Strindberg's post-inferno mystical theater – a Damascus drama transposed into a folksong key, linked thematically both to

Swanwhite and *A Dream Play* (which were published together with it) by a renewed sense of spiritual peace and of the redemptive power of certain characters. In its simplest outline, the complicated action of the play supports either view – or both, for they are not mutually contradictory. Kersti, a young peasant girl in the idyllic province of Dalarna (Dalecarlia) who has secretly borne a son with Mats, drowns the baby to be able to marry her lover as a legitimate "crown" (i.e. virgin) bride. Tormented by the demons of a guilty conscience, she confesses her crime at her own wedding feast. In the midst of her despair and disgrace, the penitent shepherdess meets a Child in White – the image of the Christ child – and gains spiritual solace. Meanwhile, the ancient feud between Mats' family and hers has now flared up again. On Easter morning, as she is making her way from prison to the church to perform penance, Kersti falls through the ice on Krummedikke Lake as the quarrelling parties fight, and her "sacrificial" death works their reconciliation. In Bergman's theatrical paraphrase, however, the action of *The Crown-Bride* was presented in an entirely new and often surprising perspective. Not only was the play's superstructure of romantic folklore and fairy tale dismantled and its use of traditional Swedish folk melodies discarded. The consoling facility with which the sinner moves toward atonement and redemption from the powers of darkness (through the epiphanic device of the Child in White) was also drawn into serious question. In what a program note for the Bergman production (November 14, 1952) referred to as "a world where the powers hold sway and a dreaded God drives man to penance and destruction," Kersti's destiny seemed, almost to the final moment, "a Damascus pilgrimage" toward a very ambiguous salvation at best. "A paroxysm of somber nocturnal and fertility rites, a cross between Garcia Lorca's Spain and Bergman's own Barjärna" was how Ebbe Linde chose to describe the atmosphere evoked by the production – an atmosphere that indeed had much in common with the mood of darkness and evil prevalent in Bergman's own "passion play," *The Murder at Barjärna*, which he had staged in Malmö eight months before.

The intense, defiant performance by Karin Kavli as Mari-Gaila in the Gothenburg production of *Divine Words* had given only a foretaste of her deromanticized, virtually demonic characterization of the title figure in Strindberg's play. The traditional perception of this character's development – from the selfish and hardhearted peasant girl of the opening scenes to the grieving, repentant woman who atones before the church door – had been epitomized in Gerd Hagman's mimically expressive performance in the Molander production of the play at Dramaten eight years earlier: "There is an untamed animal's glint in her eye – and it gleamed fatefully in the beginning – but afterwards we saw the look change to horror, in preparation for reaching the great atonement at the end," critic Nils Beyer had declared on that occasion.[12] By contrast, Kavli presented – both physically and temperamentally – a much rougher and blacker Kersti, in a performance that led this same critic to observe (in *Morgon–Tidningen*) that the audience felt itself "considerably nearer to the sulfurous lakes of hell than to the shining waters of Lake Siljan" (the quintessentially idyllic body of water in the heart of the Dalarna district). This unrelenting Kersti seemed driven to her actions more by an innate compulsion for evil than by any misguided sense of social pressure. As such, she seemed scarcely to require the assistance of Naima Wifstrand's sinister Madame Larsson, the Mephistophelian midwife who is obviously a witch when "seen from behind," to accomplish her dark deed. In this atmosphere of heady diabolism, the figure of the Child in White was completely eliminated and replaced by a demonic figure that sprang from the orchestra pit to disrupt and scatter the bridal dance. Needless to say, neither the uncomplicated Mats nor any of the other characters in the play was any real match for this passionate demon-bride – with the result that, as Henrik Sjögren observed, "even the basic concept of the production was for a long time overshadowed by this robust leading performance, which in the beginning stood far too close to hell and toward the end never really did succeed in coming nearer to heaven."[13] Only in the closing sequence on the ice of Krummedikke Lake, when the sunken church rises (like a Flowering Castle) to signify peace in Dalecarlia and on earth, did the director finally resolve and reaffirm the major tonic chord of redemption in Strindberg's work.

Unquestionably the main source of critical interest and excitement in conjunction with Bergman's *Crown-Bride* was, and in retrospect still is, the imaginatively simplified mise-en-scène with which he conclusively established his undisputed mastery of the formidable stage dimensions of the Malmö City Theatre.[14] Strindberg's stage directions for this play are often very detailed and specific, and, even as late as 1942, Vagn Børge's influential dissertation would maintain that, in staging it, "there must be the aura of pine forests, of resin and wild roses, over everything, with the great lake in the background and the blue mountains on the opposite side, and then the church in the distance."[15] Without a sense of this realistic pastoral environment, runs such an argument, the basic tensions in the play – between dream and reality, nature and society – will not become clear in performance. Bergman has given his answer often enough: "The theater calls for nothing. TV includes everything, film includes everything, there everything is shown. Theater ought to be the encounter of human beings with human beings and nothing more. All else is distracting." His unadorned, conceptual approach to *The Crown-Bride* dispensed with traditional pictorialism and local color almost completely – with the result that, in many ways, the inner essence of the work revealed itself more clearly than ever before. "Bergman has by and large eliminated the realistic elements," Per Erik Wahlund observed in *Svenska Dagbladet*. "In his hands, the latent dreamplay technique is laid bare and accentuated by the shadowy half-light and a radically stylized décor."

In the first two scenes before the single intermission, Per Falk's stage settings still incorporated realistic elements that evoked that sense of specific – and extremely ominous – places. The craggy, darkly forbidding mountain pasture where Kersti first appears was already set up on the forestage when the audience took their seats, and she made her entrance through their midst. "An enormous romantic spruce of supernatural dimensions lay, felled by the wind, across the proscenium, threatening to crush the performers to dust," Linde remarked. The subsequent and fairly detailed setting for the family council in the millhouse, placed back on the large revolving stage, was dominated by a gigantic open fireplace that perhaps most of all suggested a gaping hellmouth – though none of Strindberg's suggested emanations from the spirit world were allowed by Bergman to make an appearance.

Following the intermission, however, the depth of the stage

was increased, and it was gradually and deliberately stripped of all objects and details as the action progressed toward Kersti's humiliation, penance, and death. The fateful bridal procession, during which she is forced to confess her perfidy and forfeit her crown, was choreographed (to music from Ture Rangström's opera on the subject) on a virtualy bare and somber stage illuminated only by what Wahlund thought of as "the moon's gigantic, flame-colored stratospheric balloon in the background." Surpassing all else in terms of effectively suggestive simplicity was the climactic scene – very often cut because of its presumed technical difficulty – in which Kersti attempts to cross the treacherous ice on her way to church to perform public penance. The rival factions of the millfolk and the outsiders, for whose sake the girl becomes a divine sacrifice for reconciliation, clashed and fought with oars on a storm-lashed stretch of lake ice that was neither more nor less than the bare floor of the stage itself, which had been opened up to its full, spectacular width of thirty-six meters (117 feet). Using only this immense space and the chiaroscuro effects that are obtained when darkness is penetrated by scattered shafts of light, Bergman literally conjured forth what Wahlund called "the gloomy, perilous emptiness of a darkness-enshrouded, frozen expanse of sea." By no other means than lighting and screening, the empty stage floor was transformed, in the minds of the audience, to what Linde described in *Dagens Nyheter* as "a limitless ice field with a swirling snowstorm coming toward us."

The lesson learned was a profound one that has had far-reaching effects on everything that Bergman has since directed. In an interview many years afterwards, he reflected on the implications of the sweeping dematerialization and elimination of scenery to which he began to turn in this pivotal production:

One of the reasons why I have dispensed more and more with scenery is in fact because I believe that every stagehand on the stage, every use of the curtain, every raising and lowering of settings is a disruptive occurrence. Because the actors have that wonderful ability to suggest directly. I thought about this very intensively while I was rehearsing the closing scenes of *The Crown-Bride*. Everyone went around in rehearsal clothes and we had only rehearsal lights. It struck me that absolutely no more was needed, no lighting was needed, nothing was needed – nothing more than the performer [*artiste*]. It is that simple.[16]

To be sure, there were reviewers of this version of *The Crown-Bride* who complained that its innovations were mere borrowed finery, and who drew parallels – rather vague and unspecific in character – between Bergman's style and the "German expressionist theater" of the 1920s. *Aftonbladet*, for instance, described the staging as "a gigantic apparatus suffused with mass scenes, ballets, and stage groupings that would have been greeted with genuflections by theatergoers at Am Grössten Schauspielkomplex in Berlin at the beginning of the 1920s. The spectator was taken on Gulliver's travels to the land of the giants, with Ingmar Bergman in the coachman's seat." It is hardly surprising to find that Bergman himself reacts with undisguised impatience to the implied comparision to the more spectacular aspects of Max Reinhardt's style. "I had seen no German theater before 1952. If there was any expressionism in me, it was home-grown." And indeed, if by "German expressionism" we mean such specific traits as the maintenance of a subjective, single-character perspective, the distortion of settings and fracturing of reality that reflect this perspective, and an open or implicit criticism of the prevailing social order, then it is difficult to feel persuaded of any significant link between this (so decidedly outmoded) mode and the increasingly uncluttered and simplified style of Bergman. The latter's primary aim as a director is the intensification of the audience's involvement with the living actor, placed for the purpose in an ever more direct, more emphatic, and hence more hypnotic position in relationship to it. In a word, Bergman's method in the 1950s does not seem to look backward to Reinhardt, but ahead toward a revolution in the way we perceive the theatrical experience.

Bergman's radio productions of Strindberg during these years add an interesting dimension to this preoccupation with an elimination of external detail and a consequent tightening of focus on the personality of the actor. During the year of *The Crown-Bride*, his radio production of *Crimes and Crimes*, which eliminated the factors of time and the play's Parisian milieu altogether, created an intense concentration – virtually the equivalent of the closeup technique in film – on the individual vocal nuances of Anders Ek's hesitant and inquisitive Maurice and the seductive, glass-hard Henriette of Gertrud Fridh. In *Easter*, also broadcast in 1952 with Maj-Britt Nilsson (*To Joy, Smiles of a Summer Night*) as a completely down-to-earth, even mundane Eleonora and Gunnar Olsson as an overpowering Lindkvist in dialect, the director "tried to cut away all sentimentality, eliminate all sound effects, and bring forth a nakedly oneiric tone."[17] The following year, he succeeded even more conclusively in translating to the radio medium the dreamlike transitions and word music of *The Dutchman*, Strindberg's long lyrical fragment about a latterday Flying Dutchman and his search for love in a loveless world.

Yet it would be totally misleading to leave the impression that Bergman's splendidly eclectic seasons in Malmö were somehow characterized by a tediously single-minded quest for the grail of a more restrained and more austere theatrical syntax. If he shares anything in common with Reinhardt (apart from great theatrical genius), it is the crucial conviction that no one method is sufficient for staging all plays, that "there is no one form of theater that is the only true artistic form," that each play presents a new and distinct problem. Therefore, Reinhardt continues, "do not write out prescriptions, but give to the actor and his work the atmosphere in which they can breathe more freely and more deeply. Do not spare stage properties and machinery where they are needed, but do not impose them on a play that does not need them."[18] Precisely in this spirit, Bergman's directional approach has at all times been conditioned by the particular work at hand. In Malmö, moreover, he was able to adopt and maintain a satisfying alternation – akin in a sense to Reinhardt's tandem operation of the Deutsches Theater and the Kammerspiele in Berlin at the beginning of the century – between the large main stage and Intiman, the theater's small studio stage. On this intimate chamber stage in 1955, for example, he could present *Leah and Rachel*, the Vilhelm Moberg dramatization of the biblical story of the fertile and barren daughters of Laban (Gen. 29–30), with effective simplicity – on a sculpturally lighted circular platform accented only by a suggestive runic block of stone. Yet, earlier that same year, he was as fully prepared to offer his audiences a gracefully oriental *Teahouse of the August Moon* that was as commercially "authentic" (down to the real jeep on stage) as it was entertaining. While working on the Max Brod dramatization of Kafka's *The Castle* (Intiman 1953) he reached a last-moment decision to dispense with the intended stage design completely, and this production was eventually acted on an essentially bare stage finished only with the barest of necessities – a table, a bench, a pair of chairs, a bed. But, on the main stage a year later, he then treated his public to a spectacularly decorated and festively choreo-graphed rendering of Franz Lehár's *The Merry Widow* that called forth delighted critical comparisons with Reinhardt's legendary staging of *Die Fledermaus*. Examples of this flexibi-lity of approach could easily be multiplied. (It might be misleading, however, to overlook Bergman's own staunch preference for a more broadly based popular theater, illus-trated by a remark made just before he began rehearsals for *Cat on a Hot Tin Roof* in 1956: "It is more fun to work on the big stage, where one program can draw 100,000 spectactors. Of course there are plays that demand a chamber format, but I find it very difficult to feel much satisfaction in putting forty or fifty intensive rehearsals into a production that will play for only a couple of weeks to 200 people. And Intiman does not accommodate more than that."[19])

The principal point to bear in mind, however, is that no single method or sameness of style rules Bergman's work as a stage director. Nowhere is the adaptability of his creative method more evident than in the productions of his Strind-berg cycle, in which approaches to different plays – or even different productions of the same play – display such abun-dant variety. Hence when *Erik XIV*, Strindberg's study of the "characterless character" of that moody and indecisive Vasa monarch, reached the Malmö stage in 1956 as the third major Strindberg revival of Bergman's career, the result was once again boldly different in concept and technique from either *The Pelican* or *The Crown-Bride*. In this production, praised by many critics for its remarkable union of poetic power and formal restraint, the director took full advantage of the theater's imposing spatial potential from start to finish. Although Ebbe Linde commented in *Dagens Nyheter* that "what must have fascinated Ingmar Bergman were the possibi-lities of making something spectacular out of a text that has so often been regarded as virtually unplayable," it is essential to understand what constitutes "spectacularity" in this regard. A single massive vault spanned the full width of the stage in Per Falk's setting, and this fixed arch, combined with etchinglike projections on the cyclorama, communicated succinctly the drama's predominant mood of impending doom. No solid, ponderous physical apparatus was allowed to divert attention from the human character study that Bergman perceived as the true focus of this parable of destiny. Accordingly, the succession of seven specific, representational interiors and exteriors that the playwright describes in his stage directions was eliminated, and hence no revolving stage was needed to facilitate disruptively complicated changes of scene. Instead, large portions of the play were acted on the projecting forestage, where the magnificently costumed historical characters appeared against the simple background as "a multicolored gallery of Breughel-like figures" (*Sydsvenska Dagbladet Snällposten*).

At the core, then, of Bergman's highly stylized and physically simplified mise-en-scène was his emphasis on dynamic, swiftly changing compositions of colorful human figures. The focal point of these compositions was the intricately shaded and incisively analytical closeup of Erik created by Toivo Pawlo. The sharpness of the focus was accented and locked in place by the mute presence of a club-footed, hunchbacked court fool, whom Bergman introduced into the play to accompany the king as his ever-present mirror image, observing him and the world around him with silent but suggestive contempt. Pawlo's portrayal of Erik emphasized, with constantly accelerating force, the dangerous capriciousness of the king's moods, the ominous tension between humanity and inhumanity in his personality. His intense characterization built steadily toward the climactic moment of his abject humiliation, when his boycotted wedding banquet turns into a nightmarish orgy of rabble. In Bergman's hands this scene – which provided an interesting foretaste of the wildly grotesque surrealism of the goldmaker's banquet in his much later production of *To Damascus* – became a veritable danse macabre, led by a ghostlike band of black and plaster-white human marionettes whose ghastly figures supplied a mocking contrast to the splendid attire of the bewildered royal couple. Spectacular the production surely was at moments such as this – but it was, at the same time, forcefully simple and direct in its quest for an uncluttered illumination of the inner spirit of the work.

In this sense there is a steady gravitation in these early Strindberg productions, noticeable from *The Pelican* on, toward that strictly controlled, tightly focused form to which both Bergman and Strindberg have given the name "chamber play." Bergman the film maker has, as we know, applied this term to a number of his best-known works for the screen:

Through a Glass Darkly and *Winter Light, The Silence* and *Persona* I have called chamber plays. They are chamber music. That is, the pure cultivation of a certain number of themes for a strictly limited number of voices and figures. Backgrounds are abstracted. They are veiled in a kind of mist. One makes a distillation.[20]

This definition in turn calls to mind Strindberg's own explanation of a chamber play, in his *Open Letters to the Intimate Theatre*:

in this kind of drama we single out the significant and overriding theme, but treat it with moderation. In handling it we avoid all ostentation – all the calculated effects, the bravura roles, the solo numbers for the stars, and the cues for applause. The author rejects all predetermined forms because the theme determines the form.[21]

The broad features that align these two definitions – the distillation of a single unifying theme, its muted, unhistrionic expression in a compressed and fluid form, and the suppression of all distracting effects and disturbingly ostentatious backgrounds – are the very same preoccupations that tend to define the basic contours of most of Bergman's subsequent experiments with Strindberg.

THE GHOST SONATA: THREE PRODUCTIONS

In themselves, Bergman's three separate productions of *The Ghost Sonata*, the third and most demanding of the Chamber Plays, might be said to epitomize the changing nature of his continuous effort to evolve a dynamic theatrical style commensurate with the complexities of Strindberg's dramaturgy. His first *Sonata*, significant mainly for its historical rather than its artistic interest, was staged in Stockholm, in the tiny ninety-nine seat playhouse in Medborgarhuset that he had organized as a children's theater, in 1941. His intimately conceived and meticulously orchestrated production of the play at the Malmö City Theatre in 1954 was of a markedly different professional quality, and represents a notable milestone in his artistic development. Nearly two decades later, at the Royal Dramatic

Scene from *The Ghost Sonata*, the ghost supper, with *right*,
Benkt-Åke Benktsson as Hummel. Malmö, 1954.

Theatre in Stockholm in 1973, Bergman presented his favorite Strindberg play ("the most remarkable drama ever to be written in Swedish," he likes to call it) for a third time, in a memorable and controversial stage interpretation that has even enjoyed the distinction of having had an entire book written about it.²² Each of these three productions of *The Ghost Sonata* has been dependent on a very different set of human and physical circumstances, and each has reflected changes in the director's attitude toward his subject. At the core of that attitude, however, is a wonderfully lucid, antimelodramatic sensitivity to Strindberg in general and to this play in particular, perhaps best articulated in the remarks made by Bergman to his cast at the beginning of rehearsals for the Dramaten production in 1973:

> Everything in this production must be close to us, naked, simple. Simple costumes, hardly any makeup. The characters in the play are not monsters. They are human beings. And if some of them – the Cook, for instance – appear to be evil, it does not follow that they must look evil. The point is that they behave in an evil way toward the figures on the stage, and we must perceive the evil through the reactions of these figures. If we underrate the audience's ability to take note of reactions, we corrupt the theater.²³

Clearly, the long shadow that had been cast by the terrifying *Gespenstersonate* of Max Reinhardt and the magnificently grotesque performance of Paul Wegener as Hummel had vanished conclusively from the face of Strindberg's theater.

Extraordinarily enough, Bergman's intelligent amateur production of *The Ghost Sonata* in Medborgarhuset (September 21, 1941) evidently marked the first real revival of the play in Sweden since Reinhardt's touring performance of it startled Stockholm twenty-four years before. (Photographs of the event convey no hint whatever of Reinhardt, meanwhile, but bear instead a strong family resemblance to the old pictures of the simple, rather cramped productions of Strindberg's own Intima teatern, where the play had had its inauspicious premiere in 1908.) In a long program note written for the revival in Malmö (March 5, 1954), Bergman describes with infectious enthusiasm his earliest experiences with this key work. By the time he was twelve he had seized upon it avidly, with an eye to realizing its strange, hallucinatory images of "childhood terror" – "these suggestions that strike us, powerfully and disturbingly, far deeper than reason and analysis, this scenic music that has imparted to our theatrical feeling its basic features" – in his puppet theater. The inspiration to use the tiny stage of his children's theater in Medborgarhuset for an adult performance of the play was a bold one ("we were in fact a first harbinger of the later so popular cellar and attic theaters") but it met with only limited success and closed after four performances:

However, I recall how the fragile ensemble was lifted as though on a wave by the immensity of the drama, we found ourselves part of the theater as magic: to be cast beyond our own limitations, to be supported in our inadequacy and not dashed to pieces by it.

Then, continues Bergman in his program article, "came the great, totally shattering experience" – the first of Olof Molander's five major productions of the play, seen at Dramaten in October of 1942:

Probably never has a fledgling rooster choked on his own cock-crow as emphatically as I did that night, and during a dark and rainy walk in Djurgård Park I resolved to abandon the player's road and heed the wishes of my good parents – to continue my studies. What I experienced that night in the theater seemed to me absolute and unattainable. And it seems so still.

The eloquent tribute to the acknowledged master should not obscure the fact that Bergman was, by then, very much his own man, and that his Malmö production of *The Ghost Sonata* was far from a deliberate repetition of the Molander method – though most reviewers were more inclined to stress parallels than to discover differences. One exception was the Danish critic Svend Kragh-Jacobsen, whose review drew upon first-hand comparisons to the Molander production of the play at the Royal Theatre in Copenhagen in 1948:

Ingmar Bergman acknowledges his debt to Molander, but this new mise-en-scène possesses his own personal strength, his intensity, and a discipline that is impressive. The first and last acts are perhaps lacking just a bit in atmosphere, but the middle act – the core scene – has shattering power in the Malmö performance and is done with an imagination that at the same time subjugates the stage space and fills it, inspires the actors and drives them to their uttermost limits (*Berlingske Tidende*).

The point is well taken, for the ghastly, festering confines of the "ghost supper" – where (as Bengtsson, the valet explains)

A comparable scene from the Stockholm production of *The Ghost Sonata* in 1973. *Right,* Toivo Pawlo is Hummel, with Gertrud Fridh as the Mummy and Anders Ek as the Colonel. The figure of the Student can be glimpsed in the background. Dramaten.

the living dead "sound like a pack of rats in an attic" as they munch their biscuits and crackers in unison – provided an ideal field of play for Bergman's unique personal ability to stimulate his actors to the most intense and physically emphatic expression of scenic emotion.

In this scene of exhumation and psychic murder, all that is purely verbal in Strindberg found fiercely concrete physical articulation in Bergman's interpretation. Benkt-Åke Benktsson's voluminous Hummel was a "Big Daddy" of a vampire – "a colossus on light feet, a perverted Prospero, an evil God the Father," Ivar Harrie called him in *Expressen* – whose character was delineated in terms of sharply etched emotional peripeties. His muted, scheming tone in the first scene, as he sits in his wheelchair in front of the house, gave way to the overpowering cynical force with which he laid bare the hypocrisy and mendacity of the Colonel and his household – to be displaced in turn by tragic helplessness and terror as he is himself unmasked and destroyed by the Mummy, once his young love Amelia. "His powers were first unleashed in the second act," observed Kragh-Jacobsen: "the frightening, almost magical gleam that is suggested in his glance catches fire; his voice turns to thunder." Once he has systematically and conclusively drained the Colonel – Georg Årlin's "marionette on wooden parade" – of his property, his rank, and even the dignity of his title as father, the vampire himself falls victim to the vengeful fury of Naima Wifstrand's Mummy. No grotesque parrot-woman now, Wifstrand became the avenging dead who remorselessly settles accounts with Hummel, tears the mask from the face of this "stealer of souls," and sends him to die in the closet where she has sat for twenty years to atone for the past. "Her expression as he went, and his tottering along on crutches toward the background were shocking and fascinating – this was great acting, a brilliant dramatist's powerful scene executed so that every strand of meaning and dramatic action stood out," Kragh-Jacobsen declared – and most other reviewers concurred.

Yet, as Henrik Sjögren points out, even this unremittingly bleak climax was relieved, in Bergman's interpretation, by the lighter, conciliatory tone of the Mummy's thematically crucial speech about human compassion and atonement:

I can wipe out the past, and undo what is done. Not with bribes, not with hatred – but through suffering and repentance. We are poor miserable creatures, we know that. We have erred, we have transgressed, like all the rest. We are not what we seem to be. At bottom we are better than ourselves, since we abhor and detest our misdeeds.

This speech – accented in the Malmö performance "as a breathing space that pointed ahead toward the third act"[24] – provided a touchstone for the director's structural image of the play as a progression toward purification and redemption. In his subsequent revival at Dramaten, which in so many other respects differed radically from its predecessor, the Mummy's second-act speech continued to hold the key to his thinking

"But I can stop Time." Naima Wifstrand as the Mummy. Malmö, 1954.

about the work – to the extent that it even prompted him to assign the play's closing words of benediction and peace to the Mummy as well. During rehearsals for the Dramaten production, he commented: "In the end, I have stressed the fact that the only thing that can give man any kind of salvation – a secular one – is the grace and compassion that come out of himself."[25]

In technical terms, Bergman's approach to a key speech such as this is fascinating. His direction, Egil Törnqvist remarks in his rehearsal diary of the Dramaten performance, "suggests parallels with the work of both a conductor and a choreographer. Frequently he demonstrates how a speech can be broken up into shorter movements, each one with its own particular tone, so that the speech as a whole is molded into a word-melody, rich in psychological nuances. And on the stage he demonstrates, usually by applying his hands in various ways, the positions, gestures, and movement patterns of the actors."[26] A glance at the production script itself (in Törnqvist's scrupulous transcription) provides an excellent beat-by-beat illustration of just how the Bergman technique of detailed textual orchestration affects the speech we have been considering:

THE MUMMY (*frankly and seriously*): But *I* can stop time in its course. *I* can wipe out the past, (*looks at the Colonel*) undo what is done.
(*The Colonel, the Fiancée, and the Baron raise their eyes to the Mummy. The Mummy crosses to the clock, lays a hand on the dial. The ticking stops.*)
THE MUMMY: Not with bribes, not with hatred. But through suffering . . . and repentance.
(*The projection of a brickwall* [which had appeared earlier on Hummel's sarcastic lines about "this estimable house"] *dims.*)
(*The Mummy crosses down behind the Colonel, lays hold of him, looks at Hummel. The Colonel takes her hand.*)
THE MUMMY: We *are* poor miserable creatures, we know that. We *have* erred, we *have* transgressed, like all the rest. We *are* not what we seem to be. At bottom we are better than ourselves, since *we* abhor and detest our misdeeds. (*Crosses down behind Hummel. Fighting back tears, spitefully:*) But when you Jacob Hummel with your false name . . .
(*The Colonel, the Fiancée, and the Baron begin again to raise their heads.*)
THE MUMMY: . . . come here to sit in judgment, *that* proves that you are more contemptible . . .
(*The brickwall projection vanishes. The chairs in the round salon* [on which the actors in the scene are seated] *are lighted very strongly from the back and the front.*)

THE MUMMY: . . . than we are. And you . . . you . . . you are not the one you seem to be [. . .]²⁷

During rehearsals, Bergman provided an additional note that enlarges our sense of Hummel's physical reaction to the Mummy's coming assault in this sequence:

When Hummel, in his long speech, reveals the hidden crimes of everyone present, the audience must be able to feel how he grows and grows, like a frog blowing himself up, while the others keep shrinking. Then comes the counter-attack from the Mummy. She gives Hummel three pricks ["you . . . you . . . you"]. Now it is his turn to shrink. When he has just received the third prick, he thinks: all right, I can stand all this, just as long as you don't start talking about the Milkmaid I've murdered. At this point the Milkmaid appears. Produced by Hummel's anguish.²⁸

The lattice of dynamic human relationships into which Bergman translated Strindberg's text in this scene – for example, the obvious bond of tenderness and loyalty between the Mummy and the Colonel, the continuous, oscillating struggle

The assault of the Mummy on Hummel. Dramaten, 1973.

between Hummel and his victims, the role of the Mummy as both prosecutor and executioner – is conceived, here as always in his work, primarily as a concrete, physical pattern of movements and gestures. Inevitably, Elia Kazan's observation that directing "finally consists of turning Psychology into Behavior" comes to mind. One fundamental difference here, however, lies in the nature of the material itself: "Remember, we are not playing psychological theater, but something higher," Bergman told the cast at Dramaten. "The rhythm of the play is tremendously important. Here there are no connecting links, as in Ibsen's plays, which are much easier to act. Here you have to turn on a dime."[29] Nevertheless, the aggressiveness and sheer emotional vehemence that he injected into the ghost supper scene in the 1973 revival of the play might equally well have found a place in a performance of Williams or Albee – as indeed they did, in his own lacerating productions of these two playwrights at Dramaten during the 1960s.

The intense, Shylock-like Hummel of Toivo Pawlo was not the tottering, shattered giant that Benkt-Åke Benktsson had created twenty years before in Malmö. Strindberg's stage directions describe the old man in the black frock coat as basically passive, shriveled up "like a dying insect," once his past is brought to light. By contrast, Pawlo's image of Hummel was a poisonous pistachio-green spider who fought actively and desperately to the last, and who had literally to be dragged to his extermination by Johansson, the servant whom he had enslaved by blackmail. When the Mummy ordered him into the closet to hang himself, he attempted several steps without his crutches, fell, and then rolled sprawling on the floor in an effort to escape, uttering unintelligible noises all the while. Johansson, sensing his slavery at an end, leaped brutally on his struggling master, dragged him bodily into the closet and shut it. As the Mummy ordered Bengtsson – portrayed in this production as an old enemy of Hummel's – to place the death screen before the closet door and he then stepped ominously behind it, cold light filled the stage and the "normal" projection of a heavy, cluttered drawing room interior reappeared. A snapping sound was heard from the closet, followed by a death rattle; the Mummy, who opened the closet door and looked inside to be certain, spoke her lines to the others with quiet satisfaction: "It is finished. May God have mercy on his soul."

Hummel's destruction of the Colonel (Georg Årlin), who holds the paper disproving his right to his name. Malmö, 1954.

Ek and Pawlo in the same situation in 1973. The Colonel is stripped not only of his name, but also of his hair piece, his false moustache, and finally even his uniform.

Their "Amen" was not spoken in unison as the text prescribes, but was repeated in turn by the Colonel, the Fiancée, Bengtsson, and "very brightly" by the Baron: "It must not become too ritualistic," Bergman explained. When the final Amen was uttered, the sound of harp tones broke in as the Young Lady, seated in the background with Arkenholz, began to accompany the first of the Student's two recitations of the so-called Song of the Sun.[30]

What might seem like harsh usage of Hummel in this production was fully prepared for, however, by the excruciating sequence that Bergman composed to illustrate, in concrete terms, Hummel's brutal "unmasking" of the Colonel – played by Anders Ek in an almost caricatured parade-dress uniform of scarlet and gold braid – earlier in the scene. What is in the text a short, rather inert speech about stripping the pretentious Colonel naked became a starkly physical torture scene – "and the old man greatly enjoys prolonging the torture." Once again, a Törnqvist transcription of the production book affords a very illuminating illustration of Bergman's method of translating text into action:

HUMMEL (*leaps up, pushes the Colonel down on a chair which overturns, landing the Colonel on the floor*): Take off that hair of yours!
COLONEL (*on his knees, groans, and obeys*).
HUMMEL (*points*): Have a look at yourself in the mirror! Take out your false teeth while you're at it! Tear off that moustache! (*The Colonel obeys. Hummel thrusts him over to the left.*)
HUMMEL: Let Bengtsson (*slits up the Colonel's uniform so that a corset is exposed*) unlace your metal corset . . .
COLONEL (*closes his eyes*).
HUMMEL: . . . and then we shall see if a certain valet, Mr. XYZ, won't recognize himself! A valet who used to flirt with the maid in order to scrounge in a certain kitchen.
COLONEL (*takes hold of the bell on the table and rings*).
HUMMEL (*grasps the Colonel by the neck and pushes him so that he falls forward on the floor*): Don't touch that bell! If you call Bengtsson, I'll have him arrested! (*The clock strikes six.*)
HUMMEL (*standing over the Colonel with his crutch*): Here come the guests! [. . .][31]

At that point the terrorized and decimated officer crawled on his knees to the table, and began to replace his social mask – his wig, his glued-on moustache, his false teeth – before the eyes of the audience. Seldom has the critical commonplace "spiritual striptease" acquired such tangible reality in a theater. "When this overstuffed peacock with his center-parted wig, stupidly slack jaw, and a waxed moustache that resembles a question mark is stripped bare before our very eyes by Hummel, he is transformed into miserable, quivering human wreckage," declared Leif Zern in *Dagens Nyheter*.

It is not, of course, the macabre universe of the ghost supper in itself that constitutes the severest challenge to a director undertaking Strindberg's *Sonata*, but rather the requirement that the mood of this dark middle movement must be convincingly integrated into the overall melodic pattern of the composition. Allan Bergstrand observed, in conjunction with Bergman's Malmö production, that any director who attempts this play is in a sense faced with a basic choice: "whether to stage it, as Molander has done with all his Strindberg productions, in terms of naturalistic scenes into which mysticism and unreality are blended as completely natural elements – as they seem to be for all believers in spirits – or, instead, to opt for an undecorated expressionism in which characters appear out of or disappear into the darkness." Gunnar Ollén, who uses the observation in his well-known study of Strindberg, adds that Bergman chose "by and large a middle road" in his 1954 production[32] – a kind of conflation of Reinhardt's unadorned expressionism and that "fantastic realism" of Molander that moved in three deliberate tempi, from the dream-sharp everyday details of the first-act setting to a much more stylized milieu of heavy drapes in the second act and, finally, to a starkly simplified, symbolic hyacinth room in the last movement. By the time of the 1973 revival, however, the "middle road" had led Bergman far beyond the confines of either conventional expressionism or the traditions of the Molander style, to the adoption of his own highly expressive, interpretative mode of staging.

In none of Strindberg's later plays is there any hard and fast distinction between what is real and what is not – life, for Strindberg, *is* a dream, and hence the dream (the play) is life itself – not a conceptual comment on "the dreamlike nature" of reality but a projected image of a psychic dynamism, an exteriorization of *what it feels like* to experience existence in this way. As a result, Molander's most strenuous objection to Reinhardt's style was its failure to perceive and come to grips with Strindberg's view of life, and hence his own productions strove to reincorporate the razor-sharp fragments of observed (autobiographical) reality that are embedded in this playwright's vision. Thus, the "facade of a new house on a city square" that is described in such close detail at the beginning of *The Ghost Sonata* was identified by Molander as Karlaplan 10, the stately mahogany-and-marble entrance to the building in the Östermalm district of Stockholm in which Strindberg had resided (with an entrance at the much less patrician address of Karlavägen 40 "around the corner") following his marriage to Harriet Bosse in May of 1901.[33] His first production at Dramaten, which had impressed Bergman so profoundly in 1942, incorporated all the essential details and the characteristic sounds (church bells, horse-drawn carriages, steamship bells from the Nybrovik docks) of this turn-of-the-century Östermalm milieu. The impressionistic projection of the red building on Karlaplan might, remarked Herbert Grevenius in *Stockholms–Tidningen* (October 17, 1942), "at first seem like a color photograph, but there is a slight overexposure that quickly emerges with dreamlike clarity in the colors and contours."

It was with this potent visual treatment of the opening scene that Molander ultimately left his clearest "fingerprint" on his disciple's revival of *The Ghost Sonata* in Malmö. Bergman had once again reshaped the huge stage of the Malmö City Theatre to his own purpose – this time, by narrowing the proscenium opening to forty-six feet (from its usual seventy-two), reducing the seating capacity to a "mere" 1,100 (from the customary 1,700), and raising the stage and extending it out into the auditorium. He thereby succeeded in creating an unexpectedly intimate atmosphere in the vast theater. Behind the proscenium masking on either side of the stage, special light towers were erected to provide for sculptural backlighting of the actors and to facilitate the use of the projections on which Martin Ahlbom's scene design for the play depended. The first of these projections left no doubt about the Molander influence: "Not the walls of Karlaplan 10 – that would have been copying – but in any case a tautly realistic Östermalm prospect with banal doorway statues on guard outside the aristocratic residence, with the advertisement kiosk and drinking fountain, with Oscar's Church projected in the background, and with church chimes and steamship bells as atmospheric sound

Hummel and the Student (Folke Sundquist) at the advertisement kiosk. Malmö, 1954.

effects," wrote Per Erik Wahlund in *Svenska Dagbladet*. However, although there was nothing ostensibly abstract or
"strange" about the milieu into which the Student innocently
wanders, a distinctly hallucinatory, film-gray ambience was
created by the lighting and sustained by the eerie, puppetlike
movements of the peripheral characters. These individuals,
preoccupied with themselves and with life's trivial tasks,
seemed to move like ghostly marionettes about the large
gray-white house. As Hummel told the Student about the
unfortunate inhabitants of the Colonel's house "and they
appeared in their windows, nodding, laughing, watering
flowers," the critic for *Stockholms–Tidningen* felt himself faced
with "a perfectly staged marionette number: Hummel sits at
the outer edge of the stage as the coldly calculating director."

The focal character in *The Ghost Sonata* is, of course, Arkenholz, the clairvoyant student whose "progress" we follow from
his initial meeting with the scheming Hummel outside the
house to his final encounter with the Young Lady in the
symbolic hyacinth room. But in this dream play is the Student,
then, the Dreamer? Bergman's production of it in Malmö was
clearly conceived to suggest so, by dissociating Arkenholz
from the other characters in terms of tone, makeup, gesture,
and general appearance – although the concept caused its
share of critical confusion. The idea of the play as a dream was
reinforced by a curiously old-fashioned staging device. Behind
a neutral front curtain ("smooth and rat-gray like the human
consciousness just before sleep comes," thought Wahlund)
hung a transparent scrim that actually was kept in place
throughout the performance, "as a barely visible veil between
the stage reality and the auditorium." Swirling clouds of
"mind-mist" were projected on this curtain at the beginning
and between the acts, as a pedagogical reminder of the dream –
in emulation, it might almost seem, of the film maker's
custom-honored semiotic indicators for flashback and dissolve.

The basic concept of the play as the Student's dream did not,
however, fully succeed in welding the potentially anticlimactic
third act – the traditional stumbling block in most interpretations – to the rest of the play. "Life is terrible and we must
toil through it. But since it is at bottom only a nightmare,
dreamed in this case by the young student, the last human

being in a dying world, then there is redemption to be found beyond time and space," contended Nils Beyer in *Morgon–Tidningen*. Many of the critics took a different view of the conclusion, however. "The lyricism, the Buddhistic doctrine, and the beautiful words about a heaven that shall grow up from the earth are completely lacking in the dramatic bite that the damnation of the ghost supper in the Colonel's salon possesses," declared Kragh-Jacobsen in *Berlingske Tidende*. "It is finely conceived but it is dramatically pale – besides which it follows the bitterest of Strindberg's denunciations of life's most banal vexations." Deliberate paleness seemed in fact to dominate the setting – a severe white interior in elegant *Jugendstil*, furnished chiefly with strongly denotative object-symbols: a white harp (frozen music), a marble statue (petrified beauty), a slender white chair (loneliness), and the obligatory image of Buddha.[34] The complacent vision of Arnold Böcklin's Island of the Dead, which Strindberg's stage directions suggest as the final image following the death of the Young Lady, was banished by Bergman, who considers the painting "a hideous work of art" – perhaps not unexpectedly so, since a reproduction of it hung conspicuously in his childhood home in Uppsala. In his Malmö production, he chose instead to punctuate the play's progression toward purification and atonement with a more human – although perhaps no more dramatically logical – visual effect. In this final tableau, Folke Sundquist's Arkenholz drew aside the death screen once more, in order to take the Young Lady's head in his hands: "The light went down on the Student holding Gaby Stenberg's magnificent face in his lap," Ebbe Linde observed in *Dagens Nyheter* – and one of his colleagues even thought he caught a glimpse of a single ray of golden sunlight playing on the young' man's face.

It was clearly his own sense of dissatisfaction with this approach to the final act of *The Ghost Sonata* that animated the radically revised interpretation that Bergman presented at Dramaten almost twenty years later (January 13, 1973). The accomplishment of three basic objectives seemed to underlie this new approach: the forging of an organic relationship between the last act and the rest of the play; the articulation of a less artificially "symbolic" and hence more meaningful resolution to the last act, in line with the concept of "secular

Gertrud Fridh as the Mummy in the 1973 production. Beside her, the marble statue of her former youth.

salvation"; finally, the adoption of a far more simplified, actor-oriented approach to the production as a whole. The first two of these objectives are related to the specific play. The third point, however, is more general and is related to the radical change in Bergman's directorial outlook that first became evident in his famous open-stage production of Büchner's *Woyzeck* in 1969. A published rehearsal diary of that production makes it abundantly clear that Bergman himself saw it as a turning point. "We in the theater have always sought the best possible circumstances: in terms of staging, acoustics, audience," he told the *Woyzeck* cast at their first meeting:

That is precisely what we have contributed to year in and year out: a theater of circumstances. The time has come for us to skip all that, to be strong enough to compel the audience. We can do that if we are sufficiently convinced, if we perform with sufficient awareness.

All true actors . . . have magnetic power built in. They need only to reveal themselves on the stage for tension to be created. They themselves create the magic.

A busy director can destroy that magic in an instant with too much scenery, lighting, and so on. He can detheatricalize the actors.

The fantastic thing about theater is the communication between the audience's longing and the actors' urge to meet it.

I have myself previously preached theater of circumstances. But during the two years I have been away [following a critical failure with Molière's *The School for Wives* in November 1966] I have come to realize that this is a mistake. We must abandon that sort of thing if the theater is to survive.[35]

These principles had an immediate and startling practical effect on the style of Bergman's Strindberg productions at Dramaten during the 1970s – an effect that became apparent at once in the radically simplified, chamber-play adaptation of *A Dream Play* that he presented in 1970, and that was, if possible, even more pronounced in his revival of *The Ghost Sonata* three years later. In the latter case, the play was performed on a virtually bare stage that had to be stripped of every object and every item of scenery that might, in the director's opinion, "block the action or make it heavy." His designer, Marik Vos, devised a remarkable response to this challenge – a permanent, open acting-area enclosed in a semicircle by two towering, almost Craig-like screens, and flanked by low risers at the sides and a sloping platform at the back between the screens

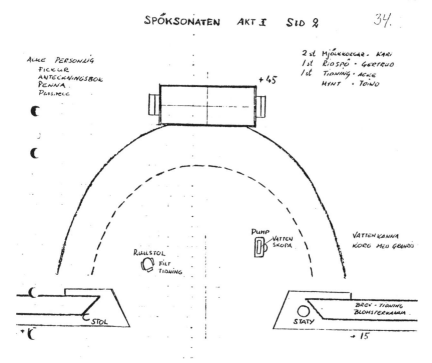

Figure 1 Floor plan, *The Ghost Sonata*, act 1.

(see Figs. 1–3). Two significant objects were positioned at either side of the proscenium, as suggestive physical reminders (not symbols) of key psychological impulses in Bergman's interpretation: an antique standing clock (Time, the passage of which the Mummy is able to halt in the second act), and the marble statue of a young and attractive woman (the Mummy as she once was in the past, just as she is in the present what the Young Lady, her daughter and alter ego, will eventually become). Other objects were used with extreme economy, and their rigorously symmetrical placement underlined the basic thematic relationship of one act to another.

Hence, in the first movement only Hummel's wheelchair and the street fountain at which the ghostly Milkmaid offers the Student a drink of water stood on the empty stage; in the last movement these were replaced, in precisely the same relative positions, by a chair in which the Student sits and the white harp and chair of the Young Lady. In turn, the arrange-

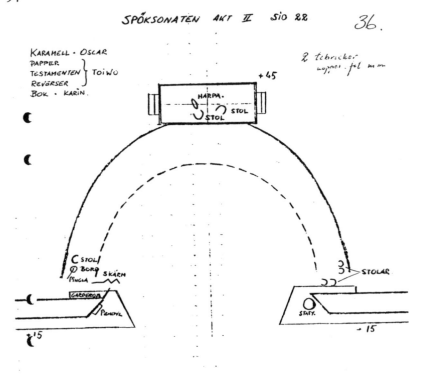

Figure 2 Floor plan, *The Ghost Sonata*, act 2.

ment of the hyacinth room in this act, with the slender white chairs and the harp occupying the foreground, presented a precise mirror image of the Colonel's salon, where heavy black chairs stood in a somber semicircle for the ghost supper. There, the audience had been able to see Arkenholz and the Young Lady seated on the raised platform at the rear of the stage. When the young couple's turn then came in the final movement, these positions were simply reversed and the room was shown, as it were, from the opposite angle: The audience could now see the funereal chairs of the Mummy and the Colonel on the platform in the background – and could draw its own conclusions about the interchangeability of roles in Strindberg's dream universe.

In general, human figure composition rather than inert scenery was the raw material of Bergmnan's directorial concept for this production of *The Ghost Sonata*: "The important thing

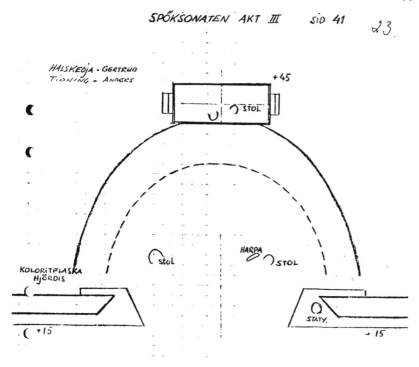

Figure 3 Floor plan, *The Ghost Sonata*, act 3.

is what happens to the bodies. No furnishings that over-shadow the action, nothing that stands around anywhere unless [it contributes to] a choreographic pattern that must be able to move with complete freedom in relation to space and scenery. Nothing must get in the way."[36] The ultimate success of this strategy is illustrated in the very observant description offered by the critic for *Göteborgs–Posten*, Åke Perlström: "The characters are at all times forcefully liberated from the setting. They stand close together on the forestage, and we perceive them in closeups. Stronger than this concentration can hardly become: Bergman has created a pressure from the stage toward the auditorium, eliminating all distance."

"Scenery," as such, was suggested entirely by means of lighting and projections on the two concave screens on the cyclorama visible beyond them in the background. (Originally, even the marble statue and the standing clock were conceived of by Bergman as projections only; ultimately, the tangible reality of these two properties was attenuated in a more unusual way, by means of projected shadows of palm fronds that played over them.) In the first act, the projections of an actual turn-of-the-century Stockholm house and church facade might at first glance have seemed yet another repetition of that familiar Molander trademark, Karlaplan 10. But Bergman's distinctively stylized, antinaturalistic approach to the play soon adjusted this impression. The *same* film-gray house facade projected on each of the mammoth thirty-foot screens evoked the half-real feeling of a dream. Moreover, during Hummel's descriptions of the blighted fates of the residents, both he and Arkenholz faced the audience continuously and located the imaginary house *in the auditorium* (where, at the same time, the audience continued to look at a distorted mirror image of the house behind the actors). Typically, Bergman explained this Pirandellian maneuver in purely practical terms – as a device to enable the spectator to see the faces and reactions of the actors, rather than just their backs. Just as typically, a number of critics were inclined to attach deeper significance to it as well: "We, the audience, are like the bogus colonel and the other inhabitants of the house – counterfeits with ugly secrets and a guilt-ridden past," proposed the reviewer for *Sydsvenska Dagbladet Snällposten*.

In general, the use of light and of projection techniques in this production reflected, perhaps more strikingly than many previous stage productions by him, the director's extraordinary sensitivity to the atmospheric properties and nuances of the photographic medium. Like the house and church in the first act, both the heavy, picture-cluttered salon interior projected for the ghost supper and the high, drapery-festooned windows that signified the hyacinth room in the last act displayed the same soft, dreamlike diffuseness of focus. One is reminded of Bergman's remark that "there is no art form – painting and poetry included – that can communicate the specifically oneiric quality of the dream the way the art of the film can."[33] Cinematic, too, were the fades and dissolves that were interpolated at intervals. At a crucial point in each of the three acts – when the Milkmaid whom Hummel has presumably drowned emerges (out of a trap in the stage floor) before him; when Hummel begins his denunciation of the household

Stage setting for the first scene of *The Ghost Sonata*, designed by
Marik Vos. Dramaten, 1973.

Setting for the third scene in the 1973 production of *The Ghost
Sonata*, with the brickwall projection seen on the high screens in the
background.

at the ghost supper; and when the Student in turn lashes out at the decay of the house and the Young Lady – the projection denoting place (street, round salon, hyacinth room) faded and was replaced by a purely connotative projection of a high, bare brickwall. The Student's remark about "the penal colony, madhouse and morgue of a world" acquired, in these moments, graphic substantiation. The implications of this recurrent and evocative image are fascinating, however, precisely because they are multiple and unattached to a simple, singular meaning. (At one stage, Bergman had evidently intended to project gradually withering hyacinths as an "illustration" of the hyacinth room; his excision of illustrative projection is characteristic of his resistance to overt, directly attached symbolism. Ultimately, only the bluish white lighting of the scene and the hyacinth blue of the Young Lady's costume were used to convey what Bergman perceived as "a sense that she has surrounded herself with a barrier of color and warmth and fragrance."[38])

As had been the case in the earlier Malmö production, projections were again used to sustain a hallucinatory, dreamlike atmosphere in the auditorium during the brief intervals that were needed for changes of scene and costume. In this instance, however, a much more abstract "snowfall" comprised of rising and falling dots of light projected on an opaque scene curtain took the place of the swirling "mind-mists" of the previous version. With regard to the identity of the dreamer of this dream play, however, a more fundamental change had occurred in Bergman's thinking. Although it is perfectly possible to identify the figure of the Poet in *A Dream Play* as Strindberg's alter ego and then proceed, as Bergman had done with success in his 1970 production, to present him as a connecting and controlling consciousness in the play, the character of the Student in *The Ghost Sonata* is not – as Bergman himself had now come to realize – particularly adaptable to this role of omniscient observer. "No, it is Strindberg himself who is the dreamer," he told his cast at Dramaten. "Notice the inward movement of the play, from the street to the round salon and finally to the hyacinth room. Strindberg takes us by the hand and leads us ever deeper into the dream."[39] A fleeting visual sign of this idea was the out-of-focus image of the elder Strindberg that materialized on the scene curtain between the second and third acts – almost a reminiscence of the crepe-hung portrait of Strindberg that had decorated the setting for *The Pelican* over thirty years before.

In itself, of course, a visual effect such as this would do little to accomplish what one takes to be the primary objective of this reinterpretation – namely, the forging of an organic relationship between the first two acts of the play and its potentially anticlimactic conclusion. The theatrical solution that Bergman offered to this dramaturgical problem was audacious and, to some minds, even extreme. As always in his work, however, his "solution" was designed to clarify emotional responses rather than to address abstract symbolic considerations; as such, it found expression first and foremost in a realignment of internal character relationships rather than in external visual or aural effects. "The fact that the Young Lady is slowly turning into another Mummy is a fundamental idea in my production," he is quoted as saying. "This is what is so horrifying in the whole situation."[40] To project this idea on the stage, he at first had intended to let the actors who played the Mummy and Hummel also take the parts of the Young Lady and the Student in the last act. Ultimately, only the female half of this astonishing twinning operation was put into practice, and the brilliant and versatile Gertrud Fridh (helped by a nonspeaking stand-in as needed) assumed the exceedingly demanding double role of the mother and daughter – the Mummy of the middle act thus became the Young Lady of the first and last movements. Mathias Henrikson's Arkenholz was also provided with enough facial resemblance to the Hummel of Toivo Pawlo (beard, moustache, even eyeglasses in common) to suggest the director's view that the Student was in reality a Hummel in embryo: "He is no longer the pure-hearted young man who dashes on the stage in the beginning. In that he has taken Hummel's hand, he is initiated."[41]

These role realignments brought about in turn a full-scale reassessment of the basic tone and the emotional configurations of the difficult final movement of the sonata. "In the third act, Bergman believes, we are led into the deepest part of the dream, the infantile, where all normal proportions have ceased to operate," declared the reviewer for *Svenska Dagbladet*. "The intense aspirations and the everyday torments of human life are here compressed into a single scene of exorcism, supplication, damnation, lamentation, and lyricism." Perlström's fine analysis in *Göteborgs-Posten* came straight to the emotional point of the Mummy's transmutation: "She returns again in the third act, the same person trapped in the daughter's destiny, to become a new sacrificial victim. The Student, the young hero of the first acts, cannot help her, on the contrary he drives her to her death with his absolute demands. He has in fact taken on the role of Hummel, and the Colonel reaches out toward his dead daughter as someone might stretch out a hand to a drowning man."

At the very core of Bergman's remarkable paraphrase is a statement that he made to his cast at an early rehearsal:

And this we must bear in mind continually, that the Student kills the Young Lady. And this is an unpleasant and terrifying scene of unmasking and murder. It corresponds to the unmasking of Hummel by the Mummy in the second act, but here it is enormously much more freed of every shred of reality . . . Here it is only with ugly words that he touches her, he makes violent gestures toward her, doesn't he, he seizes hold of her, he tears off her clothing. And this kills her.[42]

"That 'doesn't he' is truly disarming," the eminent Strindberg scholar Gunnar Brandell later declared. "Not many would in reality go along with the validity of this interpretation, yet no one in Bergman's ensemble seems to have registered a divergent opinion." Brandell goes on to make a lucid intellectual case for the "traditional" interpretation of the Young Lady's death: in addition to the Hummels of this world, there are in Strindberg also "human beings of a more delicate fibre, who never have been able to harden themselves to live, to withstand the truth of life. This is the Young Lady's situation, and her death in the third part is intended as a liberation, a wandering into the Böcklin picture toward a nothingness that is worth far more than blood, dirt, and tears." The Student, the Sunday child, is "the wanderer, perhaps the poet, standing halfway outside as so many figures in Strindberg do, with traces of the Good Samaritan and perhaps even of Christ." He does not join the living dead nor does he die at all, because "he is essentially just a student on a field trip to 'this penal colony, madhouse and morgue of a world.'"[43]

Bergman's radically divergent and very much harsher stage interpretation of these characters and this scene should not, however, be misconstrued as deliberate critical "revision" of some established view of literary scholars – indeed, the fundamental irrelevancy of such a view to the purely practical concerns of the director is the essence of his adamant objection that "absolute word fidelity is trumpery in the theater. The text is not a prescription but raw material, a frequently hidden path into the writer's consciousness."[44] Rather, he must make choices that can help to articulate, in theatrical terms, the basic thematic transitions in this scene, from the tenderness of the hyacinth poetry to the bitterness of the household concerns introduced by the Cook and back to the tenderness of the final benediction. The path that he charted for the actors was signposted by the simple active verbs (touches her, gestures toward her, seizes her, strips her, kills her) that are the most striking feature of the particular directorial comment cited previously and of his instructional method in general.

An intricate rhythmic pattern of movement, gesture, intonation, and tempo changes – supported by suggestive changes in the lighting and the projections – rendered transparent the moment-by-moment process of gradual "mummification" in Gertrud Fridh's performance. "She develops backwards," observed Zern in *Dagens Nyheter*: "the role of the mother is taken over by her step by step in a process that the actress reproduces with alarming precision." A vocabularly of expressively repetitive gestures was devised to reinforce the growing resemblance of the Young Lady to her grotesque parrot-parent. When she had to answer a question, for example, Fridh thrust her head out in front of her shoulders, while her hands fluttered helplessly up under her chin. At other times, her fingertips were seen pressed against her forehead as her hands covered her face – a movement, one critic thought, "in which the full impression of a sleepwalker on the verge of the fatal awakening is concentrated" (*Göteborgs Handels – och Sjöfartstidning*).

The apppearance of the monstrous Cook, who "belongs to the Hummel family of vampires" and cannot be dismissed, touched off the final disintegration:

YOUNG LADY (*grabs hold of the Student*): Don't be angry . . . Practice patience. She's part of the trials we have to endure in this house. (*with slight "mummy intonation" and parrot gestures*) But we have a housemaid, too. Whom we have to clean up after.

THE STUDENT: I can feel myself sinking. *Cor in aethere.* *(sits)* Music!
YOUNG LADY *(covers her face with her hands)*:   Wait!
THE STUDENT *(passionately, desperately)*:   Music!
YOUNG LADY *(takes her hands down)*:   Patience . . . *(matter-of-factly)*
This room is called the testing room. It's beautiful to look at, but it's
full of imperfections.[45]

As the desperation of the Student and the defensive "mummy" reactions of the Young Lady grew more emphatic, a cold, harsh light began to dominate the forestage. The long monologue with which Arkenholz "murders" Adele began as a purely verbal threat, made menacing by his alternating moves of approach and withdrawal. The image of the naked brickwall that replaced the hyacinth room interior on the screens was a direct visual response to the Student's bitter description of the madhouse where his father died for truth – but it also carried broader connotations in Bergman's concept: "The Student and the Young Lady," he explained, "are now in the same prison in which the others have lived all their lives, those who have deformed them. They are locked together in a kind of hell, and it is not until she dies that the air and light return."[46]

The brickwall projection, silently proclaiming the prison-house in which the young couple found themselves, signaled an emotional change in the Student's monologue, which now acquired a new tone of increased aggressiveness: "If you keep silent too long, stagnant water accumulates and things begin to rot. That's what's happening in this house." His struggle to regain the air and the light became more physical and more overtly violent – while, on the platform in the background, the Colonel and the Mummy (i.e., Fridh's stand-in) began, for the first time, to take notice of the events occurring in front of them in the hyacinth room. The Student's implied sexual challenge to the Young Lady – "speaking of which, where can one find virginity?" – marked another important transition. It was given graphic and savage physical expression by Arkenholz, who brutally spread her thighs and thrust his hand between her legs. In Bergman's dynamic orchestration, the monologue reached an explosive climax on the key line that follows the Student's futile attempt to coax music from the Lady's mute, deaf harp: "To think that the most beautiful flowers are so poisonous. They are the most poisonous." At this juncture, in a paroxysm of anger and frustration, he dragged his adversary forcibly to the front of the stage; as she sank to her knees in anguish, her hyacinth blue dress tore loose and fell from her in tatters. Beneath it, she wore a ragged and soiled undergarment of grayish white – virtually a mummy's winding sheet – streaked with red down the sides and in the outlines of the crotch.

Unmasked and literally put to death by the lacerating truth that the Student has compelled her to face ("There are poisons that seal the eyes and poisons that open them"), the Young Lady calls for the death screen – and at this moment in Bergman's version the wall projection vanished, leaving an empty background bathed in the soft, mild light of liberation (the equivalent of Strindberg's problematic direction that "the room vanishes"). In view of the conception of the Student as the Young Lady's "murderer," he was poorly suited to be the speaker of the closing lines of consolation to her – and one of the director's most interesting moves in this production was to divide these concluding lines between the Colonel and the Mummy. The Colonel, who had undergone a startling change from the stylish, red-uniformed martinet of the second act to a Beckettian old man in a worn gray bathrobe and slippers, delivered the first portion of the Student's speech, "Your liberator is coming – welcome, pale and gentle one," as he gently and affectionately covered Adele with the screen. All religious references were now excised from this moment of purely secular salvation, however, and the only Buddhistic intimation was created by such suggestions as the old man's humble sitting position on the stage floor and by his mild tone of resignation. The Song of the Sun was again spoken by the Student, but the poem's tone of optimistic affirmation was now deliberately undercut by Mathias Henrikson's reading of it, reflecting Bergman's own conviction that the poem is ultimately "nonsense" for a modern audience: "If the Student reads the poem with a skeptical tone the second time he recites it and recognizes that it turns to dust, then it seems to me meaningful . . . Every second comment in that verse seems dubious. And especially after Strindberg himself gives a brilliant demonstration of man's gruesomeness and madness, I think it is quite right that the Student reaches this conclusion."[47] Unlike the production in Malmö, no touching tableau was struck and no ray of sunlight played on Arkenholz's face.

After finishing his recital, he repeated the last word of the poem, "innocent," with utter disbelief in his voice – and then simply walked away into the darkness.

In this version, Strindberg's final words of consolation were spoken instead by the Mummy, and the effect thus created became one of the most arresting moments in this remarkable production. Concealed by the death screen, from behind which an outstretched female arm protruded, Gertrud Fridh exchanged places with her stand-in and was able to resume her Mummy costume during the delivery of the Song of the Sun (certainly one good reason for retaining this troublesome speech). Just as Arkenholz concluded his poem, the Mummy entered and slowly removed the death screen to reveal the prostrate form of the "Young Lady." As harp music sounded from an unseen Toten Insel, she then spoke the concluding lines of benediction over "this child of the world of disappointments, guilt, suffering, and death" – in essence, a benediction over the corpse of her own former self. "The third act no longer appears as a romantic appendage to the first two acts," Zern declared in his review. Rather, the harsh and bitter tone of the ghost supper reasserted itself "according to the eternal law of repetition," thereby reshaping the play "into a whole in which everything is accomplished with remorseless dramatic logic."

The savage emotional vehemence of the Student's psychic and sexual assault on the Young Lady in this final scene can best be likened to Jean's brutal humiliation of Julie in Bergman's more recent productions of *Miss Julie*. After presenting this play for the first time at the Residenztheater in Munich in 1981, he returned to it on several subsequent occasions, each time with a different actress in the title role. While each new approach yielded its share of subtle differences in shading and tone, however, his ruling conception of Strindberg's modern tragedy and its doomed protagonist remained basically unchanged. Staged in an unexpectedly naturalistic setting reminiscent of Alf Sjöberg's famous old film of the play, Bergman's *Julie* employed a cool, camera-sharp exactness of detail to create a magic realism – a distillation of reality, as it were, constantly perforated by an introspective, dreamlike tone that became steadily more insistent as Julie's ordeal continued, until at last it completely suffused her long, exhausted revelations about her ingrained family heritage of sexual strife and man-hatred.[48] Her destruction at the hands of the "real" world of Jean and Christine thus became a gradual process of growing disillusionment and revulsion on her part, orchestrated by Bergman much as a conductor would orchestrate a musical score. As he and his actors rendered this text (more effectively in the Munich production than in the somewhat less precise Swedish restagings of 1985 and 1991), a distinctly musical rhythm governed its emotional design – a rhythm built upon deliberately sustained phrasing, lighter and more acute stages of dissonance, beats of rest, changes of tempo, and what can only be described as monologue-arias. As a result, a form of progression emerged that was associational and expressive rather strictly literal or sequential. Scenes

Jean (Michael Degen) quarrels with Christine (Gundi Ellert) as Julie (Anne-Marie Kuster) sits exhausted at the table in the Munich production of *Miss Julie*, 1981.

of explicit and often violent reality were thus infused with an atmosphere of unreality and dream – one in which Christine's kitchen-world was transformed, for Julie, into a prison-world of the spirit in which she must act out a dreamlike and hopeless struggle to exist. Rarely, if ever, has the dreamplay texture inherent in Strindberg's "naturalistic tragedy" been revealed in the theater with such unexpected clarity.

DREAM PLAYS

Ultimately, it has been the inspiration of *A Dream Play* itself which has exerted the profoundest influence on Bergman's search for a performance style for Strindberg. In the first and freest of his three stage productions of this difficult masterpiece (March 14, 1970), nearly all of the philosophical and mystical elements in it were either omitted or transposed. In a performance in which stage settings as such played no part at all, the fifteen scenes into which this reconstituted but poetically faithful version was divided established a swiftly paced rhythm of juxtaposed images and contrasting moods, uninterrupted by the distraction of an intermission. "There are remarkably few extraneous elements in it, no convulsions, no exertion – all that seems to have been left behind," Zern declared in *Dagens Nyheter* following the premiere at Lilla scenen, Dramaten's 350-seat studio theater. "In itself this represents an essential part of Bergman's method. He has produced an adaptation of the play that is in part quite radical, in part extremely cautious. But in both cases it is a matter of changes that find their basis in the text."

In its style and method *The Dreamplay* (as Bergman chose to retitle his new stage version) represented an astonishing departure from virtually everything that had gone before – including his own television production of the play in 1963, which he now considers a comparative failure. The traditional identification of the Dreamer, in all three of his voices (Officer, Lawyer, and Poet), with Strindberg himself was abandoned, as were all the elaborate visual effects and atmospheric back projections that had by now become fixed conventions of the Molander school. "No castle burns on the stage, no rhetoric flames in the dialogue," Bo Strömstedt wrote in *Expressen*.

"Nor is it a biographical Strindberg Show in Molander fashion. Some wear masks in this production – but no one wears a Strindberg mask." Within the stark and utterly simple physical framework devised for the production, no attempt whatsoever was made to reproduce, in literal terms, the many different localities and spectacular stage effects called for in Strindberg's complicated stage directions. Instead, observed Åke Perlström in *Göteborgs–Posten*, "the only thing we see – and hear – are the actors, who create the illusion that all these places are there on the stage. It is a brilliantly executed activation of the audience that we experience." The end result of this dematerialized, actor-oriented approach was, as Per Erik Wahlund remarked in *Kvällsposten*, to give the text a primacy "it seldom can acquire in more monumental productions; anyone who truly wants to listen to what is being said in the play has a unique opportunity here."

A closely knit ensemble of twenty-four performers, who had been in rehearsal – as is often Bergman's custom – for more than three months,[49] played the forty-three different characters identified in this version. All but nine principal actors took on two or, in a few cases, even three roles apiece. As the performance began, the entire acting company – including five extras and even the prompter for the production – were summoned to the gray-black, curtainless stage, which stood furnished with only a scattering of plain wooden chairs, a few screens, and a single table (see Figs. 4, 5). One by one, the actors emerged in twin streams from the circular (under normal circumstances backstage) staircases located at either side of the playing area, and, moving to lively waltz music from a barrel organ, they flooded the stage in a carefully choreographed but apparently random pattern (Fig. 6). A few busied themselves rearranging bits of scenery; meanwhile, the Poet (the fourth figure to emerge from the staircase stage right, numbered 20 in the diagram) moved to the table at the center of the stage, where he drew up a chair and seated himself with his back to the audience. Then, once the prompter and the black-masked Quarantine Master (numbered 10 and 11) had reached their positions, the company joined to form a ring. Slowly the characters circled before the gaze (in the consciousness?) of the meditating Poet seated at his desk. "A metaphysical picture of mankind's shadowy wandering in the

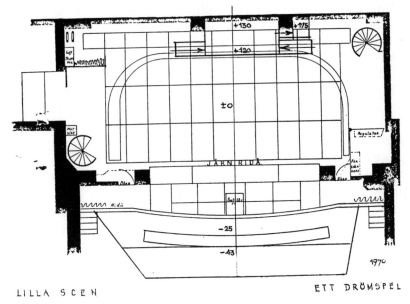

LILLA SCEN

ETT DRÖMSPEL

Figure 4 Plan of the stage (Lilla scenen), *A Dream Play*.

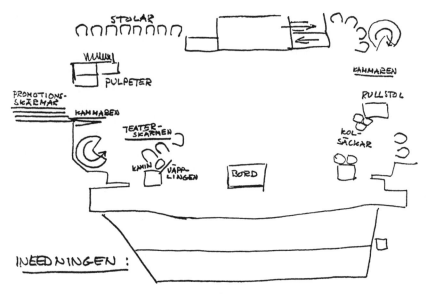

Figure 5 Floor plan, *A Dream Play*.

wilderness" was the description that *Svenska Dagbladet* applied to this evocative image.

After fifteen seconds, in the midst of a step, the rotating circle of dream figures suddenly froze in position. Quietly, the Poet read to them the six simple lines of verse that were to set the tone for all that followed in Bergman's *Dreamplay* – familiar lines that belong in the original to Indra's Daughter in the second of the scenes in Fingal's Cave:

> The earth is not clean.
> Life is not good.
> Men are not evil.
> Nor are they good.
> They live as they can,
> One day at a time.[50]

The reading of the verse dissolved the magical circle. Some of the figures disappeared once more down the circular staircases, but the majority simply took seats all around the periphery of the action (Fig. 7) – where they became both characters waiting to be called into being by their creator and actors awaiting their entrances. Agnes, the earthly counterpart of Indra's Daughter, and the Glazier sat silently in a corner,

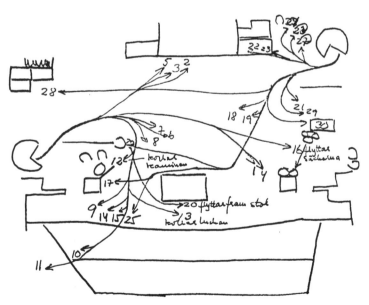

Figure 6 The entrance of the actors in *A Dream Play*.

eating. In a whisper, like a prompter feeding an actor his cue, the Poet spoke again – "Agnes, the castle is still rising from the earth" – and only then did the characters in the opening scene achieve speech and dramatic life, as Agnes, looking about her, began to discuss the Growing Castle and the prisoner who waited there for his release.

In a graphic but unpretentious manner, this opening sequence established the metaphor of deliberate theatricality that governed Bergman's production from its beginning to its end. His *Dreamplay* was anchored firmly in a world of theater that became, in turn, a *theatrum mundi*, a poetic and deeply ironic image of the world we live in. The austere and eminently flexible stage setting designed by Lennart Mörk was, in effect, hardly a stage setting at all. The playing area was opened to the full width of the building, and the bare fire walls and rows of projectors were as fully exposed to view as the players themselves. Any separation between actor and specta-

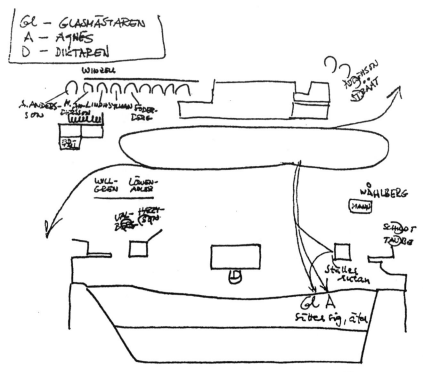

Figure 7 Taking positions for the first scene of *A Dream Play*.

tor was obliterated completely by eliminating the dividing line of the proscenium and extending the floor of the stage out over the first rows of seats. The single, fixed point of focus in the setting – that indispensable "magnetic point of energy" around which Bergman customarily plans all his moves in a particular mise-en-scène – was in this instance obviously the simple table placed at the front of the stage, squarely in the middle of the proscenium opening. Around the Poet's table – beneath which he occasionally crept to eavesdrop on "his" characters – most of the scenes in the play were arranged. "Time and place do not exist," writes Strindberg in his foreword. In this production the places themselves – the theater corridor, the cathedral where the degree ceremony is held, the Lawyer's suffocating chamber, even the enigmatic cloverleaf door itself – were always represented in the simplest possible manner, by means of rudimentary, rehearsal-type screens that could be easily put in place and as easily removed. A small platform at the rear of the stage was its only elevation, and behind this one glimpsed a large red, nonfigurative design that contributed the one patch of color in an otherwise gray-black void. (Mörk's tantalizing optical rebus led to a desperate guessing game among the critics, who professed to discover in it a picture of everything from "the burning castle of the dream" or "the human circulatory system" to "flickering flames from the earth's interior" or, in the case of one especially lively imagination, even "the inside of the eyelid as we see it when we doze off, when we dream.")

"All this with a curtain, blackouts, illusion – this is a profound depravity in the theater," Bergman had declared during the rehearsals for *Woyzeck*,[51] and that production, with its circus-ring staging, its commitment to intense audience contact, and its use of boldly anti-illusionistic scene changes, clearly foreshadowed the theatricalist approach adopted by him in *The Dreamplay* only one year later. Most observers agreed, however, that his newest Strindberg production represented a significant turning point and achieved a completely new level of emotional communication, less stridently expressionistic and hallucinatory than in *Woyzeck* and far more firmly and concretely human. "There is a proximity here to the characters and to their world, an unmitigated sensitivity to them that Bergman never abandons, even when he depicts

their darkest aspects, their torments and their pitfalls,"
remarked Leif Zern.

In this lucid, down-to-earth interpretation of the play as an
unadorned depiction of the human condition – of human
beings like ourselves "who live as they can, one day at a time"
– the divine presence of an omniscient Indra and his Daughter
inevitably became a sublimely absurd poetic irrelevancy. The
metaphysical apparatus of Eastern mysticism in the play –
itself an afterthought on Strindberg's part – was largely abandoned, but what remained of it became a deeply ironic
comment on the spectacle of human sorrow and suffering,
rather than merely a convenient "explanation" of it. Taking up
the playwright's own reminder that "the characters split,
double, and multiply" in this drama, Bergman elected to
divide the composite character of Indra's Daughter into two
distinct and independent roles. The utterly vulnerable Agnes,
played by the young Malin Ek with poignant openness and
clarity, was wholly and defenselessly human, stripped of the

Only simple rehearsal-type screens and a few pieces of furniture are
used to suggest the Lawyer's suffocating chamber in *A Dream Play*
in 1970. Kristin ("I'm pasting") peers over the top of the screen.

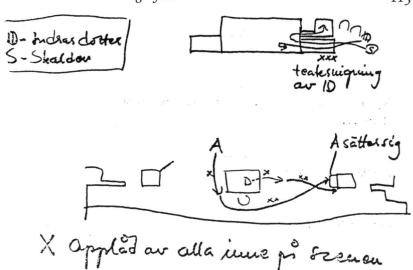

Figure 8 The entrance of Indra's Daughter in the third scene of *A Dream Play*.

divine power to reascend from earth that renders the Daughter's suffering so much more equivocal in the original. By contrast, the stately and dignified portrayal of the Daughter – the divine half of the equation – created by Kristina Adolphson emphasized the aloofness of that shadowy deity. She and Indra (renamed the Scald here) remained, throughout the play, remote presences from a rhapsodic, scaldic world of fantasy that existed, perhaps, only in the Poet's vivid imagination.

Ironically, Bergman chose not to eliminate the expository prologue in heaven – as Molander, for example, had done in his final production of the work five years before. Instead, his purpose was perfectly served by abruptly interjecting this scene (slightly cut and rearranged) into the midst of the ongoing action, just before the episode in the Theater Corridor, as a bit of theater-in-the-theater. "Yes, life is hard, but love conquers all. Come and see!" the bewildered Agnes is told by the Poet (who borrowed these lines from the dialogue of Indra's Daughter). Then, as these two sat to one side, Indra and his Daughter rose from their chairs in the background and, in full view, mounted the raised platform-stage at the rear, accompanied by the sound of polite applause from the other characters (Fig. 8). Mörk's enigmatic red pattern glowed obediently. A gushy romantic adagio was played on an old piano.[52] At the end of the prologue scene, when Indra had completed his imperious brief of instructions to his Daughter ("Have courage, child, 'tis but a trial"), she sank to her knees ("I'm falling!"). A moment later, as the divinities left their platform and retired to other seats in the background, a swirl of players again filled the stage (see Fig. 9) and the action continued without interruption. The appearance of the Bill-Poster with his placards and his green fishing net, the Prompter carrying a piece of scenery, and the Stage-Door Keeper with her unfinished star coverlet and her heavy shawl of sorrows[53] proclaimed the beginning of the Theater Corridor scene. And here, the tragicomic spectacle of the Officer (Holger Löwenadler), waiting patiently for Victoria with his bouquet of withered roses, became a hieroglyph of human disappointment and self-deception that gave the lie to all the spurious metaphysical consolation of Indra's divine design. "The entire Indra phenomenon is transformed by Ingmar Bergman into the supreme theatrical gesture," declared *Svenska Dagbladet*. "But perhaps Bergman feels that Indra's Daughter is no more than the dream of someone who knew that Indra never had a daughter, and that Agnes is in reality something quite different: the mortal woman, imperturbable in her endurance and her humanity."

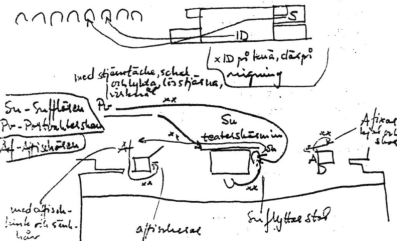

Figure 9 Taking positions for the Theater Corridor episode in the fourth scene of *A Dream Play*.

Specifically, Indra's Daughter seemed the Poet's dream in this production. Her later appearances at the close of the play were likewise removed from the reality of the situation and remained expressions of the Poet's creative imagination. Seated at his table, he began to read aloud the strophes on poetry, dream, and reality in the Fingal's Cave scene, and alone his reading called forth the Daughter's responses and her presence – although no "soft music" accompanied their recitation, no rolling billows were seen or heard and no leisurely discussion of "life's unsolved riddle" was allowed to interrupt the insistent flow of the drama toward its conclusion.

In this respect and in others, the greatly expanded role of the Poet – played with effectively restrained intensity by Georg Årlin – replaced the figure of Indra's Daughter as the controlling consciousness in the work. His was the only character to be given a function more important than that in the Strindberg text. He was present throughout but seemed more often to be a detached observer wandering through the proceedings than a participant deeply engaged in them. At times, he appeared to listen to the conversation of the characters as if to a play that he himself might have written. And he, rather than the Officer, became Agnes' guide for the brief, dazzling white glimpse of the "paradise" of Fairhaven that was, in this production, instantly shattered by a bombardment of harsh, visually concrete realities: the palpable dirt and poverty of the Coal-Carriers, the misery of ugly Edith, the pathetic plight of the Blind Man (acted by Hans Strååt, who also played Indra) who possesses everything except his sight, and finally the relentless drudgery of domestic life, which Agnes – deprived here of the comforting ability to "return to the place from which [she] came" – is condemned to resume.

Perhaps the best single illustration of the ironic tone and highly theatricalized style of Bergman's conception is his treatment of the Degree Ceremony in the Cathedral. This remarkable pantomimic tour de force was singled out by virtually every reviewer of the production as one of its most expressive moments. All traces of the grandiose formal trappings that had traditionally encumbered this scene were systematically eliminated, so that only a stark, forceful dream image of the sensation of human humiliation remained. Chopin's Funeral March – the favorite musical choice of

The appearance of Indra and his Daughter in Bergman's reinterpretation of *A Dream Play*. Dramaten, 1970.

The Officer, Agnes and the Stage-Door Keeper in the Theater Corridor scene from *A Dream Play*. The cloverleaf door, represented by a free-standing screen, is visible behind the Officer.

Molander for this episode – was turned into a rowdy academic fanfare for the occasion. The "cathedral" itself was indicated by the simplest of devices – a contorted tableau of human figures was composed on the Poet's table to suggest an altar painting of the crucified Christ, arms outstretched and head bowed beneath a crown of thorns. Behind this Crucifixion tableau, shadowy figures crept forward with long black screens – the pews of the church – from behind which they watched. The academic procession, too, had the distorted proportions of a dream. The standardbearers of the four faculties were tiny minischolars, played by children, wearing formal attire and student caps, while a dignified gnome assisted the Chancellor in his duty of conferring laurel wreaths on the doctoral candidates. Entering this bizarre scene, the Lawyer (Allan Edwall and, later in the run, Max von Sydow) found himself literally trapped in a nightmarishly logical Chaplinade from which he could not extricate himself. This "terribly ugly, unsuccessful, embittered character in an old tailcoat, shiny with use, that hangs around his shoulders" (Zern) stumbled onto the stage, bowed to the assembly – and then discovered

A comparable scene from the Munich production of *A Dream Play* at the Residenztheater in 1977.

that he was still wearing his galoshes. Desperately, he tried to unbuckle and remove them – only to be assaulted by the foul smell of his wretched old coat, heavy as all his clothes are with "the stink of other men's crimes." Quickly the sniffing spread; soon everyone present was holding his nose. In his mortification the Lawyer then tried to remove the offending coat – with the result that his trousers fell down, and he was reduced to the ultimate indignity of hopping about, unable to pull them up again. All the other candidates were crowned with laurel; the Schoolmaster even did an ecstatic war dance of joy. Only the humiliated advocate was turned away and obliged to rest content with a more "appropriate" crown – the crown of thorns, which Agnes took from the crucified Christ in the tableau and placed upon his head. One final ironic pirouette punctuated the scene. After the crown of thorns had been cast aside, the Poet strolled forward from the background, picked it up and tried it on for size before a mirror (the audience!), cocked it at a rakish angle, like a *chapeau claque*, and strolled away.

The play concluded – in a scene Bergman entitled "Many Persons become Visible" – as it had begun, with the assembling of the characters around the Poet's table. Each one brought forward his or her emblem of suffering to be burnt – the Stage-Door Keeper's shawl, the Officer's roses, the Glazier's diamond, the black mask that made the Quarantine Master "a blackamoor against his will" (but beneath which his face turned out to be just as black as ever). "Instead of casting their masks or their symbols into the fire," observed Wahlund in *Kvällsposten*, "the figures stepped forward one by one to the poet's desk and laid them there. The play has ended, the vision has vanished, and the characters who searched for their author can wander back into the darkness." Once again, the Poet's concluding lines – spoken by Årlin "with moving restraint, as a confidential message directed straight to the audience" – were "borrowed" from the dialogue of Indra's Daughter:

> In the moment of goodbye,
> When one must be parted from a friend, a place,
> How suddenly great the loss of what one loved,
> Regret for what one shattered . . .

"He steps forward to the edge of the stage, all the others gather around him, as he contemplatively and quietly speaks of parting and of the process of living," wrote the Norwegian reviewer for *Dagbladet* (Oslo). "Because all ornamentation has been eliminated, the words, the actor's voice, and the faces – so far forward on the stage that they appear as close-ups – succeed in engraving the Poet's visions upon each spectator's imagination."

Silently, the actors left the stage. The spotlight on the Poet's table was extinguished. The final image was certainly no symbolic depiction of a flowering castle of redemption and deliverance, but simply a glimpse of Agnes, the woman who had taken upon herself all of mankind's suffering in her heavy gray shawl, still seated alone on the empty stage, her hand pressed convulsively to her face in speechless anxiety.

When Bergman returned to *A Dream Play*, for the fourth time, in his 1986 production at Dramaten, his conception of it as thematically structured "chamber music" was firmer than ever. This time, however, looking back on his stripped 1970 version as too "pure" and "dogmatic," he had made up his mind to try to perform the play virtually uncut. Conceived in the same intimate and rather primitive surroundings of Lilla scenen, this revival successfully avoided the monumentality and solidity of design that had worked against his idea of dematerialized simplicity in an intervening production by him at the Munich Residenztheater in 1977. Instead, utilizing a bare minimum of actual scenery, the new production revealed the inner landscape of the play as a fluid, densely layered montage of images and impressions. It seemed, in the words of *Sydsvenska Dagbladet* (April 26, 1986), "literally scored in musical terms," developing "from a single note on a piano into progressively richer harmonies" that spanned a wide register from the poignant and the tragic to the grotesque and even the absurd. In a graphic but unpretentious way, Bergman's approach once again stressed the dimension of conscious enactment, of theater-in-the-theater. "By emphasizing everything in the play that is 'theatrical,' he allows its vision of human reality and the human condition to emerge with even greater clarity," wrote *Berlingske Tidende* of the intense actor–spectator relationship which this production and the proximity of its close-up scenes fostered.

Quite unlike his earlier *Dreamplay*, however, Bergman's newest version was specifically intended to integrate the work's complicated visual syntax more clearly and directly into his overall concept. "I wanted the audience to experience the back-alley stench of the Lawyer's office, the cold beauty of the snowy summerland of Fairhaven, the sulphurous shimmer and glimpses of hell in Foulstrand, the profusion of flowers surrounding the Growing Castle, the old theater behind the Theater Corridor," he remarks in *Laterna Magica*.[54] In practice, this kaleidoscope of moods and impressions was evoked by a virtually cinematic sequence of back projections, ranging from the luxurious color of the Growing Castle's garden to increasingly bleaker nuances of black and white. The end result was a fluid, rapidly shifting stream of sensory images, flowing together to reinforce the emotional mood of a given scene and producing a sense of "the gliding, illogical simultaneity of reality and unreality" (*Göteborgs–Posten*).

In this demystified, staunchly down-to-earth interpretation of Strindberg's dream of life, the presence of the god Indra and his Daughter – taken as a kind of absurd irrelevancy in the 1970 version – was now dropped altogether. Instead, a few more cuts and transpositions than first anticipated were introduced to make the figure of the Poet both the drama's controlling consciousness and also the active intermediary between the actors and the audience. As played by Mathias Henrikson, he became the performance's co-director, as it were, present from the very beginning in his "domain" at the front of the stage. The corner he occupied here was a segment of turn-of-the-century *Jugendstil* reality defined by a cluster of objects (writing table, oil lamp, bookcase, stained glass window, potted palm strung with colored lights) that alluded unmistakably to Strindberg's room in the Blue Tower. Opposite him, in the downstage left corner, Ugly Edith sat pounding out dissonant chords on an old piano, almost buried in a clutter of paraphernalia from the Poet's dream – a damaged crucifix, the figurehead of a ship, the cloverleaf door, a ticking clock, even the marble statue of a young girl (a greeting straight from Bergman's production of *The Ghost Sonata!*). Between these two poles of poetry and music, in an open, magical area that reached to the back of the stage, the action of the Poet's drama unfolded – as "his mise-en-scène, his poem, his dream, fragments from his life that materialize on the inner stage stretching into the deep-blue space behind him"

Agnes is led by the Poet to the Lawyer's office, in the new
production of *A Dream Play* at Dramaten, 1986.

(*Expressen*). For, very much like the young Alexander in *Fanny
and Alexander*, he was both the captor and the observer of his
dreamed existence. At times, he sat bending over his manuscript or listening silently to the conversation of "his" characters as if to a play he himself had written. At other times, he
intervened directly in his mise-en-scène, moving a bit of
scenery, directing Agnes, or comforting her by stroking her
hair and drying her tears.

For, in this context, the Daughter (as she was still called in
the production script) was above all the child of the Poet's
creative fantasy, rather than the offspring of some remote
Eastern deity. Bergman's most decisive move in his new
version was to divide Agnes' role into three distinct voices and
ages. In the opening scene (here called Awakening: The

Growing Castle), it was as a child that she conjured up for the Poet, through the strength of her unspoiled imagination, the unseen vision of a flowering castle that grows out of the earth. In the play that was the Poet's dream of life – his and hers – it was simply as a human being that the adult Agnes (played in these scenes by Lena Olin) was taught life's suffering and bitter adversities, without the luxury of a goddess' ultimate invulnerability. Instead, the very notion of divine creation ("human existence under the fumbling supervision of a distracted God," as Bergman puts it in his *Laterna Magica*[55]) was seen, in the Fingal's Cave episode, as no more than the subject for an ironic performance within the performance, eagerly stage-managed by the Poet and declaimed by him and his protégé to "soft music" from an old Victrola, as they posed before a photographer's screen depicting Böcklin's Toten-Insel (yet another signal from *The Ghost Sonata.*)

At the moment in the play when the Daughter's earthly tribulations reach their climax (as the Lawyer returns to chide her fiercely for neglecting her "duty"), Bergman's Agnes was suddenly transformed into an old woman. In the twelfth and final scene of this version (also called Awakening: Outside the Flowering Castle), it was this older, wiser Agnes, played by Birgitta Valberg, around whom the forty other members of the cast assembled. Weary and resigned now, she took leave of life and of her Poet, whom she in turn comforted as her own child, cradling his head in her lap as she explained life's mystery to him. Within a circle of fire suggested by six lighted candles arranged on the stage floor, she placed her shoes and the other characters in turn laid their various emblems of human suffering – the shawl of sorrows, the roses of withered hope, and all the rest. After the three Agneses and the others had disappeared into the darkness, the Poet remained behind. His play had vanished, his waking dream had come to an end. In this production, the final image was simply this last glimpse of the artist-dreamer, seated in "Strindberg's corner" in front of his stained glass window, alone on the deserted stage. That single evocative image could, in turn, be said to hold the essence of this director's special insight into Strindberg's poetic vision – the perception, shared by both these artists, of the dreamlike quality of reality that is at the same time always conjoined with the insistent reality of the dream. It is this insight which has governed his determination, noticeable in different ways in all his major Strindberg productions, to anchor vision and dream in a firm, tangible bedrock of heightened reality.

TOWARD A NEW DAMASCUS

For Bergman, the one true basis of all reality is to be found in the direct confrontation between the audience and the living actor. The spurious realism of a physical setting that purports to be a "facsimile" of life holds no interest for him. "Once you agree that the only important things are the words, the actors, and the audience, then it isn't the setting that matters," he reminds us. Hence, even in the face of the severest technical challenges, he has remained steadfastly committed to a style cleansed of everything that would dissipate or detheatricalize the hypnotic presence and power of the performer. At the front of his own script for *To Damascus* – an epoch-making production regarded by many as the most representative and fully realized of his Strindberg revivals – one finds an informal memorandum which sheds very revealing light on his method in this respect. This memorandum, entitled simply "Technical Solution," reads in part as follows:

It is always best if one uses for the setting nothing other than lighting, which always indicates the distribution [of scenes]. But I cannot do that here, where all sorts of things have to be shown and must appear and disappear. Therefore I see that we must avail ourselves of our stage platform and a few precise elements and pictures and *four young men who will sit on the stage throughout* and will carry things in and out . . . Then, the problems are eliminated. All the things are there, standing right there from the beginning.[56]

Bergman's production of the first two parts of the *Damascus* trilogy, which opened at Dramaten on February 1, 1974 to a tumultuous reception, provides in many ways a representative synthesis of the aims and techniques we have observed at work in the other productions of his Strindberg cycle. The scheme of visual presentation that his technical memorandum describes is, as always in his work, intimately related to his overall directorial image of the play. In practice, this scheme proved to be in perfect harmony with the mutational dream rhythm that Strindberg's mystical drama of pilgrimage establishes – a drama regarded by the playwright himself as the beginning of "a new genre, fantastic and shining as *Lucky Per*, but playing in a contemporary setting and with a full reality behind it."[57] The scenography, Alf Thoor declared in his review in *Expressen*, "consists of some few, easily portable things that are carried in and out swiftly and noiselessly – here a screen, there a sofa – together with projections on a black wall. In the nightmare scenes, the background is suddenly and silently drawn aloft to reveal a ghostly banquet or a wretched barroom on the outskirts of hell. And then, gone again. Completely without effort, one scene glides into the next in a matter of two or three seconds." Marik Vos, also Bergman's designer in *The Ghost Sonata*, created in this instance a far more complex collage of giant back-projections, consisting for the most part of stylized white-on-black drawings projected on the cyclorama or on a high screen in the center of the stage. (Strindberg, too, had hoped that his backgrounds "could be produced by a shadow picture painted on glass and projected onto a white sheet," but the bold attempt by Emil Grandinson to use sciopticon projections in the first production of *To Damascus I* [1900] had been too far ahead of its time to be technically feasible.) Small movable screens and other portable elements had, of course, earlier been used by Bergman to great advantage in *A Dream Play*. In his *Damascus*, however, the neutral and rather colorless quality of the setting was offset – particularly in such vividly phantasmagoric episodes as the Goldmaker's Banquet – by strong color accents created by the costumes, masks, and figure compositions of the characters. The one other significant detail to which Bergman's technical memorandum makes reference is the low "stage platform" that is clearly visible in several of the production photos reproduced here. This raised, rectangular platform – specified in Figure 10 as measuring 6.4 m in width and 3.6 m in depth, placed 3.0 m from the background but only a bare 20 cm from the forward edge of the stage – deftly established the requisite "magic" point of focus and concentrated energy in Bergman's stage space. Its use has been a hallmark of many of his classical productions in recent years – but in this particular case its presence also seems a direct response to Strindberg's own vigorous plea for a simple, neutral platform stage ("something in the style of Shakespeare's time") that would help to eliminate "all this theatrical

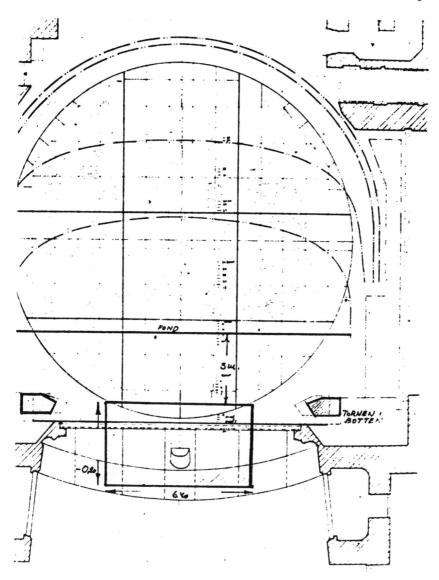

Figure 10 Blueprint plan of the stage (Dramaten) for *To Damascus*.

tinsel that now engulfs the stage and makes a play heavy without increasing its believability."[58] Indeed, this playwright's ceaseless campaign for the dematerialization of the theater has had no more ardent or intelligent champion than Bergman. Thoor's remark in his review of *Damascus* is characteristic: "This is theater that interests itself almost exclusively in human beings and hardly at all in the things that surround them."

The "full reality" that, Strindberg insists, underlies the anguished pilgrimage of his protagonist toward a distant and elusive salvation is an inner reality – a spiritual, magic realism of the soul that Bergman's interpretation delineated with laser-sharp clarity and with a powerful undertone of black humor and irony. "Strictly speaking only one character in the play is real, and he is called the Unknown," observed the critic for *GT* (Göteborg). "Whatever else happens on the stage may appear more or less real, but in the last analysis it is all a projection of the fantasies, memories, dreams, and imagination of the Unknown." The painful journey of this figure through a private, subjective Inferno was amplified, in Bergman's evocative production, into "a thrilling voyage of discovery into a spiritual landscape . . . where no values are constant, and where reality changes shape with all the remorseless, unpredictable logic of a nightmare. Figures, thoughts, situations recur, lines of dialogue rebound among the characters like symphonic leitmotifs. It is a drama that embraces wisdom and madness, werewolves and beggars, hell and heaven."[59] As this comment suggests and as we might also expect of Bergman, the director appeared relatively uninterested in a conventional religious approach to *To Damascus*, as a drama of conversion and atonement, and was far more concerned with the emotional, lyrical, and even social aspects of the central character's spiritual torment. "He demystifies the drama," wrote Bengt Jahnsson in *Dagens Nyheter*. "At times the projection screen in the background is filled by a searching eye. But this is not God's eye watching the Unknown and us. The memory of the past watches over the actions of the Unknown, intensifying his terror and anxiety. Our victims watch over us." Accordingly, Jan-Olof Strandberg's virtuoso performance as the Unknown carved out an intensely human and existentially divided protagonist, vacillating in an instant from tenderness to savage sarcasm, hopelessly trapped between rebellious arrogance and a gnawing self-torment. "Not infrequently he is so naive and comical that we laugh at him," commented *Expressen*. "But then suddenly the poetry in his words blossoms forth, the magic is there, and it falls silent around him." The end result became, in the opinion of many observers, "a drama of atonement in which the central character never repents." Both in Bergman's direction and in Strandberg's acerbic performance, the closing moments of Part Two, as the Unknown passionately embraces the Lady before leaving her to follow the mysterious Confessor ("Come, priest, before I change my mind!"), provided no clear or firm assurance that this ferocious struggle with the riddle of existence had been resolved. More than one critic called the ending "only the beginning of a new round." And yet the experience of the struggle itself – the sense of having gone through a trial that may turn out to be a blessing in disguise – inevitably does suggest its own kind of purification and reconciliation, in Bergman's world as in Strindberg's.

This three-and-a-half-hour stage adaptation of *To Damascus I–II* was, in strictly technical terms, an astonishing feat of dramaturgical compression that rivaled Per Lindberg's legendary one-evening production of the entire trilogy, seen in Oslo more than forty years before. The arrangement of Bergman's nineteen compact and tightly focused scenes is given in outline in the following table:

To Damascus

Bergman	Sequence of scenes	Strindberg
1	At the street corner	act 1, scene i
1A	At the cafe	
2	The veranda (At the Physician's)	act 1, scene ii
3	By the sea	act 2, scene ii
4	On the highway	act 2, scene iii
5	The kitchen	act 2, scene v
6	The Rose Chamber	act 3, scene i
7	The asylum	act 3, scene ii
8	The Rose Chamber	act 3, scene iii
9	The kitchen	act 3, scene iv
10	On the highway	act 4, scene ii

While faithfully mirroring the sequential logic and flow of Strindberg's original creation, this skillful reorchestration infused the two parts of it with a remarkable new sense of coherence and organic interrelatedness. Those critics who objected to the disruption of Strindberg's satisfying symmetrical design in part 1 – eight scenes leading up to the pivotal episode in the asylum, followed by exactly the same number and sequence of scenes in reverse order – were evidently overlooking the fact that an analogous and no less deliberate formal design governs Bergman's repatterning. Although four short and relatively inconsequential scenes (in the hotel room [2.i and 4.iv] and in the mountain pass [2.iv and 4.i] have been eliminated in his scheme, the centrality of the Unknown's unnerving experience in the asylum is still manifestly emphasized by the arrangement of the incidents. Following this episode, the Unknown retraces his steps exactly. Four scenes later, he is reunited with the Lady at the very spot – by the sea – where they first began their wearisome journey as man and wife, after leaving the home of the Lady's former husband, the Physician.

Part 2 thus emerged as the direct, infernal consequence of this reunion. "I have at all times seen the second part as [a vision of] the depths of hell. Just as in a spiral, one sinks ever deeper, at last giving up the struggle and going over to religion, to the church," reads part of a note in the director's script. With this clue before us, it is not difficult to discern the logic of Bergman's decision to eliminate the final three scenes of Part 1 (4.iv, 5.i and 5.ii) and proceed, with the master film maker's uncanny sense of an effective cut, directly to the much more harrowing domestic and emotional conflicts that culminate in the appalling ritual of humiliation known as the Goldmaker's Banquet. "The effect is so strong and the decision so obvious that we only ask ourselves why it had never been done before," *Expressen* was brought to conclude. "For here we have a pattern that is eternal, a structure that will never weaken. It begins with their meeting. It ends with their parting. 'Scenes from a marriage' would not have been a bad subtitle for *To Damascus* in this interpretation." One might add, though, that it was after all Strindberg himself who first recommended the sort of dramaturgical conflation that Bergman so successfully accomplished.[60]

Each individual scene in this production stood out with a sculptural clarity, like a figure cluster on an ancient frieze or vase. One distinct group of scenes were "close-ups" very tightly focused within the defined limits of the small raised platform, utilizing only a back projection or a screen or two (often to facilitate entrances or exits) and the barest minimum

At the street corner. The first meeting of the Unknown and the Lady in *To Damascus*. Dramaten, 1974.

At the Physician's. The Unknown's first encounter with Caesar, the madman, in *To Damascus*.

of furniture. Four of the most striking of these moments are captured in the accompanying production photographs.

The initial, hypnotic encounter between the Unknown and the Lady ("At the street corner") was played against a projected background that evoked a dreamlike, spiderweb image of a Gothic church portal and a house facade. The sole piece of furniture on the stage was a simple wooden bench, around which the rhythm of the moves of approach and withdrawal, union and separation, was choreographed with all the precision of a pas de deux. Helena Brodin, dressed in cool green as the Lady, created an intense but restrained impression in this scene as a listener holding back her passion, "a well-dressed woman of the world who watches this strange and singular man with interest. Later, love and hatred alike obliterate this restrained facade, and the strife between the man and pregnant woman takes on that frenzy that we usually call Strindbergian."[61] As their first meeting drew to a close with the Lady's impulsive kiss and passionate declaration ("Come, my liberator!"), an inquisitive human eye gazed down ironically from the projection screen. The reason was a very practical

The suggestive, semiabstract setting for the Kitchen in *To Damascus.*

one: "It is essential to finish on the Unknown," the director noted, for in this version the Unknown remained throughout the play the controlling consciousness through which all its events are perceived and recorded.

The first station on the couple's journey is the home of the Physician – the "werewolf" husband from whom the Unknown has rashly vowed to free his fairy princess. The "veranda" setting for this scene consisted of no more than a trio of low screens and three simple chairs, arranged to enclose and confine the action. A naive triptych depicting Swedish country scenes adorned the rear screen, as the merest hint of the elaborate milieu that Strindberg describes in his stage directions. Here in this haunted house of ticking death clocks, the demonic, vengeful doctor ("bizarre at first, later terrifying in his threats and hatred" in Ulf Johansson's performance[62]) confronted the Unknown with the most sinister of his exhibits – Caesar, the laurel-crowned madman who dwells in the cellar and in whom the Unknown is horrified to recognize a grotesque mirror image of himself. "Why does it all come back again – corpses and beggars and human destinies and childhood memories," he cries as he falls to his knees in desperate supplication.

Unlike the localities of these first two incidents, the "kitchen" of the Lady's childhood home becomes a recurrent station on the Unknown's journey, reserved in particular for his humiliating confrontations with the Lady's taunting and remorseless Mother. Bergman returned to this setting four times in his production, for it was also here that, in part 2, the vindictive mother-in-law robbed the Unknown of all joy in his newborn daughter. Each time the kitchen reappeared, the sparse furnishings of the scene were slightly rearranged but one strongly connotative element remained constant – a plain white screen upon which, as its sole adornment, a large crucifix was prominently displayed. (When turned around the screen had a rose-colored reverse side, for use in the Rose Chamber scenes.) The illustration in which the Mother and the Maid are seen joined with the old Grandfather in prayer depicts the opening moment of the fifth scene in Bergman's version (Strindberg's 2.v). In his use of a suggestive, semiabstract setting such as this, the aim of the director is obviously in no sense to provide a picture of a recognizable place – that is, Strindberg's "roomy kitchen with white calcimine walls" in all its details. Instead, the spectator is faced with an evocative and disturbing image of a state of mind – a recurrent visual image of the harsh, hell-fire religious orthodoxy that the Unknown encounters in this place. What this particular illustration omits to show is, incidentally, the highly theatricalized use that Bergman invariably makes of his total stage space. Although "offstage" while their predicament is being so unfeelingly discussed by the others, the Unknown and the Lady were, in fact, already standing in full view to the right of the platform at this very moment, waiting silently to make their "entrance" and place themselves at the mercy of the family's grudging charity.

Often, the most effective of these "close-up" moments in the *Damascus* production made use of no scenery at all. Such an instance was the moving scene in which the Unknown is reunited with the Lady ("By the sea") – "a scene of great tenderness, closeness, desperation, and love," Bergman describes it, with which he concluded Part 1 in his adaptation. The stage was completely open and empty. The overall visual impression was, at the outset, one of winter whiteness and extreme cold. The only scenographic accent was provided by projections of shifting cloud formations in the background. Among these was perhaps the most striking of all of Marik Vos's projection effects in this production – the haunting impressionistic image of shipmast crosses that loomed up on the horizon during the closing moments of the episode:

THE UNKNOWN: Put your hand in mine, and let us leave this place together. (*He reaches out his hand. She takes it. He lowers his head, she kisses him on the mouth, and he rests his head against her shoulder.*) Are you tired?
THE LADY: Not any longer! (*Music*)
THE UNKNOWN (*facing the sea*): It's growing dark and the clouds are gathering . . .
THE LADY (*quietly consoling him*): Don't look at the clouds . . .
THE UNKNOWN: And over there? What is that?
THE LADY (*consoling*): Only a sunken ship!
THE UNKNOWN (*in a whisper*): Three crosses! – What new Golgotha awaits us now?
THE LADY (*consoling*): But they're white: that's a good sign!

By the sea. The reunion of the Unknown (Jan-Olof Strandberg) and the Lady (Helena Brodin) on an empty stage, accented only by Marik Vos' evocative background projection.

The Confessor (Anders Ek) and the Unknown in the Asylum scene from *To Damascus*.

THE UNKNOWN (*looking at her*):   Can anything good happen to us ever again?

THE LADY (*consoling smile*):   Yes, but not right away.

THE UNKNOWN (*laying his arm on her shoulder*):   Let us go![63]

The illustration that captures the final moment of this exchange may inevitably cause some to recall its famous counterpart – the old rehearsal photograph of August Palme and Harriet Bosse, at the same moment, in the world premiere

The Asylum scene from *To Damascus*, with the soup-eating participants in the ghostly supper.

to *To Damascus I,* in which Carl Grabow's heavily pictorial backcloth now seems to much at odds with the fleeting, visionary character of Strindberg's first dreamplay.

A dynamic rhythm of contrasts was established in the *Damascus* production between the intimate, close-up scenes and another kind of stage composition entirely. In these latter *changements à vue* (so Bergman himself calls them), nightmare penetrated reality in an instant, and the Unknown suddenly found his private demons and innermost fears transmogrified into hideous scenes of public condemnation and disgrace. The background opened, the small platform stage was absorbed into the new figure composition, and the Unknown found himself at the focus of a mass spectacle that was always different and yet always the same. Each new public mortification became an amplification of the previous one. And, in one form or another, the Unknown's constant companion in these ordeals was the shadowy dual character of the Beggar-Confessor created by Anders Ek. "Visible or invisible he is always present, prodding or provoking the Unknown," remarked one observer. "Ek holds the stage with a combination of the clown's jesting – the trait that seems to run through to the very core of his personality – and a massive, almost annihilating authority" (*Nerikes Allehanda*). It was he who guided the Unknown on the road to Damascus, he who commented on every station along the way. In the role of the Latin-quoting Beggar who bears the mark of Cain upon his forehead (and hence is the Unknown's grotesque double), his presence first brought down public ridicule on the Unknown in the crowded cafe filled with brown-clad pallbearers that suddenly materialized and just as abruptly disappeared during the opening scene on the street corner. As the Dominican confessor in the asylum scene, his attack became fiercer and more harrowing as he intoned the litany of curses from Deuteronomy over the Unknown, who sat virtually like a condemned prisoner. (His chair, Bergman noted, "must have a high backrest and high armrests so he sits cramped.") At a long table in the background sat the ten spectral, soup-eating participants in the ghostly supper – Caesar, the Beggar, the Physician, the grieving parents, the cruelly treated sister, the abandoned wife and her two children, and farthest to the right, the Lady, who sat knitting rather than eating. "Decide whether they are the same [i.e., identical to the actual characters from the Unknown's past]! No, they should wear masks and [different] costumes," reads an interesting memorandum in the director's script.

The most crucial scene in Bergman's theatrical paraphrase of *To Damascus* was, however, not the Unknown's confrontation with his past sins during his ordeal in the asylum, but rather the garish, trenchantly satirical episode of the Goldmaker's Banquet, which occurs toward the end of part 2. Previously in the laboratory scene – condensed by Bergman into a brief, somnambulistic dream sequence that began *allegro furioso* and concluded with the tempo indicator *retard* ("the dream that you cannot stand up and cannot speak") – the Unknown had revealed to the Lady his true motive for attempting to make gold:

. . . so as to destroy the world order, to bring chaos, you see! (*more heavily*) I am the destroyer, the annihilator, the arsonist of the universe, and when everything lies in ashes, (*more heavily*) I shall run *hungering* through the ruins and rejoice in this thought: (*more heavily*) that *I have done* this, I who have written the final page of the world's history – which can now be regarded as finished.
(*The face of the Dominican appears in the open window, unnoticed by them. They fall silent.*) Who's there? Who is that terrible being who follows me and paralyzes my thoughts? – Did you see anyone? (*She only looks at him.*)[64]

The Unknown is crowned with laurel and hailed as the Great Goldmaker in *To Damascus*.

Absorbed in his own rebellious vision, the Unknown readily permits himself to be acclaimed and decorated at what he conceives of as a glittering testimonial banquet held in his honor. It was composed, in Bergman's production, of a smirking, bugeyed troll court of absurdly uniformed gentlemen and enormous barebreasted society ladies – a fantastic vision that seems more reminiscent of earlier productions like *Peer Gynt* or *Caligula* than of anything he had attempted before in staging Strindberg. No sooner had the unsuspecting Unknown been crowned with laurel and hailed by the tawdry multitude as the Great Goldmaker than this bizarre assembly began to undergo a metamorphosis. Swiftly, in accordance with a carefully choreographed four-stage pattern of visible transformations, the beribboned officers and gentlemen were turned into beggars, vagabonds, and *clochards*, while the fine ladies became whores and other more disreputable (unfortunately unprintable) types. By the time Caesar, the Physician's madman, had launched his terrifyingly irrational, virtually Hitlerian tirade against the Unknown, the change was complete. What the latter had perceived as a "royal celebration" and a "sincere tribute" that had restored "[his] faith in himself" was now an ugly, shabby, and distinctly hostile collection of ruffians gathered in a dingy cafe.

Virtually every reviewer had words of praise for the startling visual effect created by this scene ("altar painting" is perhaps the term that crops up most frequently). One or two critics were even prepared to congratulate the director on having made, for once, an acceptable anticapitalistic comment on the hollowness of the ruling classes: "As far as one can remember, this is the first time that Ingmar Bergman has uttered a word in the sociopolitical debate – the scene is a comment on the representative establishment and its relationship to those it represents," ventured Åke Perlström in *Göteborgs–Posten*. However, these generalizations are of little help in understanding the thematic relevance of this episode to Bergman's directorial image of *To Damascus* and, indeed, to his conception of Strindberg's drama as a whole. One might well argue that, above all, the Goldmaker's Banquet became in this production the ultimate nightmare of humiliation – in this sense it bears a direct relationship to the scene of the Degree Ceremony in Bergman's *Dreamplay*. In it, the ridicule and scorn heaped upon the dreamer are exacerbated and confirmed by his own innermost sense that they are justified and represent the truth about himself. Transformation was the governing theatrical technique in the production, and this served to establish irony as its predominant mode of communication.[65] With the swiftness and logic of a dream the Unknown found himself cast, without a transition, from the happy illusion of the banquet into the inferno of degradation. As such, this scene represented the culmination of a perpetual ironic process in which every potential happiness in the Unknown's existence – love, family ties, children, success, even royalty statements – had been suddenly transformed into dust and ashes in his hands.

A projection of dissolving, disintegrating house facades in the background provided a concise visual image of the aftermath of the grotesque banquet. In the final "public" scene, the Unknown returned to the wretched cafe, hopeful that "a mud bath" might "harden [his] skin against the stings of life." Instead, in a macabre atmosphere filled with the sprawling, writhing shapes of beggars, cripples, and whores, his spirit was poisoned and his life virtually sucked out of him by the savage, hypnotic power of the "werewolf" Physician. The ceremonial entrance of the hooded Confessor, carrying the monstrance to "a dying man inside," coincided with the Unknown's horrified realization that he, too, was perhaps dead without even knowing it. "The dead claim that no one knows the difference," agreed the venomous Physician "with ghastly emphasis."

In Bergman's radical abridgment of the remaining episodes in the drama, the last stages of the Unknown's journey were swiftly covered, and they led toward a distinctly and deliberately arbitrary resolution of his plight. Several intermediate, explanatory steps in the process – his anguished dream-encounter with his abandoned children, the destruction of Caesar and the Physician, the consultation between the Lady and the Confessor about his salvation – were omitted. Instead, the closing moments in this version were tightly concentrated on the last of the "scenes from a marriage." Our final glimpse into the connubial Rose Chamber revealed a deadlock from which there could be no escape – a timeless, airless domestic hell of hatred and guilty conscience, from which the Unknown was powerless to extricate himself. ("The Unknown is locked into his position. He cannot move an inch. He is in catatonic paralysis," reads a characteristic note in the director's script.) Hence, the Confessor's mystical option represented at least a kind of exit visa – in Bergman's distillation a very simple, open alternative to the ironies and torments of this life's Inferno. This concluding scene, which condenses some two pages of discussion in the original into six emotionally expressive speeches, provides a forceful example of this director's determination to forge a living theater text that "listens" to the inner emotional consciousness – "the poet's anxiety-driven fever pulse," as he called it back in 1945 – that is the authentic core of the Strindbergian dramatic vision:

"The dead claim that no one knows the difference." In the wretched cafe filled with beggars and cripples, the Physician (Ulf Johansson) destroys the Unknown with his psychic power.

(*The Confessor enters, carrying a small, open prayerbook.*)

THE UNKNOWN: Why, it's the beggar, isn't it?

CONFESSOR: Yes. Once, you forswore your soul to me when you lay sick and sensed madness approaching. You promised then to serve the powers of good. But when you became well again, you broke your promise.

THE UNKNOWN: Come, then, before darkness falls!

CONFESSOR   (*When he begins to read, he goes forward to the Unknown and shows him the text. Possibly it is he himself who reads the last line*): "Over all the earth shone a bright, clear light, and men laboured without hindrance, doing their work. Over them, night spread its thick blackness – a foreboding of the darkness that was to set in over them! *But they themselves were harder upon one another than the darkness.*"

(*When they finish reading, they intend to leave. Before they can take any steps, the Lady speaks.*)

THE LADY: Let no harm come to him!

(*He goes forward to her and falls to his knees, but not too close. Concerned about the child she places a finger on her lips.*)

THE UNKNOWN (*passionately*):   Listen to her: how kindly she can speak, and how evil she *is*! Look at her eyes: weep they cannot, but they can caress and can sting and can lie! And yet: "Let no harm come to him!" – Look, now she's afraid that I will wake her child, the little mischief that took her away from me!

(*She goes forward to him, falls to her knees, embraces him and kisses him lingeringly on the mouth. Then she rises. Still kneeling, he lifts a hand to his mouth. Then he rises and goes toward the priest. He reaches out his hand.*)

Come, priest, before I change my mind!

FINIS MALORUM[66]

One detects no single "formula" at work in the Bergman cycle of Strindberg productions. Each play in the canon has stood for him as a new and unique challenge, calling for a fresh perspective and a renewed creative response. The intuitive daring of his interpretations of Strindberg's plays has, however, been coupled with a staunch loyalty that is typical of his directorial method in general. "I cannot and will not direct a play contrary to its author's intentions," he has said. "And I have never done so. Consciously. I have always considered myself an interpreter, a re-creator."[67] The last word in this remark is, of course, the operative one. If the text is, as Bergman insists, "a hidden path into the writer's consciousness," the director must ultimately translate the explicit or implicit choices and values he discovers there into his own theater language – which is, in the final analysis, the only language in which a playwright can be heard by a living, contemporary audience. The act of producing a play on the stage creates a new organism, an integral work of art responsive, by definition, to a whole new set of circumstances. "In my case it has always been a matter of reading closely. And interpreting in the same way a conductor interprets a score," Bergman has reminded us. "My intention is not to be an innovator. I want only to present the play and make it live in the hearts of an audience." For, as he yet again reminded his public at an open rehearsal of his newest *Miss Julie* in 1991, "it is in your hearts, in your imagination that the performance must take place."

4   A theater for Molière

In the succession of provocative revivals of Molière that Ingmar Bergman has given us over the years, the manifest authority of his approach to classical comedy has derived from his recognition of the complementary significance of innovation and tradition in the theater. Like Louis Jouvet before him, whose own revivals of Molière were always animated by a vigorous sensitivity to this playwright's distinctive theatrical heritage, Bergman, too, regards Molière as, above all, an artist "who truly commands the vocabulary of the stage; he is to the very fingertips a man of the theater."[1] Theater as motif and metaphor is indeed present everywhere in Molière's bitter comedies. Throughout them we are made to witness the triumph of theater, of make believe, in a cardboard world where the ability to don a cloak and mask and play a double game seems the one sure prerequisite for survival. Bergman's successive explorations of these plays over the past four decades – seven major revivals since his first production of *Dom Juan* in Malmö in 1955 – have consistently exploited a consciously heightened theatricality intended to amplify this deeply ironic dimension of Molière's comic vision.

Accordingly, his method of presenting a Molière play has invariably been to remind the spectators that they are in a theater and that these are actors performing before them. In general, his aim is always to establish a mutual pact, as it were, between actor and spectator – a pact that recognizes and depends upon the spectator's willing participation in the creative process. In his Molière productions in particular, the machinery of the stage stands exposed; changes of scene are handled by costumed stagehands or even by the characters themselves; the actors can sometimes be glimpsed at the outskirts of the playing area, waiting quietly for their cues; and even the prompter occasionally takes a hand in the action. The end result of all such devices is that never for an instant in such a performance is the audience permitted to lose sight of its role as an informed and active witness to an amusing but unsettling masquerade – one in which the masks do not conceal reality but are in themselves the only reality.

Above all, the style that Bergman has developed for Molière seems rooted in the impressions of Jouvet, Barrault, and the French comic tradition that he derived during his first visit to Paris in the autumn of 1949. "The experience was indescribable," he writes in *Laterna Magica*. "The dry alexandrines blossomed and thrived. The people on the stage stepped through my senses into my heart: that is how it was, I know it sounds silly, but it was like that."[2] The question of how accurate or inaccurate such recollections may be need not concern us here. What is significant is Bergman's own obvious predilection for what he calls the self-confident "brutality" of French comic acting and direction – "their incredible brutality and power and tempo and then their black, savage humor that suddenly becomes absurd," as he says in an interview with the authors. Precisely this sense of savage, potentially absurd comedy has set the dominant tone for most of Bergman's own productions of Molière. In them, the broad farcical spirit of the *commedia dell'arte* that lies so close to the heart of Molière's comic theater has exerted a strong and pervasive influence, and hence the exuberant *lazzi* and burlesque *coups de théâtre* associated with this performance tradition have almost invariably occupied a central place. The one exception has been his harsh and relatively unsuccessful production of *The School for Wives* and its *Criticism* (Dramaten, 1966), which remained coldly impervious to the more carefree blandishments of the commedia tradition.

Otherwise, however, Bergman's various interpretations of Molière's plays have differed widely in concept and design, ranging from the rough-hewn, improvisational texture of his first *Dom Juan* in 1955 to the cool, stylized formality of his two highly successful revivals of *The Misanthrope* (at the Malmö City Theatre in 1957 and at the Royal Theatre in Copenhagen in 1973). Of particular interest are his two German-language productions of Molière, both as example of the general tendencies already noted and also as evidence of a new, deconstructive impulse in his interpretative approach to this playwright. If his production of *Tartuffe* at the Residenztheater (January 13, 1979) can be seen as his most extravagantly farcical Molière revival, his third *Dom Juan*, which opened the Salz-

Orgon (Walter Schmidinger) as the madcap bourgeois whom no one – not even the charming Dorine (Gaby Dohm) – can rescue from his folly in *Tartuffe*. Residenztheater, 1979.

burg Festival on July 27, 1983, is unquestionably his blackest. In both cases, moreover, the extremeness of the interpretation was clearly deliberate, intended (and taken up) as a challenge to accepted critical and popular assumptions about these two sharply contrasted but related comedies.

Bergman's vigorously unorthodox *Tartuffe* – consciously designed, as he himself explained, to emphasize the "ironic charm" of the play rather than its "blackness," and consequently featuring an undangerous Tartuffe, whom some German critics went so far as to call "closer to Nestroy than to Molière" in spirit[3] – took no notice of the familiar notion of the work as a moral comedy, a bitter satire of religious hypocrisy and deceit. As a result, the leading Munich critic Joachim Kaiser found himself lamenting the lack of "a warm-hearted understanding of humanity" in Bergman's approach,[4] while other reviewers spoke variously of an absence of "seriousness" and an indifference to "the tragic side" of Tartuffe's character. In fact, however, this astringent production's main concern was not with the imposter who hoodwinks everyone around him but rather with the nature of the absurd society – epitomized by the incurable madcap Orgon (Walter Schmidinger) and his topsyturvy household – that allows such a creature as Tartuffe to flourish. Neither the coaxing of his wife Elmire (Rita Russek) nor the plain common sense of the saucy Dorine (Gaby Dohm) could deflect this folly-fallen bourgeois from the path of his appointed destiny. He virtually demanded to be gulled and plundered by the oily religious hypocrite, who very nearly takes over the world in the process.

From the outset, the animated family conference with which this performance began firmly established the atmosphere of parody and accelerating absurdity that prevailed to the end. This domestic "portrait" – the matriarchal Pernelle (played by the burly actor Franz Kutschera!) with "her" lap dog, Orgon's blue-eyed and empty-headed daughter Mariane with her baby doll, and his whining son Damis with his yo-yo – presented a bizarre, virtually Ionesco-like image of a family. Although the more solemn of the critics protested Bergman's lack of "veneration" for "these golden roles," these and the other characters in the comedy were in fact conceived by him not as more or less rationally motivated human beings, but rather as grotesquely exaggerated masks of human folly who inhabit an artificial world of duplicity and painted canvas. Not a trace of seriousness was permitted to overshadow the astonishing foolishness of almost everyone – with the exception of Laurent, Tartuffe's manservant, who here became a stern, omnipresent watcher whose silent presence commented on both the folly of Orgon's lunatic household and the fiendish intrigues of his unscrupulous master. Here as elsewhere in Bergman's work, this figure of the "watching" character – a silent actor-spectator whose presence in itself implies an objective critical comment – was a focusing device used to control and adjust the intensity of the communicative relationship between actor and audience.

The dominant mode of *theatrum mundi* – the world as a stage, the stage as an image of the world – was deftly supported by Bergman's physical mise-en-scène. From the moment the actors made their entrance onto a raked platform of rough boards erected in the middle of the stage and illuminated by the obviously artificial glow of old-fashioned footlights, the audience was continually and wittily reminded that this was a piece of theater they were watching. Once the actors had appeared, a painted canvas backing was carried in and put in place – and their world was created. Charlotte Flemming's stage design was a primitive pastiche of a baroque theater set, made up of canvas-covered screens at the sides and back that were painted with light gray, Watteau-like motifs on a white ground. Whatever changes took place in this décor were integrated into the action as ironic punctuation marks. As the comic intrigue became progressively more entangled, appropriate rearrangements of the screens offered telling visual comments on the reigning confusion. Orgon's bewildered universe became one in which pieces of the setting occasionally stood, defiantly, upsidedown, or else were placed with the unpainted side of the canvas (neatly stenciled "Tartuffe" for easy identification!) facing the audience. And when the tumult reached panic proportions – as it did when a thoroughly beguiled Orgon departed with Tartuffe in a whirlwind of ecstatic glee to draw up the deed at the end of the third act, or when the imposter later made his hilarious attempt to seduce Elmire – the actors gave way to their high spirits by virtually toppling the painted screens.

Charlotte Flemming's pastiche of a baroque theater set for *Tartuffe*. Note the exposed footlights and the upsidedown piece of scenery in the far background.

The highly theatricalized stage setting, designed by Sven Erik Skawonius, for Bergman's second production of *Dom Juan*. Stockholm, 1965.

Another variant of Bergman's deliberate theatrical artifice is his staging of *Criticism of the School for Wives*. Dramaten, 1966.

Small wonder, then, that Orgon's cautious brother-in-law Cléante (Karl-Heinz Pelser), the weary spokesman for rationality and order in this absurd society, needed first a cane, later a pair of crutches, and finally even a wheelchair to get around in a world in which reason is crippled, sanity paralyzed. To Molière's highly satirical resolution, in which justice is reimposed and the victims of folly are saved from Tartuffe's clutches through the intervention of their gracious monarch, Bergman added one final commedia touch. Here, the King's Messenger rattled off his improbable proclamation, *in French*, like a tape recorder on rewind; Cléante, as Reason, sprang up from his wheelchair, magically restored to health; and Orgon and his dispossessed household were restored from their madness – if only barely. The mocking, farcical note on which Bergman ended his *Tartuffe* reflected the mood of ironic absurdity that had prevailed throughout it – a mood for which the skeptical Cléante seemed to supply the perfect motto: "Les hommes la plupart sont étrangement faits!" – or, in good German, "Gott, sind die Menschen komisch!"

Dom Juan, written in great haste in 1664 after *Tartuffe* had raised a storm of indignation and had been banned, is sometimes seen as its frustrated author's angry rejoinder – his means of squaring accounts with the malicious enemies who had robbed him of a great popular success. "Molière had only his own weapons to combat this injustice," Meyerhold writes in conjunction with his own spectacular production of the play in 1910. "In order to ridicule the bigotry of the clergy and the hypocrisy of the nobility which he despised, he clutched at Dom Juan like a drowning man at a straw."[5] It is interesting that Bergman's German revival of this work in 1983 adopted a remarkably similar point of departure. "There is something mystical and magical about *Dom Juan* that isn't found in other Molière plays," he said in an interview at the time. In this swiftly composed comedy, written in a turmoil of severe financial and marital crises, Bergman finds that "an angry genius wields the pen. A man who felt the pain of death and who, at the same time, is obsessed by his love of life. So, when all is said and done, it is really a play about life and death." In an unsigned program article, entitled "Das Spiel der Verlierer" (The Play About the Loser) and added by the director when his production moved to Munich for the regular season, he asks why Brecht, Vilar, Strehler, and Bergman have all been drawn to this particular work. "What attracts them? The realism of the play. Mingling several styles, it tells a story in which nobody has a chance. A fairy-tale. But one in which the princesses dissolve into skeletons. It is hard to imagine the despair that drove Molière to write this play."

Led by Joachim Kaiser, the Munich critics voiced general approval of Bergman's "denunciation" of the myth and his exposure of Dom Juan's "other self."[6] Yet the crux of this interpretation was not Brechtian social criticism but the delineation of an existential state of soul-sickness that bordered on death-in-life. Michael Degen, shaved bald for the role of Dom Juan, portrayed an antiheroic sufferer who was, as Bergman pointed out during rehearsals, "a man already on his way to invite the Commander. When we see him for the very first time, he has another twenty-four hours or so to live. About twenty hours before he invites the stone statue to supper."[7]

Hence, from the very beginning, a stifling atmosphere of weariness and human despair hung heavy over the title character and all his actions. In both of his earlier revivals of this play, Bergman had introduced a seriocomic pantomime in which a yawning, scratching, barelegged, and ludicrously unromantic Juan was dressed up in his seducer's costume of silk and ruffles by his totally illusionless servant, Sganarelle. This amusing visual conceit made its point with perfect graphic clarify: the falsity of the mask which Molière's cynical deceiver knowingly adopts. In the third and much darker version, however, this opening pantomime was transformed by Degen and his director into a grotesque, Hoffmannesque ritual of mock resurrection. In it, the *only* reality was the fashionable wig and rich costume worn by a Dom Juan who was, for all intents and purposes, already dead. Slowly, this absurd Lazarus arose from his bier-like bed – gargling, expectorating, urinating in a chamber pot, all under the watchful and solicitous scrutiny of Sganarelle and La Violette. Facing the audience with a blank, lifeless stare, he let himself be hoisted by his two servants into a pair of gaudy yellow tights; garters, shoes, an elaborate corset device, a sumptuous wig, and a splendid golden coat all followed in due course. A complicated routine of painting, powdering, and perfuming ensued. In his comically anxious scrutiny of his image in the looking-glass – first a little hand mirror and then a huge pier-glass, held at crazy angles by Sganarelle – this glittering marionette seemed to be searching for some affirmation of a living reality. Instead, what he saw reflected in the mirror and in the eyes of others – the myth of the irresistible lover and seducer – was no more than that: an empty fiction.

The point of Bergman's concept was not, however, the difficulty with which this weary Dom Juan assumed his false role, but rather the utter revulsion with which he now regarded it. His erotic exploits (whether real or imaginary) had long since ceased to interest him. When, for instance, the outraged and humiliated Dona Elvira (Birgit Doll) arrived to demand an explanation for her husband's abrupt desertion of her, his reactions reflected, above all, disdain – a reluctance to participate any longer in the wearisome masquerade of living. His face as he listened to her pleas, eyes closed, was a shuttered mask that barely concealed his self-disgust and

Watched closely by his servant Sganarelle (Hilmar Thate), Dom Juan (Michael Degen) studies his face in the glass. Salzburg, 1983.

inherent incapacity for love. "Dom Juan is a totally negative person," Bergman declared at rehearsals. "He is already an exhausted man whose only pleasure lies in manipulating other people. Everyone around him is manipulated by him."

In a charged atmosphere of theater-in-the-theater, the last day of Dom Juan's life was enacted on a simple, wooden platform stage. The reality of the event was created – as it had been in Meyerhold's theater – in the minds of the audience rather than on the stage. The raised, slightly raked platform, erected within a neutral framework of burgundy-red walls and overlooked by four small balconies, evoked the flavor of the primitive itinerant stages of the Renaissance and of Molière's own day. ("You cannot play Molière without bearing in mind how he was once played – and it certainly wasn't aestheticized," Bergman insists.) The utterly flexible setting, designed by Gunilla Palmstierna-Weiss, needed and used only the most basic objects – chairs, a table, a succession of simple back-screens, the familiar Bergman looking-glass – and these things were moved about at will by costumed servant–stagehands or by the actors themselves. As a result, the play's twenty-two short scenes came together in a swift, uninterrupted flow of juxtaposed images. The commanding dissonance of a trumpet and drum signaled each new act; stylized front curtains, carried in and held up by four "curtain boys," were drawn across the scene and then quickly whisked aside again, like a conjurer's cloak, to disclose a fresh constellation of figures. It was in this conscious, seductive arrangement of shifting and colliding images that the hand of a great film maker was most readily apparent.

The fixed comic focus in this fluid theatrical montage was provided by Sganarelle – for, as Bergman maintains, it is essentially through the undeceived, ironic perception of Sganarelle that Dom Juan and his exploits are viewed. "This servant is a strange figure," the director explained. "We know that he was played by Molière. Accordingly, he has surely taken the admonitions about decency, ethics, and conscience seriously. At the same time, he sees how absurd they are in this context, in this society."[8] Hilmar Thate's portrayal of Sganarelle shrewdly preserved the contradictions and ambiguities lodged within this fascinating character, without trying either to oversimplify or resolve them. Servant and master were plainly polar and complementary opposites, locked together in a curiously symbiotic relationship. Sganarelle possessed all the vitality and virility that Dom Juan so manifestly lacked. In the outlandish adventures with the peasants in the second act, he even took over Dom Juan's part as the anonymous "dashing gentleman" whom the simpleton Pierrot has pulled from the sea and saved from drowning. With effortless virtuosity, *he* proceeded to accomplish the twin-handed seduction of the gullible Charlotte and her tempestuous rival Mathurine, while his strangely silent master looked on with vicarious pleasure and even sexual excitement.

Ultimately, however, the basic premise of this production was neither the comic interchangeability of Sganarelle and his master nor even their symbiotic union, but rather the gulf that separates them, in Bergman's view, as representatives of the opposed forces of affirmation and negation, human compassion and its denial. It was Dom Juan's final, fiercely cynical espousal of a religion of hatred and hypocrisy that conclusively placed him beyond the reach of even his faithful companion's

To Sganarelle's horror, the stone statue drags his master to eternal reckoning in *Dom Juan*, 1983.

fellowship and sympathy. Yet, as four spectral figures, each wearing a grinning death-mask, appeared on the balconies overlooking the stage and called the offender to repentance and reckoning, the compassionate Sganarelle rushed impulsively to Dom Juan's side and held him in a close, protective embrace. During a long, dreamlike instant of suspended time, servant and master merged into a single, extraordinary figure, hurling painfully slow, hallucinatory gestures of blind defiance at the four spectres. Then abruptly, like someone drained of life, Dom Juan collapsed in Sganarelle's arms as the stone statue of the Commander broke in upon them, striding straight through the violet screen at the rear of the platform to deliver (in the unmistakable voice of Dom Luis, Juan's tyrannical and morally outraged father) his infernal summons.

In this performance, Sganarelle remained, above all, an actor, continually taking the audience into his confidence and often addressing it directly, in that familiar conspiratorial tone of his, *inter nos*. After his death-marked master had been dragged through the jagged, gaping hole in the screen and had disappeared into "Hell" amidst billows of smoke and a roar of dissonant sounds produced by dimly visible stagehands, Sganarelle, the actor, was left alone with his audience for the last time. The sense of critical distance inherent in Thate's handling of this scene created a depth of perspective that reached beyond the simple fact of his reprobate master's damnation. His ritualized punishment had now been accomplished, to the universal moral satisfaction of the offended parties. But the very artificiality of the ritual thrust the reality of Sganarelle's pain into the foreground in this production. For here it was he, rather than the sinister seducer-marionette, who became the real victim of the world's perfidy and perplexity. "Now all the world is content and only I am miserable," he cried out in bitter desolation – and as he spoke, the stage behind him darkened, the smoke cleared, and all that remained was an empty hole in a ruined theater flat. With a last, mournful glance at the dark stage, he walked into the wings, from which he had emerged at the beginning of the play, and disappeared from sight. "My wages!" he continued to shout, again and again, as his voice receded into the bowels of the theater. The unanswered cry became a demand for an explanation, a meaning in the midst of absurdity. Above all, perhaps, it was in this performance the outcry of the actor who is also the poet; for whose suffering and humiliation there can be no adequate recompense, either in Molière's world or in Bergman's.

Throughout his various productions of Molière in general, engagingly broad slapstick effects on the one hand and strategies for establishing critical distance on the other have been combined as related aspects of Bergman's deliberate design upon his audience, from whose point of view every move and every effect in his mise-en-scène is calculated. For him, as for the other modernists whose views have helped to reshape theatrical art in this century, the vocabulary and craft of the theater are inextricably bound up with its audiences – with their active involvement and spontaneous reactions, with the dynamic interplay that is established between stage and auditorium. In Bergman's case, perhaps the most interesting practical application of this theoretical preoccupation with the role of the audience as an active collaborator in the creative process has been his previous custom of holding open, public rehearsals for certain plays. The idea was first tried in conjunction with his radically experimental, open-stage production of Büchner's *Woyzeck* in 1969. "It is essential to undramatize the whole system of theatrical distribution, the hysteria surrounding dress rehearsal and opening," he declared on that occasion. "I now believe that all this atmosphere of secrecy that surrounds us, and that I myself have enthusiastically supported, is finished."[9] The inspiration for his open-rehearsal concept has been his determination to break down the sense of a barrier separating the actor from the audience. In brief, unabashedly hortative speeches delivered to the audience at these public rehearsals, he has usually tried to explain this aspect of his attitude in these terms: "Remember that every performance is dependent upon involvement. You come here with a longing to experience something. The actors are trying to meet that longing, and they perceive how you react. Try to experience the play as intensely and directly as you can."[10] The audience has an active job to do on such occasions, he insists, and the price of admission is its undivided and unbroken concentration. Seen in this way, a theater performance is indeed "to an exceptional degree a matter of give and take."[11]

From the point of view of the actor, meanwhile, these open

rehearsals help to prepare the ground upon which these two vital forces in the creative process, the performer and the beholder, will encounter one another in the finished performance. As training exercises, these occasions are arranged by Bergman – sometimes quite spontaneously – as a means of helping the actors to maintain a healthy, "unneurotic," and disciplined attitude towards their work in this respect. "The audience comes to be influenced, not to influence us. We are the ones who give; we must radiate strength, self-confidence, joy in our activity on stage," he explained to the *Woyzeck* cast, who faced the unusual prospect for the first time. "No private neuroses must be allowed to come between us and the audience. It is a terrible mistake to confuse private neuroses with talent. It is significant that the more firmly the details are implanted, the stronger, freer, and happier the actor will feel."[12]

Bergman's first application of the open-rehearsal method to Molière came in connection with his notable revival of *The Misanthrope* at the Royal Theatre in Copenhagen in 1973. "According to the wishes of the Swedish director, some rehearsals were made public so that the audience (who picked up tickets at the box office) might attend a quite ordinary rehearsal of *The Misanthrope*. IB had done something similar in Stockholm," an obviously puzzled stage manager recorded in the Royal Theatre's official daybook.[13] "During the open rehearsals we perform the entire play, and we then discuss the audience's reaction after they have left," the director himself explained to the Copenhagen press at the outset of the nearly eight-week rehearsal period.[14] The first of these public sessions took place a little more than a month after rehearsals had started and only four days after the company had begun rehearsing on the stage itself. By the time of the actual opening (April 6), a total of seven such free, open rehearsals had been held – at first, with the cast in rehearsal clothing, for a limited audience of some 150, subsequently, with complete costumes and makeup, for a much larger general public. It might seem almost paradoxical that the outcome of this process was one of Bergman's most perfectly finished, precisely formed classical revivals, bearing not the slightest trace of an improvisational or "workshopped" style. In Bergman's theater, the end result is thus the product of a highly conscious, very carefully calcu-

Work photograph of Kerstin Hedeby's stylized baroque setting for
The Misanthrope. Danish Royal Theatre, Copenhagen, 1973.

lated process of give and take, in which the actors "adjust their
roles, their voices, and their spiritual processes" to their
audience – but also a process under the close and vigilant
scrutiny of the director-mediator, whose task it is "to indicate
the concept for the production and then to function as eye and
ear, security factor, stimulator, coordinator, work foreman,
and, to a certain degree, teacher."[15]

PORTRAIT OF A MISANTHROPE

The three elements that Bergman regards as the only essential
ones in the theater – a subject, actors, and audience – confront

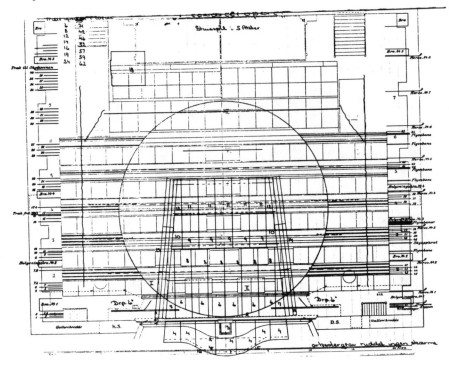

Figure 11 Plan of the stage (Danish Royal Theatre) for
The Misanthrope.

and interact with one another continuously. The nature of this
interaction is, in turn, invariably influenced and conditioned
by the physical space that contains a performance, and which
thereby becomes, for the actors, "a co-performer in visual and
acoustical terms".[16] In his Copenhagen production of *The
Misanthrope* – which may be said to exemplify his vision and
method as a classical director perhaps better than any of his
other Molière revivals – the immediacy of the contact between
stage and auditorium was strengthened by eliminating the
front curtain and constructing a raked platform that reached
out over the orchestra pit to form a roughly semicircular
forestage. Figure 11 illustrates both the shape of this construc-
tion and the disposition of the twenty-nine platforms needed
to create the gently sloping stage that Bergman required. To
achieve the same purpose in the earlier production of the play
at the Malmö City Theatre in 1957, Bergman and his designer
had actually moved the backdrop forward almost to the pro-

scenium opening, and had extended the forestage so far into the auditorium that it seemed to include the audience in the same continuous space. ("Everything was faraway and yet close to us, remote and yet very familiar," one critic remarked on that occasion. "It was the kind of aesthetic distance that creates an intensified perception of what remains eternal beneath the changing masks."[17]) In the less adaptable gold-and-stucco precincts of the Danish national theater, so radical a structural fusion of stage and auditorium would hardly be feasible – or appropriate. Here, however, as the audience entered the theater the soft, subdued lighting served to erase the separation between the two spaces and make them one. The observant spectator was introduced at once to the play's visual ambience – an elegant pastiche of a baroque perspective stage, a theater erected within a theater, designed to evoke the

The stage as it appeared in the earlier production of *The Misanthrope*. Malmö, 1957.

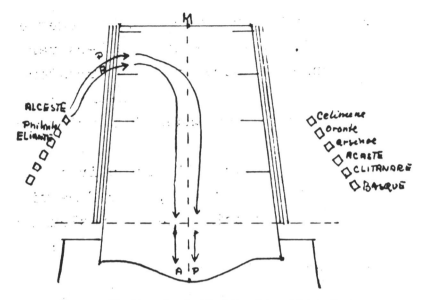

Figure 12 Blocking plan for *The Misanthrope* (V.i), indicating positions of actors' chairs in the wings.

period flavor and the sense of graceful formality of the age of the Sun King, Louis the Fourteenth. The balanced recession of parallel flat wings in designer Kerstin Hedeby's stage setting – four on each side, decorated with feather-light motifs of trees and birds seen against a golden ground – created an emphatic, deliberately stylized impression of perspective depth. Hedeby's neutral, symmetrical stage picture – which served to place the vivid costumes and three-dimensional figure compositions of the actors in high relief – was completed by a formal balustrade at the back, beyond which one glimpsed the luminous outlines of painted trees. Only a bare minimum of furnishings – a pair of baroque chairs, a bench, a mirror – occupied the stage proper. The floor of the stage was divided, by means of white lines, into a pronounced pattern of large rectangles, quite different in character from the more representational checkerboard floor employed in the Malmö production. This distinctive grid imparted to the acting area an imposing sense of choreographic regularity and formality – an impression further enhanced by the symmetrical rows of ornate chandeliers (four pairs in all) that cast their festive, subdued illumination over the action.

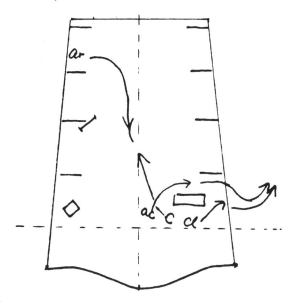

Figure 13 Acaste and Clitandre return to their chairs in the wings, during act 3, scene 3 of *The Misanthrope*.

To the atmosphere of elegant artifice established by the physical setting, Bergman added an unusual and suggestive touch to his Copenhagen revival that had the effect of deepening his comment on the intrinsic theatricality of Molière's conception. Seated on the outskirts of the stage, in the dimly lighted area just beyond the side wings, the performers involved in any given act of the play could be seen nonchalantly awaiting their entrances. When their cue came, the actors simply rose from their chairs in the wings and mounted the three broad steps that led to the elevated platform-stage (cf. Fig. 12) – while at the end of their scene they stepped back into the wings and again resumed their seats (Fig. 13). The actors "'take on' their roles, so to speak, as they enter Célimène's salon, where the audience, too, becomes a guest," noted Henrik Lundgren in *Information*. They seemed, thought Robert Naur (*Politiken*) to, be "inanimate properties until the action summons them into its living space." The striking overall impression thus created was likened by this critic to "the toy-theater effect of a magic box." In Bergman's view, the experience of watching the costumed, concentrated actor – or the circus performer – waiting to step into the performance is indeed a special, magical one. The presence of these silent, waiting actor–spectators facilitates the movement from reality into the world of the imaginary event, he feels, thereby preparing and urging the audience to take the step "from the realm of everyday existence into something extraordinary." The effect created on an audience while a large symphony sits tuning its instruments is a favourite analogy of his in this connection.

Like the stage set itself, of course, the visual perspective introduced by the presence of these actor–spectators in *The Misanthrope* calls to mind certain specific historical antecedents. In the conversation "Talking about Theater," Bergman describes the tradition that actually inspired his use of this strategy – the old custom at the Comédie Française that the actors did in fact remain on the stage, behind the scenes, throughout the entire performance of a play ("like shadows, as a presence") – each one with his own chair, with his name on it. However, the mere resurrection of an historical tradition is

In this scene between Alceste and Philinte, from the Copenhagen production of *The Misanthrope*, the costumed actors seated in the wings can be seen to the right of the picture.

obviously not the reason for Bergman's adoption of a technique such as this. Rather, it is his abiding preoccupation with the bond between audience and actor that would inevitably attract him to the device of the performer–spectator, as one of those simple, concrete "suggestions" that, taken together, "create a dimension" in his theatrical method. In *The Misanthrope*, the device was an ingenious means of sharpening the focus, thereby stimulating a climate of expectation and intensifying the communicative rapport between stage and auditorium.

From the moment of his first, fiery entrance, the figure of Alceste remained the undisputed center of dramatic interest in Bergman's production. Every development of the action was orchestrated to accentuate the potential drama around his figure. For Bergman, the key to this role – and hence to the shape of the play as a whole – is to be found in Alceste's relationship to Célimène. "I do not experience this work as a wordy play about an apostle of the truth," he remarked in an interview in *Helsingborgs Dagblad*. "I see it instead as a fascinating love story; about how love becomes one of the most important motivating forces in our lives." By locating the mainspring of the action in a concrete situation of human interaction rather than by defining it in the more static and abstract terms of a character study, the director deftly underscored the comedy's dynamic peripeties and suspense. He made of Molière's play "not merely a painting of manners, set in the superficial, make believe world of the salon," declared the reviewer for *Berlingske Tidende*, but "a drama about the love relationship between two incompatible people." The central character becomes not simply a man incapable of hypocrisy, singlemindedly upholding his ideal of absolute integrity to the very end, but more important, a man caught in an intensely human predicament. In this production a remarkable bond of sympathy was forged between Alceste and the audience, bringing the character much closer to the spectator. "The Misanthrope, as we encounter him in the black-clad figure of Henning Moritzen, is neither pathetic nor a psychological case study nor pure clown," Robert Naur observed.[18] "He is an impassioned young man intent upon changing the world for the better, intent upon transforming his beloved Célimène after his own image, and, on top of it all, quivering with

The passionate, black-clad Alceste of Henning Moritzen, who seemed "as though forever battling an imaginary head-wind," is seen here in an exchange of Eliante (Hanne Borchsenius). Copenhagen, 1973.

jealousy." This critic added an interesting visual descriptor to his analysis of the character that Moritzen drew – "he bends a little forward as he moves, as though forever battling an imaginary head-wind."

In the Malmö production of the play sixteen years before, Bergman's Alceste had been Max von Sydow, who played the character as a rebellious, restive, rather confused idealist – "a disoriented Don Quixote who is perpetually shocked to discover that people are not as noble as they are in Gothic

The Alceste of Max von Sydow, in the Malmö production of *The Misanthrope*, 1957.

romances."[19] Henrik Sjögren draws a convincing portrait of von Sydow's Misanthrope as "a relative of the angry young man who had just [1957] begun to make his presence felt in English drama. He went around, like another Gregers Werle, with his demand for the ideal; his call for absolute truth, his severe, rational absolutism obscured his vision as much as his uncontrollable love for the coquette did."[20] Harald Engberg (*Politiken*), commenting that Bergman "would not have been who he is if he had not transposed the key of Molière's comedy of manners into the tonality of a drama of passion," also aligned this Alceste with John Osborne's angry antiheroes – "an aggressive and demanding personality with a hopeless love-hatred of the circle in which he moves, a pathetic figure among the fools of his time, who wins our sympathy precisely because he does not try to but, on the contrary, does all he can to fend it off."

In the Copenhagen production, Henning Moritzen's authoritative interpretation of Alceste traced a far darker, more tragic pattern than his famous Swedish predecessor had done. Incapable of pretense and at the same time painfully aware of the compromises upon which society is based, this Alceste seemed "an awkward and paradoxical but pure soul, in the midst of a world of deceit, superficiality, and altogether too much cold detachment" (*Kristeligt Dagblad*). In spite of his disillusionment, however, Moritzen's Misanthrope shared with von Sydow's earlier characterization the quality of poignant youthfulness – "the youngest that one recalls," recorded Svend Kragh-Jacobsen, the dean of Danish critics, who added: "it is precisely this youthfulness that explains the character, the hotheaded vehemence, the intolerance, the demand for all-or-nothing." The emphatic sensation of alienation and of suffering inflicted by the searing conflict betweeen a hot heart and clear reason made Moritzen's black-clad Misanthrope seem, to many observers, a Hamlet-like figure: "Alceste is an *angry* man, not a bad-tempered one," wrote Inge Dam in *BT*. "His noble outlook on life clashes decisively with the mendacity of society. Like a young Hamlet, he is puzzled by the smiling villains who surround him."

Bergman himself once remarked, in working on *Hedda Gabler* (1964) and *The School for Wives* (1966), that he was struck by "a tremendously strong impression that Ibsen and Molière

– each with varying strength – are giving deeply personal and overt expression to a profound depression. Molière in the guise of a rather brittle humor – and Ibsen with a shocked despair that he has covered over with an elaborate superstructure, precisely because he is so desperate."²¹ Bergman's second production of *The Misanthrope* conveyed a forceful impression of this accumulating sense of outrage, bitterness, and blackness that lie just beneath the comic veneer of the play. A neatly printed exclamation in his director's script, commenting on Alceste's speech about his physical revulsion at even the slightest distortion of the truth, speaks for itself concerning the Ibsen–Molière affinity that he perceives:

> there's none I'd choose to spare.
> All are corrupt; there's nothing to be seen
> In court or town but aggravates my spleen.
>
> (I.i.87–90)²²
>
> BRAND! GREGERS!

Nevertheless, Bergman's interpretation very carefully maintained and emphasized the paradoxical syntax of Molière's play. Hence, though virtually every reviewer summed up his ultimate impression of the performance as tragic, it derived its distinctive, dynamic tone and texture from its preservation of juxtaposed and contrasted moods: pathos and comedy, a seriousness and an exaggerated humor that bordered on the grotesque.

As the house lights dimmed to half and two warning thumps of the stage manager's baton paid homage to the traditions of the Comédie Française, the performance opened on a note of high intensity. A violently agitated Alceste ("already out of balance because of Célimène," notes the director's script) rushed swiftly and purposefully in a diagonal line across the stage to the very front righthand wing (Fig. 14) – behind which he actually disappeared before speaking his first line ("Leave me alone, I beg of you"). In a production built predominantly on strong, single emotions and emphatically defined juxtapositions of mood and objective, Philinte was similarly supplied by the director with a pointedly contrasting attitude to the explosive situation: "What has caused this crisis? Philinte surprised and pleasant." Reemerging, in high dudgeon, from his hiding place behind the side wing, Alceste

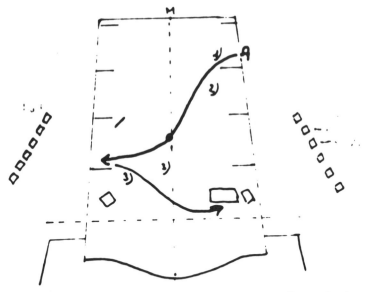

Figure 14 Blocking plan indicating Alceste's first, diagonal entrance movement in *The Misanthrope*.

again stormed across the full width of the stage in front of his puzzled friend, who remained standing calmly at its center. Abruptly, the perpetually angry Alceste sat down and deliberately turned his back on Philinte as he expressed, with a typically brusque, seriocomic gesture of finality, his firm determination to remain furious and not to listen ("I choose to be rude, Sir, and to be hard of hearing"). Move followed restless move to produce a meticulously coordinated, boldly accentuated pattern of poses, gestures, and sculptural figure compositions – a pattern governed at all times by an unfailing harmony and formal control. This strong sense of design, coupled with the astonishing visual eloquence of Bergman's attack, prompted most reviewers to comment, in one form or another, on the "classical" qualities of simplicity and clarity so evident in a mise-en-scène that "progressed in crystal-clear, almost mathematically structured scenes, amazingly controlled . . . yet saturated with vitality and dramatic tension" (*Kristeligt Dagblad*).

Although the emphatic figure clusters and movement patterns in this performance stood out on the gridlike ground of

the stage floor with relieflike definition and firmness, the
ultimate impression was never one of static tableaux. On the
other hand, Bergman made no attempt, as a naturalistic
director might have done, to animate his composition by
means of a particularized mosaic of realistic stage business or a
multitude of painstakingly detailed, fluctuating objectives
geared to the slightest nuances in the text.[23] He deliberately
placed the emphasis on the artifice and lively theatricality of
the comedy by relying throughout on consciously formalized
blocking patterns that underscored the broad tempo variations
and vigorous rhythmic flow of Molière's alexandrines. Typical
of Bergman's method as well was the fact that he relied to a
very large extent on close-up scenes, played at the front of the
stage and deepening the direct rapport between actors and
audience, rather than on the detached naturalistic technique of
locating characters within the context of a "living" environment.

Alceste's misfortunes, as the French scholar Alfred Simon
succinctly observes, seem during the course of the play "to
multiply to a tempo of burlesque that mocks his seriousness,"
as the representatives of the fashionable society that surrounds
him force him into a succession of hopeless situations. Bergman consciously broadened the comedy of these encounters
by depicting the *fâcheux* – the fops who descend on the
beleaguered Misanthrope in an apparently never-ending
stream – in a spirit of fierce, scathing parody, as representatives of the "enslaved, dangerous, and terrifying society" that
the director sees reflected in Molière's play. "The worst and
most dangerous thing that can happen," he told his audience
at the outset of one of the first public rehearsals,

is to fall into disfavor with the king and to cease to be part of the ruling
class. This can happen by saying the wrong thing, by not having the
right emotions, by having any emotions at all. Certainly one can be very
sentimental. And one can cry, provided they're crocodile tears. But one
must never display *genuine* emotion, never admit how things really
stand. One must continually have an intrigue in motion. All watch one
another, spy on one another, but at the same time smile to one another,
pay perpetual compliments to one another.

Accordingly, the vain poet Oronte, the two foolish marquises,
Acaste and Clitandre, and even the Officer of the Marshals of
France all appeared as grimacing caricatures, decked out in

colorful, elaborately adorned period costumes, topped by enormous edifices of makeup and wigs. The sumptuous riot of color produced by their parodic appearance identified these figures as a species of puffed-up, basically inhuman creatures – akin to the figures of peacocks and other birds worked into the stage setting itself – vainly and aimlessly parading themselves in their finery. "Who could forget the black figure of Alceste in contrast to the radiant color profusion of the scoffing fops. Superb," proclaimed *Berlingske Tidende*.

Only the occasional critic was inclined to object, in the name of "realism," to the broadly stylized exaggeration of the *fâcheux*. "I cannot understand why these figures and the scenes around them are made so grotesque in their humor," one reviewer had written of the Malmö production in 1957. "The comedy is not necessarily lost in a more cautiously elegant treatment, and that alternative has the added advantage of providing a better background for Alceste's betrayal."[24] Essentially the same kind of literalistic objection was raised in Henrik Lundgren's review of the Copenhagen revival: "Why has Bergman depicted Célimène's admirers and friends with so little understanding of her personality," the critic demanded. "Would she not have sensed it to be a waste of time to associate with these ridiculously caricatured marquises?" The question can have no meaningful answer, however, for it reflects a fundamental misunderstanding of the director's intent with such a strategy. "One has to be an enormously unresponsive spectator not to recognize that here is an example of theater that has nothing to do with naturalistic psychologizing," Jens Kruse declared bluntly in *Jyllands Posten*. Seen from this angle, then, the confrontation with the would-be poet Oronte (I.ii), the first of the direct clashes between Alceste and the "terrifying society" of fops that surround him, served less to establish a believable psychological relationship than to illuminate the threatening tension that Bergman perceives throughout the play between humanity and inhumanity, seriousness and near-burlesque. In Ebbe Rode's portrayal, Oronte stood out as "a monumental caricature . . . the epitome of imbecile self-confidence" (*Aktuelt*); his physical appearance was that of a fabulous monster, "a mixture between a bull and a turkey" (*Berlingske Tidende*). One purpose alone propelled this fatuous poet–monster: "Oronte's sole objective is to get to read his poem aloud," reads a characteristic note in the director's script. This single objective – the self-styled sonneteer's frantic desire to display his artistic achievement, his sonnet, and to be duly praised and admired for the accomplishment – became the motivation for his every action: the overdone, even oily respect that he pays to a decidedly reluctant and increasingly embarrassed Alceste; the kiss on each cheek with which he seals his declaration of "friendship"; not least, his unyielding determination to occupy center stage.[25] Swelling with pride at the idea of having written a sonnet, Oronte delivered himself of his masterpiece – bound in a small, elegant book – in a deep, declamatory voice, looking to Alceste for approval at every pause. As the latter, seated ("like a block of ice") at the farthest physical remove from the poetaster, tried resolutely to avert an open conflict over the "masterpiece," Oronte's blissful self-satisfaction gradually wilted until, at the end of the scene, he left the stage in a fury, yet nonetheless bowing and smiling as affably as when he first appeared. The high point in this exchange – and one of the brightest moments in the entire production – was Moritzen's sincere, unaffected delivery of the old song with which Alceste pointedly counters Oronte's bombast ("Si le Roi m'avait donné/Paris, sa grande-ville"). This verse, in whose simple, unassuming rhymes one is meant to sense something of the voice of the true poet, was first sung and then recited simply and directly by Alceste, framed by the totally immobile figures of Philinte and Oronte.

A crucial aspect of Bergman's interpretation of *The Misanthrope* is reflected in the fact that, in this scene, the vivid contrast established between Oronte and Alceste was heightened by the comic rigidity of the poses of *both* characters – a rigidity that, in Alceste's case, continued throughout the performance to be seen as a predominant feature of his character. On the one hand, this Misanthrope possessed "a basic sympathetic normality" that, as the critic for *Politiken* observed, made him "not a caricature but a portrait of a human being with whom everyone could somehow identify." On the other hand, however, Moritzen's Alceste was, from the very outset, so filled with disgust at any trace of hypocrisy, so unbendingly and self-righteously obsessed with honesty, so absolutely charged with his own integrity that the very

Right, Alceste with the would-be poet Oronte (Ebbe Rode), whose sole objective is to read his poem aloud. Copenhagen, 1973.

inflexibility of his attitude inevitably provoked laughter. This sense of rigidity was suggestively expressed in many ways in the physical mise-en-scène as well. At the close of the first act, for example, the moves and gestures that accompanied Alceste's passionate refusal to listen to the ever-patient Philinte ("Je n'entends rien") constituted a virtual replay in reverse of the very same moves and the long diagonal cross that had been used to bring him on the stage at the beginning (see Fig. 15).

Precisely this kind of carefully structured balance and design

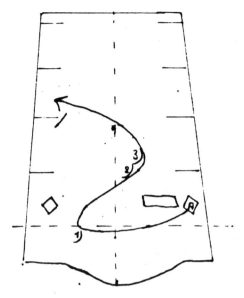

Figure 15 Alceste's exit in the first act of *The Misanthrope*, reversing the pattern of his entrance cross.

remained an abiding characteristic of the production as a whole, as it unfolded in a series of almost musically phrased contrasts and parallelisms, some lightheartedly comic, others tinged by a strong note of pathos. Perhaps nowhere was Bergman's concern for formal coherence more in evidence than in his original treatment of the intervals between the acts. These transitions were fashioned into a sequence of panto-mimic interludes that not only maintained a satisfying sense of continuity, but also accounted in themselves for some of the most entertaining visual conceits in the performance. During each of the four intervals between the respective acts of the play, Célimène's servant Basque – a virtually nonexistent role in the text, transformed by Bergman into a key one – appeared and proceeded, with great ceremony and an elaborate show of superiority and self-importance, to rearrange the few pieces of furniture on the stage, dangling his fan (in imitation of his mistress?) and flirting broadly with the audience all the while. Following each of the acts, the ubiquitous Basque, brimming with a mixture of urgency and supreme *hauteur*, would turn up to repeat his "number," and only his signal to an invisible stage manager permitted the play to proceed. Like so much else in the production, this device has its obvious antecedents in theatrical history. In the theater of the Baroque period and during the eighteenth century, as we know, the task of clearing unneeded furniture and props from the stage was left, whenever possible, to the servants and other minor figures in a play. In Bergman's hands, however, this venerable convention became far more than merely a useful practical expedient; Basque's *lazzi* provided their own suggestive comment on the motif of theatricality and role playing that is so central to Bergman's interpretation of Molière's comedy.

In another and equally important respect, moreover, Bergman's development of Basque as a dramatic character illustrates this director's scrupulous attention to even the smallest details in the overall fabric of a given work. Every one of Basque's brief appearances – which are included in the text merely as a means of announcing the arrival of a new character – was textured in such a way that the comic momentum was sustained while a new facet of the zany servant's personality was revealed. Basque's three appearances in the second act serve to demonstrate the point briefly. To announce the arrival of Acaste, he came dashing onto the stage and then stopped abruptly, interrupting a tense encounter between Alceste and Célimène with a one-word announcement spoken with an air of regretful anxiety. ("Basque is a little afraid of Acaste," was the clue provided by the director at rehearsals.) Next time, however, his behavior had altered completely, and he came tripping in on the tips of his toes to deliver his message ("Clitandre, Madame") beaming with delight, contentedly inspecting his own image in the mirror. (The reason: "Clitandre has said such fantastically nice things that Basque comes dancing in, in a tiptop mood.") The servant's last appearance in the act revealed yet another side of his temperament. Obliged to announce the arrival of the legal officer who comes to serve a summons on Alceste for allegedly having affronted Oronte, the humorously complex Basque was directed to be "virtually in tears with fear" at the very thought of this awe-inspiring individual.

At the critical core of Bergman's interpretation, imparting perspective and bitter irony to the seriocomic encounters between Alceste and the world of deceit that surrounds him, was the director's apprehension of the play as, above all, "a

The coquettish Célimène of Gertrud Fridh, seen with von Sydow's Alceste in the Malmö production of *The Misanthrope* in 1957.

fascinating love story" about a relationship between two basically incompatible people. Bergman views Célimène as "a woman who has chosen to conform, who wants to 'survive,'" Bibi Andersson (who played Eliante in his Malmö production of *The Misanthrope*) recalls. "She wants to enjoy herself and, at the same time, she is an unusual personality, more intelligent than average. Therefore she is doomed to come into conflict in her love for Alceste . . . With his striving after righteousness and his impossible ideal demands, he is doomed to succumb, no matter how right he is. He judges and condemns and becomes trapped in his own excellent intentions,"[26] Gertrud Fridh, who acted Célimène in Malmö, had possessed a quality of playfulness that lent distance and kept her from appearing overly cruel in her coquettishness. "One capitulated completely before her; we asked neither for breadth nor depth, but simply recognized that she was what she was and could not be different, almost innocently cynical, a woman who forms no attachments but captivates everyone," recorded one observer on that occasion.[27] In the revival at the Danish Royal Theatre, Ghita Nørby presented a warmer and more human Célimène, who took an almost childlike delight in game playing – a woman, Svend Erichsen called her in *Aktuelt*, who "toys with reality, with men . . . and with herself. She establishes a distance between her own life and that of others." To the critic for *Information* this Célimène seemed "not wicked, but only spoiled by her association with flatterers and rumormongers" – "not an expert but only a novice in the craft of creating scandals. She gradually feels her way forward, mesmerized by her own success." In this performance, Célimène's love for Alceste was real enough in its own way. He represented what was serious in her life, and that seriousness seemed always present behind the games she chose to play.

The first movement in their relationship, their initial encounter at the beginning of the second act in which the impetuous Alceste ultimately proclaims the utter singularity of his overwhelming passion for Célimène ("Morbleu! faut-il que je vous aime!"), established the paradoxical syntax of the conflict – the crackling erotic tension generated by the juxtaposition of Alceste's furious infatuation and Célimène's elegant, composed, invariably lighthearted enjoyment of control. The climax of their first scene was a memorable illustration of Bergman's remarkable ability to "orchestrate" a classical text – that is, to establish a swiftly but precisely oscillating rhythm of speech patterns, eloquent pauses, moves, and gestures. As Alceste's final passionate tirade of devotion soared, Célimène absentmindedly kissed her handkerchief and casually let it fall to the floor – compelling her lover to take to his knees to pick it up. His closing couplet, spoken on his knees, crystallized into a flash of pathos that was immediately counterpointed and undercut by Célimène's brittle comic rejoinder:

ALCESTE   (*kneeling before Célimène*):   Words can't describe the nature of my passion,
(*He makes a distinct pause, and passionately kisses her handkerchief before continuing*): And no man ever loved in such a fashion.
CÉLIMÈNE (*replies promptly, lightly and brightly*):   Yes, it's a brand-new fashion, I agree;
You show your love by castigating me.

(II.i.523–6)

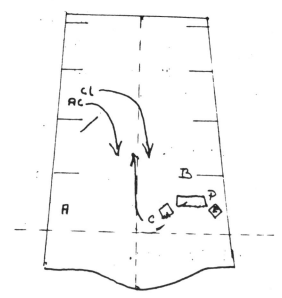

Figure 16 Blocking plan for the formal, vertical entrance march of Acaste and Clitandre in *The Misanthrope*, act 2.

The gracefully controlled erotic contest played out between Alceste and the reluctant Célimène was, however, anchored firmly by Bergman in the larger context of the "dangerous" courtly society that enveloped these mismatched lovers – the world of superficiality and duplicity to which, as Alceste must learn to his grief, Célimène ultimately belongs. With the intrusion of this world – in the person of the two marquises, Acaste and Clitandre – into Célimène's salon in the second act, the mood of the preceding love scene was swept away in a gust of broad, boisterous parody. These two sumptuously costumed gentlemen – living examples in Bergman's production of folly ripened to the point of bursting – made their pompously ceremonial entrance together, commanding a maximum of attention as they marched with great delight down the central axis of the stage (Fig. 16). Met at the halfway point by an equally delighted Célimène, they greeted her with effusive hand kisses and ecstatic outbursts of falsetto laughter. "The marquises must feel that they are a gift to the nation!" Bergman's assistant had noted during rehearsals, and their behavior throughout the performance certainly radiated precisely this point of view. Bergman, a superb director of farce (though he himself denies it and one might not guess it from his films), delineated and differentiated these gross and gorgeous caricatures of human folly with a loving eye for telling visual and vocal comic details. Peter Steen's Clitandre, propelled by an overpowering self-esteem so intense that it threatened at times to lift him off the floor, maintained a piercing falsetto voice and a laughter "that resembled the cry of a peacock" (*Fyens Stiftstidende*). His smaller, more earthbound, and decidedly more venomous colleague Acaste was acted by Erik Mørk in a contrastingly deeper tone of voice that had a grotesquely birdlike, cackling quality about it. Their exchanges with Célimène – colored by an intoxicating sense of comradeship as they joined together in the stimulating game of double entendre and murdered reputations – assumed the character of a symphonic composition for three voices and three distinct sorts of laughter. An entire vocabulary of contrasting sounds and gestures – ranging from "little-marquis laughter," and "little-marquis approval" through "great-marquis laughter," "general laughter," and a complete battery of assorted "marquis glances" – accompanied Célimène's successive attacks on the reputations of their absent "friends." (The pointers offered by Molière himself in *L'Impromptu de Versailles* for playing a foppish marquis – "with that swaggering manner they call the society air" and "with a special way of talking, to distinguish themselves from the common herd" – must surely have exerted an influence on Bergman's conception.) However else they were differentiated, meanwhile, the twin marquises moved, gestured, and reacted in perfect harmoney, united, as it were, by their mutual conviction of unmitigated superiority. Their entrances and exits and the general arrangement of their movements on the stage were all organized by Bergman in precise patterns of parallel, geometrically clean lines – a technique that might even remind one of the formality and contrived control of the entrées in a *ballet de cour*. However, in their strictly measured movements, in their deep, elaborate curtsies, and in the wide sweep of their lace-festooned arms as they gestured, these figures suggested grotesque, effeminate automatons, parodying the ideals of decorum and grace in *le grand siècle* in a capering crescendo of comic excess.

Although Bergman's broad satire of the *fâcheux* afforded a

continuous and carefully balanced comic contrast to the passionately serious tone of Alceste, the overall directorial concept of the comedy dictated a subtle but steady movement toward a black conclusion. Consequently, his treatment of the famous third-act encounter between Célimène and her older rival, Arsinoé – played with dignified composure in this performance by Lise Ringheim – deliberately minimized the scene's comic potential, emphasizing instead the essential vulgarity of the jealousy that animates their catty confrontation, the hollowness and even the brutality of the respective poses that they strike in their bid to gain control over one another.

Darker still was the tone of humiliation and suffering that pervaded the second major scene between Alceste and Célimène (IV.iii). In Bergman's view, Alceste's appeal here for compassion on the part of an unmoved and increasingly self-confident Célimène ("Good God! Could anything be more inhuman?") became "an almost Strindbergian passage," expressing the insoluble dilemma of a situation in which love and hatred are inextricably bound up together. In this scene, with its harsh and distorted resonances of their earlier encounter in the first act, Célimène seemed to be enjoying Alceste's defenselessness, as though it were a kind of applause for her performance. This time, as he fell to his knees to reiterate the absolute force of his love for her ("I love you more than can be said or thought"), she stood at the opposite end of the stage with her back turned, idly fingering one of the yellow roses in a magnificent bouquet that she had carried in with her at the beginning of the scene. In response to the "étrange manière" of her suitor and to the ideal demands that he seeks to impose upon her, she laughed harshly and then, ceasing to laugh, she threw the rose in his face. The moment anticipated Alceste's final bitter confrontation with the cardboard world of mendacity that surrounded him.

Bergman steadfastly resisted either sentimentalizing the play or distorting its basic tone into a uniformly and oppressively tragic one. Accordingly, his version did not conclude, as countless stage interpretations of The Misanthrope have done, with Alceste's angry departure from a world wrenched apart by irreconcilable contraries. It ended instead, as Molière's text of course does, with Philinte's closing lines to the effect that Alceste must be dissuaded from his purpose – a couplet that restored the sense of irony, the emphasis on a universe of paradoxes and unresolvable contradictions, on which the entire production had built. "After the final curtain has fallen," Bergman's production assistant has in fact remarked, "Philinte will bring Alceste back and the same game will begin again."[28] Nevertheless, this implied ironic repetitiveness in no way dispelled the atmosphere of darkness and finality that lies close beneath the brittle surface of Molière's bitter comedy. This mood was brought forcefully and decisively to the fore as the characters in the play confronted one another, for the last time, in a spirit no longer camouflaged by their previous gaiety.

Alceste is rejected by Célimène (Ghita Nørby) in act 4. The rose she had disdainfully flung in his face still lies on the floor, in the far left corner of the picture. Copenhagen, 1973.

The central character's disillusioned vision of the world as a jungle in which right is systematically overthrown and justice perverted, in which intrigue and self-interest alone govern and human intercourse is mere sham and theatrical make believe, was restated in the final act with the same vehemence and energy that had been dominant traits of his turbulent temperament from the beginning. "He wants to be angry," reads a note in the director's script (an echo, of course, of Alceste's own remark in the first act), and, charged with this overriding wrath, Moritzen's Misanthrope remained as trapped in the passionate intensity of his somber vision as the glittering society around him remained enmeshed in its own hollow masquerade. Locked in their single vision, the *fâcheux*, too,

The formal, frontal staging of the letter-reading scene in the Copenhagen production of *The Misanthrope*. Alceste stands in isolation to the right, his back to the audience.

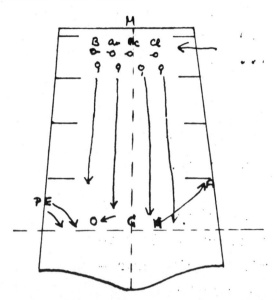

Figure 17 The inquisitorial entrance of Acaste and Clitandre,
accompanied by Basque and Arsinoé, in the letter-reading scene of
The Misanthrope.

maintained to the very end that fixity of character that they had
displayed at their first appearance. The ludicrously overblown
Oronte ("the winner of the sonnet-feud," as the production
book calls him) seemed, if anything, to have grown in stature
when he turned up again – in the scene that Bergman labels
"Alceste's humiliation" – to present his proposal of marriage to
Célimène, who haughtily declines to drop her mask or indicate
her preference. The foppish affectations of the twin marquises
were not a fraction diminished as they made their splendid
inquisitorial entrance, with Arisinoé and Basque (who came in
backwards). Marching straight down the central axis of the
stage (see Fig. 17), they triumphantly displayed the incriminat-
ing letters that expose the perfidious Célimène for what she
really is. Only when their masks momentarily slipped and the
superficiality of their own poses stood revealed did these
figures acquire a curious kind of unsentimentalized dignity;
but they quickly resumed their poses and, trapped in their
pretense, they remained to the very end of the performance
what Bergman had so pointedly made of them from its start –

players acting out their roles, playing their game of make believe.

Once they had departed, with self-possessed and greatly exaggerated salutes to a visibly chastened Célimène, and the two lovers were left face to face for the last time, the undertone of moving pathos that critics found so remarkable in Moritzen's performance reasserted itself. Utterly dejected and at a loss for words, he turned to Célimène. Admitting her guilt, she in turn faced him, head bent, as he reached out in an attempt to take hold of her hands. However, as he replied ("almost with a smile") by expressing his sense of being inescapably trapped in his irrational love ("scornfully and with self-reproach, not sentimentally"), the intensity of his anger began to return. At Célimène's subdued but firm refusal (spoken "like a child – with sincere directness") to follow him in

The receding figure of Alceste in the closing scene of *The Misanthrope*. Danish Royal Theatre, 1973.

renouncing the world (for, after all, "la solitude effraye une âme de vingt ans"), his utter contempt for her compromising spirit exploded, and in a final gesture of outrage he knocked away her outstretched hand. Seeking some support for her position and finding none, she left the stage in a hurt, childish pout.

Following Célimène's departure, the play moved swiftly to its conclusion. Burying his face in his hands as she left, Alceste turned (after "a long pause of despair") to Eliante and spoke his last lines to her and Philinte in a restrained but vibrantly emotional tone of regret and resignation. Betrayed on all sides, overwhelmed with injustices, this Misanthrope made of his final exit a striking visual image of bitterness and isolation – an image that bore the stamp of his director's astonishing ability to create an interplay of gestures and words, glances and movements. Describing that "distant place" where one might be free to be an honest man, Alceste made his way up the stage, walking slowly backwards and facing the audience directly, his hands outstretched in a final, eloquent gesture of leavetaking – a receding black figure, etched in solitary, three-dimensional relief against the flat, artificial wing-and-border world of the stage setting. And then, having made his exit, he moved swiftly to take his vacant seat in the wings.

"There are two kinds of reality, that which you carry within yourself and which is mirrored in your face, and then the outer reality," Bergman has said in an interview, shortly before beginning work on The Misanthrope in Copenhagen. "I work only with that little dot, the human being, that is what I try to dissect and to penetrate more and more deeply, in order to trace his secrets."[29] Perhaps more than anything else, it has been this passionate preoccupation with the inner, spiritual reality of the work, the character, and the actor that has been the guiding impulse behind his finest classical productions.

5   The essence of Ibsen

While at work on his 1964 production of *Hedda Gabler* at the Royal Dramatic Theatre, Ingmar Bergman recalls that, for the first time, "the poet's face was revealed behind the mask of the weary master architect. I saw that Ibsen lived desperately entangled in his furnishings, his explanations, his artistic but pedantically constructed scenes, his curtain lines, his arias and duets. All this bulky external lumber concealed an obsession for self-exposure far greater than Strindberg's."[1] This perception of an inner, hidden Ibsen has, in one way or another, governed all nine of Bergman's major revivals of this playwright's work over the years. In each of these productions, an ever freer, more immediate, and hence more expressive form has been his conscious aim. Although the fullest and most convincing realization of that aim has been achieved in his more mature work, even his very first Ibsen venture – an uncut, five-hour production of *Peer Gynt* at the Malmö City Theatre (March 8, 1957) – revealed an unmistakable determination to forge a new and less cluttered Ibsen style. Leaving Ibsen's dramatic poem "liberated in world and picture from the lyrical and musical paraphernalia of theatrical tradition," this very early *Peer Gynt* seemed, to enthusiasts and skeptics alike, "astonishing: it [was] like seeing a painting cleansed of its yellowed exhibition varnish."[2]

Musical liberation was indeed no small part of Bergman's fresh approach to the play. Ever since 1876, when it was composed for the world premiere of *Peer Gynt*, Edvard Grieg's familiar incidental music (Opus 23) has been inextricably linked to a "romantic" conception of Ibsen's work. The richly melodious, nationalistic strains of the Grieg musical score invariably endow any production in which it is used with a basic tone of lyricism and sentimentality, casting over the play a conciliatory aura of folklore and romance that obscures the sharply ironic and antisentimental undertones in Ibsen's conception of Peer and his exploits. For the poetic dreamer of dreams must also be recognized as the egoist and the self-

185

deceiver, the man who shirks responsibility and evades reality, determined instead to follow the easier course of "going roundabout." A change in attitude came slowly. By 1948, however, the Norwegian actor–director Hans Jacob Nilsen's controversial antiromantic production was ready at last to take the decisive step of replacing Grieg's inappropriate romanticism with the stark, dissonant tones of a muscular new score by Harald Saeverud (Opus 28), whose music attempted to create a coherent pattern of "musical-psychological development" for the play.[3] It remained for Bergman to conceive the bolder and simpler expedient of dispensing with the rival claims of Grieg and Saeverud alike. In his *Peer Gynt*, the orchestral element was finally silenced, and musical accompaniment was restricted to the barest minimum needed in the play. Solveig's song was sung to a simple Norwegian folk tune; Ingrid Thulin's Anitra gyrated grotesquely to the stark accompaniment of a drum solo. "He has placed Ibsen back in the poet's seat and closed the orchestra pit," declared Martin Strömberg in *Stockholms–Tidningen*. "The inner logic of the drama, carried through to the final scene, has never been made as clear on the stage as it is here."

The real thrust of Bergman's conception was to lay bare the inner, deromanticized essense of Ibsen's drama – "Ibsen looked straight in the eye, without extenuating circumstances," as one critic phrased it.[4] To this end, he endeavored to cleanse both the play and its central character of all the sentimental associations, poetic stereotypes, and conciliatory idealizations that had accumulated about them over the years – and, what is more, to do so before the very eyes of the audience. "For us," declared a program note for the ambitious revival, "the essential thing has been to present the work as it is, without expressionistic trappings and topical political pointers but also without wrapping it in a romanticism that it had broken with at its very inception." In itself, the decision to present the play virtually without cuts represented a staggering challenge. The program lists a cast of fifty-six speaking roles, only eight of which were doubled. In all, Bergman required some ninety actors and extras for his production. His motive for undertaking the challenge in the first place is characteristic of his attitude in general: "Once only every ten or twenty years does a theater possess a Peer

Gynt. Therefore we must do the play now – while we have Max von Sydow."[5]

Bergman's faith in his brilliant young star, not yet twenty-eight and fresh from his triumph as Antonius Block in *The Seventh Seal*, was not misplaced, and von Sydow's rootless, compromising inwardly self-doubting Peer provided a solid basis on which the director could plan and execute his strategy. Instead of presenting *Peer Gynt* as a traditional kaleidoscopic series of more or less lifelike scenes, the entire visual framework of the production was subordinated to a single, ruling directorial concept – that of the play as a drama of pilgrimage, of the inward, spiritual journey of Peer, the man who is lost in illusions, toward disillusionment and nothingness. To articulate this idea, Bergman gradually and very deliberately removed the various decorative physical elements from his stage as the action progressed. In the early scenes, action was supported by a mixture of solid realistic details and stylized back projections of black-chalk landscape sketches, designed by Härje Ekman. The wedding celebration at Haegstad Farm, for example, took place in a basically realistic setting, framed by a vaguely sinister and threatening vision of mountains in the background – a vision that reemphasized the predominantly antiidyllic, even demonic tone that informed Bergman's interpretation of the wedding scene as a raucous, noisy brawl that culminates in the raw brutality of Peer's abduction of the bride. "It is no idyll, this wedding at Haegstad – there is drunkenness and violence and when the folk dance sounds over the farm, malicious laughter and evil words fill the air," commented Åke Perlström in *Göteborgs–Posten*.

As the play moved on, however, a development toward greater and greater simplification and dematerialization of the stage environment became apparent. Projections alone were now used to establish, in a nonrepresentational manner, the basic mood of a given scene, until, by the end of the play, these too had been eliminated and the stage was left completely stripped and empty. In the last act, all theatrical paraphernalia had vanished; the immense stage at Malmö now became an apparently limitless, black, and empty space that accentuated the old man's spiritual impasse and intensified his isolation and despair as he roamed about near the last crossroads of life,

unable now to fantasize himself away from the reality and
finality of death. In the darkness of the void, Peer encountered
figures of an obviously and entirely symbolic character, who
threatened him with doom and final extinction in the Button
Moulder's casting ladle. The concluding moments of the play
thus resolved themselves on a bleak and extremely subdued
note of loneliness and of ultimate reckoning. "The onion had
been peeled, Max von Sydow had penetrated to Peer's innermost, naked core, the human being beneath the troll."[6]

The more perceptive critics had by this time begun to notice
and to debate with energy Bergman's unique sense of choreography, his "ability to mold a scene with many figures in
such a way that the controlling hand of his artistic intent is
evidence in every aspect" (Göteborgs Handels – och Sjöfartstidning). His use of static or animated figure compositions as the
most important decorative element on the stage was fast
becoming a trademark of his production style. "But in that
Ingmar Bergman utilizes far fewer individuals for this purpose
and often arranges them within an optically almost vacant
space, he places far more severe demands upon his super-
numeraries than, for example, Reinhardt did, and he also
achieves far more sophisticated effects," Ebbe Linde observed
in connection with Bergman's presentation of Goethe's Ur-
Faust, a kind of companion piece to Peer Gynt that he staged at
Malmö the following year.[7] In both of these productions,
gestures, movements, positions, and groupings were all integrated into an architectonic pattern that yielded a flow of
expressive pictorial compositions, each one designed to support and enunciate the inner logic of a particular scene. Some
reviewers were troubled by a sense of stiffness and construc-
tion in the very tightly stylized Faust production, but the freer
and more robust scenes in Peer Gynt stood out with an almost
explosive plastic eloquence.

The intensely colored episode in King Brose's troll court
resembled a macabre Hieronymus Bosch vision of hell, with
the trolls "grouped like grotesque, animallike creatures carved
into the very mountain walls" (Politiken). The strongly erotic
nature of the encounter between Peer and the Greenclad One
("lust ran like molten metal through her body, on which
pouting red nipples had been applied to her skintight tulle")
gave the scene the character of an orgastic, trollish amplifi-

cation of the raucous festivities at Haegstad. The restless, opportunistic Gynt of Max von Sydow seemed in danger of being virtually swallowed up by a troll court that rolled forward in a block "like an infestation of vermin, fluttering and waving in uniform reactions until it breaks up, like an avalanche of lava-colored rocks, and sucks itself firmly around [him], a sticky mass of hair and snouts that already is halfway the Boyg" (*Göteborgs Handels – och Sjöfartstidning*).

The sheer visual force of this scene lent it a nightmarish quality that continued to persist throughout the performance. This sense of nightmare recurred again and again – in Peer's horrified brush with the shapeless, faceless Boyg, whose voice drew him trancelike across the empty stage toward the background; in the writhing contortions of Anitra, who (false rump and all) bumped and grinded for him in the desert; but above all, in his Kafkaesque encounter with the madmen in the Cairo lunatic asylum.

Retention of the "detachable" fourth act – albeit somewhat shortened – was a cardinal point in Bergman's interpretation of *Peer Gynt*, and the closing scene of this act, in the Cairo madhouse, became the most harrowing experience of all in Peer's long journey through a hostile world. Here, in the realm where "Absolute Reason passed away at eleven o'clock last night," the inhabitants were "staring, yawning, half-sleeping, aimlessly revolving and grimacing monsters in the same khaki-colored institutional outfits.[8] Neither the barred windows nor the iron cages mentioned in Ibsen's stage directions were to be seen in Bergman's production. Nor were they necessary, for the lunatics themselves comprised the "scenery." In the darkness of the vast, empty stage, bare except for a few simple benches, these figures were isolated in pools of light to form a grotesque tableau around Peer and Begriffenfeldt, his guide to this chamber of horrors. A few of them demonstrated their personal specialities: "Someone hanged himself, and his neighbor, who could no longer be bothered to carry his own head, leaned it against the corpse," wrote Allan Fagerström in *Aftonbladet*. "Another lunatic in an effective Einstein mask cut his throat, while the remainder of this contorted company marched in a stately polonaise that would be unthinkable on any other stage but this one." The topical satire with which Ibsen was concerned in this part of the play was subordinated to the more coherently dramatic purpose that the scene was made to serve here – a concrete and frightening nightmare vision of an inferno of madness, absurdity, and despair that marked the outermost station on Peer's weary pilgrimage in search of his true self.

Bergman's production of *Peer Gynt* is especially noteworthy because it presented a coherent and completely unified interpretative image of the entire play – one that reached beyond the folklore and pictorialism of the first three acts into the dark and threatening dimension of the work's final movement. "Forward and back is equally far," Peer is fond of repeating – but his journey home was far bleaker and more lonely and it took him through an endlessly dark and empty universe of a stage, where menacing presences awaited him everywhere. In the depths of the darkness, Toivo Pawlo's Button Moulder crouched over his bellows, his ladle, and his doomsday book – and out of the same darkness stepped the light and redemptive figure of Solveig (played by Gunnel Lindblom). Every trace of sentimentality was expunged from Peer's reunion with her. The final picture that confronted the audience was that of "only two human beings on an immense stage, and in the background the mute, bent figure of the Button Moulder, his casting ladle in his hand and his box of tools upon his back."[9] (Always reluctant to waste a good effect, Bergman managed to give this striking tableau an effective "reprise" in his subsequent production of *Ur-Faust*. In the final dungeon scene, played by the same constellation of actors, Faust [von Sydow] tried desperately to penetrate the madness of Margarete [Lindblom] while the brooding silhouette of Mephistopheles [Pawlo] loomed ominously in the background.)

"The theater calls for nothing," Bergman has said. "TV includes everything, film includes everything, there everything is shown. Theater ought to be the encounter of human beings with human beings and nothing more. All else is distracting."[10] This expressed determination to strip away all inessential representational details in order to focus on the face-to-face encounter between actor and spectator has been a singularly persistent feature of all his Ibsen productions through the years. With *Peer Gynt*, it removed the play decisively from the realm of amiable but confused pantomime to which it is so often confined in the theater. But there is

The writhing contortions of Anitra (Ingrid Thulin) are watched with obvious relish by Peer Gynt (Max von Sydow). Malmö City Theatre, 1957.

another side to Bergman's work with Ibsen that must also be emphasized, namely this director's exceptional critical sensitivity to those details in the plays that *are* essential, but that are often overlooked by less incisive minds. When asked to give an explanation for the unusual power and effectiveness of the scene in which Mother Aase (Naima Wifstrand) dies in *Peer Gynt*, he apparently had a ready reply:

Quite simply because we followed Ibsen. It is all there in the stage directions, you see – that he must sit at the foot of her bed. He cannot watch Aase die – he dares not do so – and therefore she summons the last of her strength to help him. It isn't he who comforts her, quite the other way round. It pays to show solidarity with the playwright, especially when his name is Henrik Ibsen.[11]

It can be argued that this remark points to a more general truth about Bergman's artistic attitude, not only toward Ibsen's plays but toward any work he undertakes to present on the stage. In his drive toward simplification and intensification, certain extraneous or overtly symbolic things (vine leaves, portentous portraits, white horses, visiting cards marked with black crosses) may well risk being eliminated – but nothing is added that does not find its ultimate basis and justification in the text.

THE AIRLESS WORLD OF HEDDA GABLER

Hedda Gabler, Bergman's second Ibsen production, burst like a bomb on the European theater scene when it first appeared at Dramaten in 1964, and in retrospect it has remained one of the truly revolutionary and influential Ibsen productions of this century. As he had done in *Peer Gynt*, Bergman resolutely swept aside the dusty impedimenta of accumulated tradition – in this case the assumptions acquired through three-quarters of a century of naturalistic performances. In his hands *Hedda Gabler* emerged, with almost hypnotic intensity, as a work whose vision extends far beyond the realistic or the social plane. His starkly simplified and stylized interpretation created a tightly controlled distillation in which nothing was permitted to distract from the ruling image of the play as a drama of destiny, a cold fable of characters buried alive in a deadly vacuum. "His inspiration transformed the mathematical reality of the play into the workings of a dream, over whose outcome one has no control. He illuminated the drama in a light that was not of this world," wrote Siegfried Melchinger in *Theater heute*.[12] In no other Bergman production has his instinct for clarity and purity, his extraordinary ability to comprehend and transmit the inner shape of the drama found more pregnant expression than in his boldly untraditional *Hedda*.

Bergman, who says he envies the musical conductor his unlimited opportunity to return again and again to a favorite score, has tried to adopt something of the same approach with those plays that "pursue" him – and *Hedda Gabler* has decidedly been one of these. This particular work has been restaged twice by him since the Stockholm premiere, both times outside Sweden, and in each instance a different set of artistic and personal circumstances prevailed. In 1970 he was persuaded by Laurence Olivier to direct members of the National Theatre company in a London production, with Maggie Smith in the title role. On the surface, in terms of physical setting and details of the external mise-en-scène, little seemed to have changed since the Stockholm production (which had come to London on tour in 1968). In fact, however, having no control whatsoever over the selection of the cast and confronted with unfamiliar and extremely uncongenial rehearsal conditions, Bergman found it impossible to direct the English revival in a satisfactory manner. The inevitable outcome was a disturbing sense of discrepancy between his concept and the style and execution of the English actors: *Punch* insisted that "this is a director's idea undermining an intelligent performance," while *The Observer* was inclined to suggest that "a naturalistic production would fit most of Maggie Smith's performance better."[13] In *Laterna Magica*, Bergman takes the opportunity to provide his own lively account of the adverse working conditions that later caused him to disown this unrepresentative production.

A very different result was achieved in his subsequent production of the play at the Residenztheater in Munich (April 11, 1979), where the difficulties that had so obviously beset the English cast of the National Theatre revival had vanished completely. In Munich the play emerged once again with the full force and intensity that had made Bergman's first *Hedda Gabler* so memorable – which is not to say that this third revival was merely a replica of the Dramaten performance. In the Residenztheater production, Ibsen's four-act drama became a chamber play, an even more precise formulation than it had been before, played now as one fluid and unbroken action, without an intermission. There were also differences between the Munich and Stockholm productions both in terms of certain features of the setting and in terms of the choreography of particular moments in the play. Unlike the distinct conceptual differences that separate Bergman's versions of *The Ghost Sonata*, however, the changes made in this case concerned matters of detail rather than matters of substance. In essence, all three of these productions of *Hedda Gabler* projected a fundamentally identical vision of the play as a drama of entrapment and isolation, of ghostlike figures – "dead souls in the ashes," as *Süddeutsche Zeitung* called them – caught in a world in which there are no second chances.

To articulate this vision, Bergman relentlessly stripped away the heavy mosaic of realistic details present in Ibsen's "handsomely and tastefully furnished drawing room" – the thick carpets, the dark porcelain stove, the curtained French windows, and, not least, the portentous portrait of Hedda's father, General Gabler, were all eliminated, for much the same reason that the symbolic allusions to the Dionysian vine leaves in Løvborg's hair (pointers so dear to the hearts of literary scholars) were ruthlessly expunged by him. "No fascination with museumlike interior decorating is permitted to divert the audience's concentration away from the human drama," declared Per Erik Wahlund (*Svenska Dagbladet*) following the Stockholm premiere (October 17, 1964). The entire stage space was transformed by Bergman and his designer (Mago, in all three cases) into an immense, nonrepresentational box that reflected and contributed to the prevailing atmosphere of claustrophobia, rather than illustrating it in a photographic manner. Uniformly lined with a dark red, velvetlike fabric, this mausoleum–stage radiated an oppressive sense of enclosure and lifelessness. "One looks into this strange locale and wonders how human beings can breathe there. It is as though there is no air in this red chamber of horrors," wrote Nils Beyer (*Stockholms–Tidningen*) of this "ghostly vision." There were neither actual windows nor walls, only a succession of simple screens, all covered in the same dark-red velvet, which demarcated a shallow playing area within the empty space.

A smaller, movable screen – sometimes a door, sometimes a barrier in the central character's mind – bisected the stage vertically into two separate spheres of simultaneous action. "A red screen divides life into two compartments," remarked *Dagens Nyheter*. "In one of them the dull routine of living drags on, in the other Hedda Gabler writhes in desperation and frustration." This was the "inner room" of Ibsen's stage directions, the physical and psychcic retreat where Hedda keeps her piano and the General's pistols, which Bergman now laid bare to view. Only the strictest minimum of stylized period furniture – a dark-red sofa, a pair of red chairs, a black bookcase, a black piano on which stood a bouquet of dark-red roses, a large mirror – dotted the monotonous landscape of Hedda's prison-world. In this all-consuming red vacuum, the exits at the back and to the side seemed veiled in obscurity. Now and then during the performance, the wall screen in the background opened, as if moved by a ghostly hand, to reveal a dark void in which offstage characters were seen to move. Of the world outside, the world of reality, there was no trace anywhere. "It exists only as a quotation," observed Hans Schwab-Felisch in *Frankfurter Allgemeine*. "It impinges on what happens, and it even has the power to affect actual events, but it has no real meaning."

Perceived in the eerie unreality of this airless, timeless red inferno, illuminated by a uniformly cold light that tampered with contours and erased any secure sense of spatial dimensionality, the characters in the drama appeared like figures suspended in a void. Each was dressed in a muted, unrelieved monotone – Hedda in dark green, the others in yet more subdued color values that ranged from pale gray and olive to black. A hint of period flavor in the costumes – pointedly simplified and stylized – completed the impression of characters that existed, independent of any material surroundings, in an atmosphere in which reality had no place. ("We had no intention of making the costumes symbolic," Mago has stated specifically. "We wanted them to be simple, uniform, and suggestive of another time, only vaguely dated, vaguely period."[14]) Inevitably, perhaps, the impact created by these isolated human figures, seen against a ground of strangely menacing vacancy, evoked allusions to Bergman's own austere vision as a film maker and, in particular, to Edvard Munch's brooding studies of a mood of spiritual desolation and paral-

Hedda Gabler (Christine Buchegger) watches from behind the
screen that bisected the stage vertically in Bergman's *Hedda Gabler*.
Residenztheater, 1979.

ysis. "The memory of Munch's great canvas of humanity haunts one's inner eye: those swaying figures of women in monochrome, suffused in the color of blood . . . It is oppressive, subdued, and enclosed," remarked one critic.[15]

In Bergman's theater poetics, as we know, the various external components of a production – the setting, the costumes, the lighting design – have importance only in so far as they conspire to stimulate the imagination of the audience. This process of spectator activation – the need to make the performance "live in his heart, in his mind" – is, to Bergman, the essential requirement, the basic and immutable law of the theater. Every decision and every spatial arrangement in his mise-en-scène is calculated to contribute to a spectrum of suggestions, a visual and aural rhythm that will accomplish this end as forcefully and directly as possible. Accordingly, his conception of *Hedda Gabler* endeavored to establish, from the very outset, the strongest possible sense of an imaginative bond between stage and auditorium. In the Stockholm production at Dramaten, the theater's ornate front curtain rose – but only halfway – several minutes before the play began, allowing the audience to breathe in the atmosphere beforehand.[16] Deprived by the director of the comfortable naturalistic fiction of an invisible fourth wall, the spectator felt himself to be in the Tesman "home", virtually face to face with its inhabitants. "Everything is quiet. We experience the theatrical space as a unity. We are made to understand that actors and not real people from the nineties are about to make their entrance. The screens are not walls in a house, but rather the kind of screen that the Chinese put up to force evil spirits to alter their course," commented the reviewer for *Arbetarbladet*. In the Munich production, which was played entirely without a curtain, Bergman accomplished his purpose of establishing a sense of rapport between actors and audience by extending the stage of the cavernous Residenztheater so far forward into the auditorium that virtually all the scenes were acted in front of the line of the fire curtain. (Notice the extreme frontal placement of the sofa and Hedda's chair in the ground plan seen in Fig. 18.) In both productions the houselights were dimmed only after the play had begun, and later a glaring projection of light from the rear of the house, sweeping directly above the

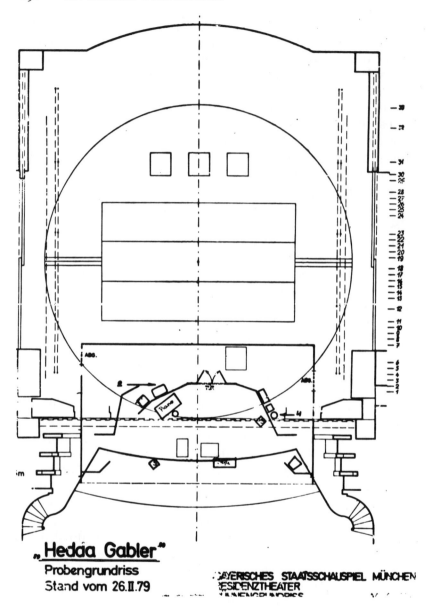

„Hedda Gabler"
Probengrundriss
Stand vom 26.II.79

BAYERISCHES STAATSSCHAUSPIEL MÜNCHEN
RESIDENZTHEATER

Figure 18 Plan of the stage (Residenztheater) for *Hedda Gabler*.

heads of the audience, further obliterated the separation between stage and auditorium.

Ultimately, however, the real impact of Bergman's interpretation of *Hedda Gabler* derived not so much from his revolutionary dematerialization of the physical setting as from his analytical, almost surgical dissection of the enigma of Hedda herself. In Bergman's version Hedda was never allowed to disappear from sight. She stood trapped before us on the stage, caught in a Pirandellian situation of having to watch her innermost spiritual agony dragged into the spotlight of public scrutiny. Even when she was not directly involved in the action, she remained a visible, restless, solitary presence isolated on her own side of the stylized dividing screen. "She is the secret director of the events, but there remains always a glass wall between her, the defeated human being, and the others," wrote *Frankfurter Allgemeine* of the Munich production. Here, Christine Buchegger established an unhysterical Hedda characterized not by frantic desperation, but rather by a strangely detached sense of composure, of authority and

The stage setting, designed by Mago, for the Stockholm production of *Hedda Gabler*, 1964. The vertical dividing screen is visible to the left of the prompter's box.

control blended with an almost cynical disdain for the destiny she knows she has chosen for herself. At Dramaten, Gertrud Fridh drew a more mature and more strikingly aristocratic portrait of General Gabler's daughter, possessed of an even greater degree of self-control and displaying an ironic remoteness from everything and everyone about her. Her isolation seemed predestined, grandiose. The common denominator of both these performances was the accumulating sensation of alienation and entrapment that they created.

From the outset, in the dreamlike opening pantomine with which Bergman prefaced and defined the play proper, Hedda's entrapment was boldly underscored. Silently, like a sleepwalker, she came on to the empty stage, her features locked in a death mask of despair and frustration. "We do not experience her as a human being of flesh and blood," wrote Nils Beyer of Fridh's extraordinary appearance: "It is a damned soul who is stirring in this strange abode, before Ibsen himself starts to speak and the intricate clockwork mechanism begins to operate." As the light focused on Hedda and the auditorium gradually darkened, she moved noiselessly towards the audience. At the very front of the stage she stopped and, for a frozen moment, she stood, utterly immobile and expressionless, staring with wide open eyes into vacant space. Melchinger provides an unusually vivid description of this moment: "For a long time to come, I will see Hedda Gabler before me: standing at the front of the stage, aristocratic, with her chin tilted slightly upwards, the Titian-red hair outlined against the dull red of the stage space, with her sarcastic, tense mouth and those eyes that stared into the darkness, where we sat." Turning away, she walked over to the (empty) mirror and began a critical examination of her person – first of her face, then her figure, letting her hands run slowly down her body to her stomach. Then, in a violent reaction of revulsion and despair, she suddenly bent double and pressed her hands to her abdomen, pounding it several times with the full force of her clenched fists. At last, in an effort to regain control over herself, she walked to the piano, lit a cigarette, stubbed it out at once, and then settled herself in an armchair. Meanwhile, the intrusion of the outside world, in the persons of Aunt Julle and the maid, began, as their expository small talk broke the silence for the first time.

Buchegger's Hedda dispassionately planning her suicide. The book she previously had dropped in boredom still lies at her feet.

Hence, the outcome was inevitable from the start. This preliminary, oneiric movement in Bergman's production proclaimed a relentlessly closed framework of doom from which there was clearly no escape. "She is forced into a corner because she is a woman who, when she is pregnant, is left with no choice. She is in a blind alley. Whether she likes it or doesn't like it, there it is. It says so in the score," Bergman himself has declared. Nor, he is quick to add, should the opening pantomime be viewed as an interpolated embellishment upon that score: "It is there in the play. Not the scene itself, but the fact that she is pregnant and doesn't want the child. It's only that it is so disguised in Ibsen that if you don't listen very carefully, it will elude you. It is precisely the same in a musical composition. If something is more weakly scored but needs to be brought out, then you lift it up. That is precisely what I have done in *Hedda Gabler*."[17] The director's point communicated itself forcefully both in the Stockholm and in the Munich productions (neither of which exhibited the risible morning sickness antics that eventually crept into the English performance). "She appears in a wordless scene that is not in the play, as a woman whose despair manifests itself only as a last and, as she knows, a vain protest against circumstances," remarked *Frankfurter Allgemeine* of the 1979 revival. "She is defeated from the very beginning."

Once established, the pattern of Hedda's alienation and spiritual nausea proceeded to grow and develop through a continuous sequence of peripheral actions, performed as she listened – or pointedly refused to listen – to the conversation taking place on the other side of the dividing screen. The spasmodic movements of Hedda in her cage – lighting and extinguishing cigarettes, biting her own hand in a sudden neurotic gesture of self-contempt, or ironically perusing a book in a parody of the manners of the well-educated nineteenth-century woman, only to let it fall to the floor a moment afterwards – were signposts marking her inexorable progress towards destruction. "One might have thought that Hedda was spying; but the impression produced was rather than the stage spied on Hedda, that she was being dissected by it against her will," observed Melchinger. The point is an essential one. Attention was fixed not on the act of Hedda's suicide – for that was a foregone conclusion from the outset – but on the existential *process* of the act, as analyzed by the character who commits it. Out of self-reflection arose Hedda's consuming soul sickness. Humiliated by the superimposed identity that Tesman's world has prepared for her, she searched in vain for some reliable evidence of her elusive self. Tormented by the thought of this incarceration in a role, she found herself drawn to the mirror – that most central of all props in Bergman's art – in which she could watch herself live and watch herself prepare to die. She was "continually shown before the imaginary mirror, striking poses, testing attitudes, examining her fading complexion, trying as it were to convince herself that she is truly real; now and then she stands so close to the mirror that it seems as if she wants to breathe away her human features," commented Wahlund. Much more important than as a device for reassuring Hedda of her reality, however, was the mirror's function as a glass in which *the actress* observes her own performance. Standing before the mirror at the end of the first act, staring at a reality that is already fixed forever, she coolly and dispassionately rehearsed the aesthetically pleasing suicide she has planned for herself. She removed her high-heeled pumps carefully, both as a gesture of fastidiousness and as a practical measure that allowed her to stand more steadily when she fired. And she again stood before the mirror when, with the utmost composure, she actually pointed the pistol to her temple and squeezed the trigger at the end.

From her first entrance into the world of the others, Bergman's Hedda stood demonstrably alone, cut off from everyone else about her. Whether reacting with disdain or thinly disguised disgust to the insinuating conversation between her husband and his precious Aunt Julle or coldly contemplating the bleak autumn landscape outside ("so golden – and withered"), her entire behavior emphasized that she was the outsider, the alien who acted and reacted on a different level and with far greater intensity than these ordinary – and in this case actually paler – figures around her did. Tesman, her husband, was in Bergman's interpretation an affable, middle-aged pedant whom she treated with bored, impatient politeness, and whose ceaseless pursuit of data from a dead and meaningless historical past epitomized the futility of her own situation. Both in Ingvar Kjellson's discretely comic performance in Stockholm and in Kurt Meisel's very sympathetic

Hedda Gabler (Getrud Fridh) with Tesman (Ingvar Kjellson), the husband she treats with bored politeness. Dramaten, 1964.

portrayal of the character in Munich, Tesman's contentedly self-centered preoccupation with his own small world lent him a certain childlike innocence that, in itself, deepened the impression of the gulf between him and Hedda. His reactions invariably reflected the egoistic simplicity of a child. "He became utterly distraught when the anticipated professorship seemed to be slipping away from him and, when Løvborg refrained from competing with him, he glowed with over-flowing, naive, and grateful happiness," remarked one reviewer of Kjellson's performance.[18] Perhaps even more strikingly in the Munich revival, as Meisel's Tesman ran excitedly towards a totally disinterested Hedda with the news of Løvborg's decision, the unbridgeable distance between them materialized with graphic clarity.

There are two other men in Hedda's life – neither one of whom represents a viable means of escape from her predicament. In Bergman's productions Judge Brack was a smiling, insolent blackguard who offered an alternative she had certainly considered and had long since rejected. This coldly detached and ruthless libertine – who like a spy or a villain in a melodrama made all his entrances and exits through a concealed door in the proscenium – was the only one to whom she could actually communicate her boredom, her excruciating sense of life as one unending and tedious railroad journey that one spends locked in a compartment with a single travelling companion. But, as she well knew, the cynical Brack was also the only one who saw straight through her at all times. As a kind of male counterpart of Hedda, he recognized the potential danger when she threatened him with her revolver – yet he was at the same time maddeningly unwilling to treat her threat as more than an empty theatrical gesture ("People don't do such things").

Eilert Løvborg, the third man in Hedda's life and, in Bergman's interpretation, so obviously her former lover, was from the beginning a man who had reached the end of his rope. This deromanticized Løvborg – played with particularly moving and passionate desperation by Martin Benrath at the Residenztheater – was no free-spirited Dionysian visionary. He possessed neither vine leaves nor a future any longer, and the "masterpiece" containing his prescription for the future of human civilization was nothing more than a pitifully few sheets of paper. (Questioned about this very suggestive detail of the strikingly thin manuscript, Bergman finds a characteristically concrete explanation, pointing out that had it been any thicker Løvborg would certainly have noticed his fatal loss of it at once.)

The fact that no one else but Hedda seemed aware of the stifling, hermetically sealed atmosphere ("the odor of death" she tries to describe to Brack) in which they moved and in which she was imprisoned heightened the sense of her alienation from the other characters in the drama. "They behave as though they came here through gardens, from animated soirees, and from the forests of the North; and they depart in due time, as a matter of course, to go out into their life again, to drink, to work, to socialize. And nobody realizes that they . . . have been drawn into a somber classical drama in which it is

A visual image of Hedda's isolation from Løvborg and Thea in act 2 of *Hedda Gabler*. Residenztheater, 1979.

impossible to be lighthearted or to maintain an everyday attitude," remarked *Süddeutsche Zeitung*. The deep irony of this tonal discrepancy (which this critic in fact failed to comprehend) was clearly a deliberate strategy on Bergman's part. This suggestion of a perceptional gulf was continually amplified by him in terms of the spatial and compositional patterns he developed. Taking the fullest advantage of the width of his stage – reinforced by a strong impression of shallowness created by the barricade of low screens encircling the playing area (and by the half-lowered curtain at Dramaten) – he stressed widely separated groups, conversations conducted from opposite sides of the stage, and vivid images of Hedda seated apart or faced away from other characters during even the tensest of confrontations (e.g., in the second-act scene in which she so ruthlessly destroys the relationship between Thea and Løvborg). Each choreographic nuance of this kind was in turn blended into a broad, firmly conceived sculptural plan, in which the creation of an illusion of reality played no part at all.

Instead, the graphic bas-relief effects that Bergman favored in his *Hedda Gabler* were at the same time both powerfully abstract and eloquently expressive of the unspoken subtext and inner rhythm of the drama. A sinuous interplay of colors, lighting changes, and figure compositions produced at times a distorted, impressionistic, even dreamlike quality in the many scenes in which silhouette or bas-relief effects predominated. In both the Stockholm and the Munich productions, for example, a chilling physical sensation of staleness and futility was conjured up for the moment at the beginning of the third act when Thea and Hedda awaken from their anxious all-night vigil. Here, low-angle projectors (so-called Bergman lamps) that hung at the back of the auditorium illuminated the forestage so glaringly and piercingly that the plastic contours of the characters" faces were momentarily obliterated. "There they sat, facing the front of the stage, opening their mouths, carefully choosing their gestures, now and then looking at each other in profile," wrote Melchinger. Bergman's antinaturalistic emphasis on unmitigated frontal playing and severely linear, flattened picture compositions was even compared by this critic to Cézanne's revolutionary redistribution of the elements of pictorial space.

Time, like space, is a dimension with which Bergman often experiments freely in his stage productions. As a film maker, of course, such an idea is very close to him: "I found out at a very early stage that time doesn't exist in films. That is: logical time ceases to exist for the spectator. In fact one can play about with time more or less as one likes . . . it's part of the magic of film, that one's awareness of time vanishes completely."[19] The translation of this line of thinking into theatrical terms has yielded some fascinating results in Bergman's work – not least in *Hedda Gabler*, where his manipulation of temporal perception played a sometimes crucial role in creating a precise atmosphere or directing audience response towards a specific emotional stimulus. The compression of hours or even days of real time into only a few moments of stage time is among the fairly routine conventions of drama and theater. Far less common, however, is Bergman's (characteristically cinematographic) attraction to the obverse process – the expansion of perhaps only a moment of real time into a much more prolonged slow motion replay of that moment on the stage. "One second of reality can be two minutes on the stage," he persuaded the cast of the Munich production of the play, and his consequent application of a kind of theatrical slow motion at times added a striking extra dimension of suspended animation to the finished performance.

Perhaps nowhere was this dimension more forcefully projected that in the first face-to-face encounter between Hedda and Løvborg (in Ibsen's second act), in which a sense of time and motion in suspension governed the expressive vocabulary of signs and gestures in the sequence.[20] As Løvborg's arrival was announced, Hedda's forcible attempt to conceal her apprehension and to remain, as always, in control of the situation found its expression in languid, automatonlike movements. She tried first to sit down dispassionately, but, unable to remain seated, she rose again "in slow motion" – watched closely by the cynical Brack who, as usual, lost no time in signifying that he, too, had taken note of her unrest. When Løvborg did appear, he stopped at once to search out Hedda; looking fixedly at her – and completely ignoring Tesman, who stood directly beside him – he walked slowly toward her and took her hand, which he held "a little bit too long." The virtually mesmeric influence that the mere physical presence of Løvborg exerted on Hedda overshadowed his subsequent conversation with Tesman about his new work ("This is my real book. The one in which I have spoken with my own voice"). As he sat down to show Tesman his manuscript, Hedda, who had been restlessly prowling in the area behind the sofa, abruptly went around it and sat down as well – clearly unaware that she was in fact copying Løvborg's movements, and narrowly observed all the while by the ever-vigilant Brack. But to this Hedda, her former lover's vision of the future obviously held as little meaning for her as her husband's empty pursuit of a dead past. Accordingly, she drifted nervously into her private sanctuary as the two men continued to talk – only to reemerge moments later, curt and determined to remain collected for the encounter that was to come.

With steadily accelerating force, Bergman's staging of this focal scene between Hedda and Løvborg articulated the

"This is my real book." Løvborg, manuscript in his pocket, is received by Hedda, Tesman, and Brack. Dramaten, 1964.

essence of the total impasse between them – not as a "break-down of communication" in conventional terms, but rather as a situation in which the unspoken communication that passed between these two was all too audible and clear. The passion-ate emotionality of Løvborg's first impulsive outburst ("Hedda. Hedda – Gabler!") was coupled with a conviction of his own strength in this encounter ("he knows he is dangerous for Hedda"). She, in turn, met this from the outset with her own determination to avoid an emotional scene altogether and, above all, to regain her dominance over him. In the initial phase of this power struggle, a variety of strategies – her calculated formality, her avoidance at first of any eye-contact, the ferocious insistence with which she concentrated her attention on the photographs from her honeymoon that she stiffly displayed for him, and the exaggerated amiability with which she greeted Tesman's interruption of their tête-à-tête – contributed to her campaign for perfect aloofness. Gradually, however, the mood of the scene began to change. As Løvborg insistently demanded to know whether there had not been a trace of love between them, Hedda's stinging retort – that their relationship had been that of "two good friends who could tell each other everything" – was spoken "to herself, full of sadism," and this marked the beginning of an emotional transition in her behavior. From this point on, as the conversa-tion drifted to remembrance of things past, she became both more responsive and also increasingly more aggressive. Her realization that "you think I had some power over you" even prompted her to smile.

As the scene between Hedda and Løvborg took on the character of a virtual reenactment of similar scenes between them in the past, Bergman's choreography and lighting estab-lished an eerie visual adumbration of unreality and déjà vu. Much as the presence of General Gabler had hovered over their meetings in the past, so too the figures of Tesman and Brack could now be seen through the open screens, as menacing presences that loomed in the background. By the time the scene had reached the point at which Ibsen's stage directions indicate that it had begun to grow dark, Bergman's lighting scheme – which was, of course, completely independent of Ibsen's naturalistic considerations, as there were neither windows nor obvious sources of light in his setting – had undergone a subtle but marked change. The penetrating light that fixed the two characters on the forestage had dimmed, and long, oversized shadows began to be cast upon the wall screen behind them. The contours of the figures themselves were erased, and for a moment the distinction between the living human characters and their own ghostly silhouettes seemed actually to be obliterated.

Immersed in this dreamlike atmosphere of brooding shadows, Hedda and Løvborg pursued their futile journey into the past with a bitterness and an increasingly overt aggressiveness that drew the scene several degrees closer to Strindberg's vision – or to the more harrowing sexual confrontations in Bergman's own films. "But tell me Hedda – the root of the bond between us – was that not love?" cries Løvborg – and that outcry became the explosive juncture at which he decidedly lost his serenity and the balance of power reverted inexorably to Hedda. Their discussion of Løvborg's new relationship with Thea was suffused with a savage, menacing belligerency on his part that communicated itself directly to Hedda and conditioned her own response. Her defiant "I am a coward" erupted into a sudden outburst of hatred, expressed both in her harsh tone of voice and in her abrupt movement as she sprang up from her chair. The struggle reached its climax when Løvborg, in a final and erotically charged gesture, impulsively embraced Hedda from his seated position, passionately pressing his face against her. For a single instant she seemed about to relax her steely self-control. Then, brutally reasserting her dominance, she thrust him away with both hands. Immediately afterwards Thea entered – "as in a dream," Bergman had observed during rehearsals, "because when you want something to happen in a dream, it does. And Hedda wants a showdown with Thea."

Hedda's ruthless determination to reassert control over Løvborg ("For once in my life I want to have power over a human destiny") stood remorselessly exposed in Bergman's interpretation, as a critical step in the progression that led with relentless dramatic logic to her own destruction. The scene, near the end of the second act, in which she goads the reformed alcoholic to drink again was more than merely an act of deliberate, malicious irresponsibility. It was also a violent metastatic eruption of the deadly cancer – the perception of entrapment and internment – that fed on her inner being. The emphatic slow motion effects that Bergman introduced again in this scene gave it both an hallucinatory intensity and also a virtually mythological signification that several critics associated in their reviews with the somber fatality of the gesture with which Isolde seals her own and her lover's destiny in the first act of Richard Wagner's *Tristan und Isolde*. "In the terrifying scene in which she sits with the glass of punch in her hand and tempts her former lover to drink it, it is her own destiny that she is preparing and not merely her lover's," Jahnsson remarked in his review of the Stockholm production in *Dagens Nyheter*. "Great catastrophes always begin very quietly," Bergman himself had explained to his cast at the Residenztheater when setting the tone of suppressed tension in this crucial incident. In the rhythm of feeling that he established for the play, this scene directly prefigured and prepared for the powerful emotional climax in which Hedda destroys both Løvborg and his manuscript.

This final, destructive encounter between the two gained emotional intensity through some shrewd editing of the text on Bergman's part. In general, although *Hedda Gabler* was presented by him substantially uncut, he was resolute in pruning away the punctilious exposition and naturalistic "small talk" that link the play to the theatrical conventions of an older period – but that, in his terms, only serve to dissipate the potential emotional impact on a modern audience. Bergman's commitment to the view that cinematic or theatrical art must speak directly to the subconscious mind rather than to the conscious intellect has provoked its share of critical quarrels, to be sure. It is a view that necessarily resists the imposition of any closed framework of "meaning" – be it symbolic, Freudian, feminist, political, or whatever – that will point the spectator in a single predetermined direction and deny him imaginative alternatives, thereby voiding his truly creative participation in the dramatic event. If Bergman has any reservations about Ibsen as a theater poet, it is, he says, because Ibsen "points the audience in the direction he wants it to go, closing doors, leaving no other alternatives." Kenneth Burke, in an essay called "Psychology and Form," has distinguished two kinds of literary composition, "syllogistic progression," in which the reader is led from one point of the composition to another by means of logical relationships, and "qualitative progression," in which the reader is led, according to a "logic of feeling", by means of association and contrast. Francis Fergusson, from whom these remarks are freely borrowed, relates Burke's qualitative progression to the compositional principles of Wagnerian music-drama – but the analogy might be extended with equal validity to Bergman's art as well.[21] "How tired I am of hearing that imagination must always be responsible to the intellect! Inspiration should be well behaved in the face of reality's accusations," he protests in *Cries and Whispers*.[22] But art, he has repeatedly insisted, is not a rational phenomenon to be comprehended by logical analysis; it is "a matter between the imagination and the feelings." Expressed with the utmost economy of means, often compressed into an arresting sensory image, each emotional unit or suggestion in Bergman's theater seeks to reach the spectator spontaneously and directly, through the medium of the senses, without an intermediary landing in the intellect.

Thus, in Bergman's editing of the hypnotic third-act scene in which Hedda finally destroys her former lover, both overt symbolism (vine leaves) and expository explanation ("you looked down its barrel once") were eliminated in order to reveal the emotional core of close, unspoken violence in the scene. First, the text as it was played at Dramaten, showing the cuts in square brackets:[23]

HEDDA: What will you do now?
LØVBORG: Nothing. I just want to put an end to it all. As soon as possible.
HEDDA (*takes a step towards him*):   Eilert Løvborg, listen to me. Do it – beautifully!
LØVBORG: Beautifully? [(*Smiles*) With a crown of vine leaves in my hair? The way you used to dream of me – in the old days?]
HEDDA: [No. I don't believe in that crown any longer. But – do it] (B)eautifully[, all the same]. Just this once. [Goodbye.] You must go now. And don't come back.
LØVBORG: Adieu, madam. Give my love to George Tesman. (*Turns to go.*)
HEDDA: Wait! I want to give you a souvenir to take with you. (*She goes over to [the writing table, opens the drawer and] the pistol case, and comes back to Løvborg with one of the pistols.*)
[LØVBORG (*looks at her*):   This? Is this the souvenir?]
HEDDA (*nods slowly*):   You recognize it? [You looked down its barrel once.]

LØVBORG: You should have used it then.
(Bergman direction: Pause. Hand-kiss.)
[HEDDA: Here! Use it now!]
LØVBORG *(puts the pistol in his breast pocket)*:   Thank you.
HEDDA: [Do it] (B)eautifully, Eilert [Løvborg. Only] promise me that!
LØVBORG: Goodbye, Hedda Gabler.

And in the Munich revival the final beat of this scene, as Løvborg takes the pistol from Hedda, became even more terse and more brutal:[24]

LØVBORG: This? Is this the souvenir?
LØVBORG *(puts the pistol in his breast pocket)*:   Thank you.
HEDDA: Beautifully, Eilert Løvborg. Promise me that!
LØVBORG: Goodbye, Hedda Gabler.

After her move to destroy Løvborg himself, Hedda's burning of his manuscript seals her own fate, by finalizing her willful rejection of the future and her election of the past and of death. This action – perhaps the most intense emotional gesture in Bergman's productions of the play – was positioned by him at the very center and forefront of the stage. Facing the audience directly, Hedda slowly knelt before the hooded prompter's box itself, which then became the "stove". As a result, every slight nuance of facial expression was remorselessly disclosed in the searching light that flooded the stage at this point. With icy determination, her face now frozen in an immutable masklike expression, she fed the "fire" with page after page of Løvborg's manuscript – his vision of the future, his and Thea's spiritual child. Just when her act of wanton destruction had been completed, Bergman added a startling touch that exemplifies his extraordinary gift for compressing the essence of a situation into one eoloquent visual image. The sorrowing figures of Tesman and the black-clad and veiled Miss Tesman, in mourning for her dead sister, appeared behind her, and at a single stroke the image of physical death merged with the image of Hedda and the motif of death-in-life, emotional sterility, and inhumanity that she embodies.

In this interpretation Hedda's implacably exposed public suicide, which Bergman considers "the most consequent of any in dramatic literature," became as logically inevitable as the solution to a mathematical problem. Nothing was permitted to mitigate the harshness or obscure the clarity of this final scene.

The sorrowing figures of Tesman (Kurt Meisel) and his Aunt Julle appear behind Hedda just as she has burned Løvborg's manuscript. Residenztheater, 1979.

The "frenzied dance melody" that Hedda plays on the piano in Ibsen's text was reduced to a few dissonant, nonmusical chords hammered out in frustration. As she stood before the mirror and quietly prepared to put a bullet through her head, her husband and the self-possessed Thea Elvsted sat motionlessly at the other end of the stage, totally absorbed in their absurd task of reassembling the dead Løvborg's notes – a deadly picture of hollow people trying to paste together a vision whose spirit they do not comprehend, clinging to a meaningless past that completely overshadows both the present and the future.

Hedda's last act before withdrawing into the ultimate isolation of death was to remove her high-heeled shoes carefully, in a final irrational attempt to control and transcend a reality that had become a nightmare. "The only thing she wants is to die a beautiful death," Bergman has been prompted to explain. "She has rehearsed the last gesture before the mirror. She knows how to use the pistol so that it becomes aesthetic. Perhaps she also takes into consideration that she wants to fall nicely. It is an uncontrollable moment that she subconsciously tries to control by taking off her shoes."[25]

Judge Brack had the last word, as of course he does in Ibsen, in all three of Bergman's productions of the play. In Munich, however, his line was reinforced by an astonishing gesture of sheer brutality. Standing nonchalantly over Hedda's outstretched corpse, Brack seized her roughly by the hair and lifted her head, as though to assure himself that she was dead, before pronouncing his cynical verdict that "people don't do such things!" Like Eilert, Hedda had found only a harsh and unlovely end. "The irony in all this," Bergman remarks, "is that she dies such an ugly death anyway – that she ends up lying there with her rump in the air."

AN ACTORS' THEATER

In some respects, the staging of Bergman's brilliant revival of Ibsen's *The Wild Duck*, which began its lengthy run at Dramaten on March 17, 1972 and was subsequently seen on tour in six other European countries, bore a distinct resemblance to the novel scenographic style that he had adopted for *Hedda Gabler*. In this new production, both of the detailed naturalistic environments described in the stage directions were condensed into deliberately incomplete settings that consisted of isolated elements on an otherwise empty stage. Simple, stylized wall screens were again used to denote the contours of these two interiors. Each of them was confined to a relatively shallow area at the front of the revolving stage, with the result that beyond it one saw only an encircling black void that was sometimes pierced by abstract projections. The atmospheric interplay of light and shadow within the setting itself heightened the semireal effect.

The "expensive and comfortably furnished study" of Haakon Werle in the first act was a relatively cold, green-tinted room of angles and corners, defined only by a back screen and completely open at the sides. An aristocratic fireplace with poker and tongs stood at one end of the room, with no wall

The study of Haakon Werle, designed by Marik Vos, for the first act of *The Wild Duck*. Dramaten, 1972.

behind it. Four upholstered chairs and an ornate writing table were the only other furnishings. A pair of tall ornamental candelabra placed in either corner, just outside the actual setting, added a note of elegance and opulence. Only one striking addition was actually made by Bergman and his designer (Marik Vos) to Ibsen's specifications for this interior – a richly framed portrait of a woman, presumably Werle's late wife, occupied a conspicuous place on the wall above the writing table. In his various productions of *Hedda Gabler*, as we know, Bergman had eliminated the portrait of General Gabler precisely because it belongs to that category of oversimplified, deterministic "explanation" that obscures the true complexity of the central character's situation – a woman who is *not* a mere product or victim of social or hereditary circumstances, but who has consciously chosen – in an existential and also a quite

The studio of Hjalmar Ekdal in *The Wild Duck*. Dramaten, 1972.

coincidental manner – her own hell. In Bergman's production of *The Wild Duck*, meanwhile, the interpolated portrait was not at all this kind of closed naturalistic symbol – although at least one bedeviled commentator professed to see in it "the symbol of Gregers' Oedipal complex." Rather, it seemed a concrete but completely open image that manifested the irrevocable presence of the past in the play, the awareness that old sins cast long shadows and that, ultimately, "the forest will have its revenge."

The forest was indeed very much a part of Hjalmar Ekdal's humbler and more comfortable studio in the acts that followed. Here the most striking pictorial addition was a large screen depicting an old-fashioned woodland scene – virtually a vision of the great forest about which Old Ekdal warns us so often – which the director introduced, with characteristic logic, as a conventional prop of the kind that one might very naturally expect to encounter in the modest studio of a portrait photographer. Where the pair of stately candelabra had stood in Werle's study, dried-out old spruce trees could now be glimpsed (the "four or five withered Christmas trees" that are, as Relling remarks, the same to Old Ekdal as "the great, fresh forests of Høydal"), reinforcing the impression of a "waking reality" suspended in a void, "an island in the sea of flight from reality" (*Göteborgs Handels – och Sjöfartstidning*). Even the rectangular screen used to demarcate one corner of the room carried, in its faintly flowered wallpaper, a tantalizing hint of this motif of the encroaching dream forest.

Other sharply defined contrasts to the more patrician Werle establishment were suggested with deft economy through the strategic placement of the sparse furnishings. The position occupied by the elegant fireplace in the previous setting was now taken by an old iron stove. At the opposite side of the stage from it, in the area formerly occupied by Werle's commanding desk, a dilapidated sofa and table arrangement served both as a work place for the none-too-energetic Hjalmar and as the center of domestic warmth where the various (indispensable) meals in the play could be served. Here in this warmly illuminated area the Ekdals gathered – frequently watched closely by Gregers, "the outsider who intrudes in order to influence the life of the family" and who hence often sat "as far removed as possible from the dining-room table, the natural gathering place of the family, with his back towards the audience so that he shared his watching attitude with them."[26]

For those familiar beforehand with the specific details of *The Wild Duck* Bergman's most unexpected innovation was doubtless his relocation of the attic in the Ekdal studio – although, once accomplished, his daring reversal of the play's perspective seemed, to informed and unsuspecting viewers alike, both completely consistent and disarmingly self-evident. Previous productions of the play have traditionally sought to fulfill Ibsen's familiar stage directions more or less to the letter, attempting to reproduce the "long and irregularly shaped loft" that lies beyond the rear wall, "full of dark nooks and crannies, with a couple of brick chimney-pipes coming through the floor. Through small skylights bright moonlight shines on to various parts of the loft, while the rest lies in shadow."[27] In Bergman's hands this fateful and fleetingly perceived interior loft, the abode of the maimed wild duck and the realm of illusion and entertainment for three generations of Ekdals, was transformed into a magical ghost-attic located in the no-man's-land between the audience and the stage. "Without stage properties and with only the aid of the lighting and the art of the actors, Bergman creates, before the eyes of the audience, that fantasy world that Hjalmar and Old Ekdal have built up around themselves," wrote Leif Zern in *Dagens Nyheter*. "Here rule the night and the dreams, in scenes of such intensity and poetry that I have never witnessed their like."

In this ingenious arrangement, characters entered the "loft" through a side door in the stage-right wall of the studio – with the interesting result that they did not thereby disappear from view but were instead seen to draw nearer, both physically and metaphorically, to the audience itself. Bergman "has with a resolute touch burst the bounds of the perspective box by placing the imaginary loft almost where the spectators are sitting," recorded Henrik Sjögren in *Kvällsposten*. "Accordingly they can observe every one of the characters who turns toward the wild duck [whose 'basket' was the prompter's box]." Only the facial expressions of the actors and projections of roofbeams on the stage floor and on the black background above them served to indicate where they were and what it was they saw in this kingdom of the imagination. The resultant sense of immediacy was truly startling. "More than in any other production of Ibsen's play that one recalls," one reviewer wrote of the touring production, the attic became "an image of that secret fantasy life that these escapists and losers have not been strong enough or courageous enough to realize for themselves. The small living room of Hjalmar Ekdal becomes a doll's house of eternal childhood above which, in the scenes with the wild duck, the roofbeams soar like the lofty vaults of a cathedral, while from afar one hears the surge of the wind."[28] The withered Christmas trees, obscured in any conventional performance by the backs of those characters who, at various times, peer into the mysterious attic at the rear, were now, for the first time, brought forward to form a profoundly expressive component of the Ekdal environment. As a result the thematic bond between studio and forest was strengthened; time pre-

"Here rule the night and the dreams." Gregers' first visit to the attic, as it was conceived in Bergman's production of *The Wild Duck*.

sent and time past were fused together in a fluid but indissoluble concurrency. "The symbolic essence of the play thus becomes central and more securely welded to the clockwork mechanism of the dramatic action than I have ever experienced it before," Sjögren concluded.

Once again, then, Bergman's technique of bringing forward exposed, close-up glimpses of peripheral or implied offstage action added an entirely new dimension to the audience's mode of perceiving the realistic action of Ibsen's drama. In this respect, similarities to his innovative staging of *Hedda Gabler* seem fairly obvious – although one basic difference between these two productions must also be recognized. In *Hedda Gabler* the "inner room" of the central character was still seen as a place. Regardless of how stylized or abstractly conceived it was, it was still furnished with recognizable physical objects – the piano and stool, Hedda's chair, the mirror. In *The Wild Duck*, however, the "interior loft" had no independent existence of its own. Its reality was created *solely* through the medium of the actor's art. As such, this production epitomizes a cardinal principle of Bergman's theater poetics – the subordination at all times of the technical dynamics of staging to the creative presence of the living actor. "Once you agree that the only important things are the words, the actors, and the audience, then it isn't the setting that matters," he argues when talking about *The Wild Duck*. Moreover, his thinking in this regard is fundamentally "simple" and practical, uncomplicated by abstract theoretical considerations. "The actors must materialize, before the eyes of the audience, the magic of the attic. And they cannot do that at a distance; with their eyes, their way of walking and standing and moving, they create it in front of you. So you can see it. That is the magic of the theater."

Indeed, no other Bergman production has more persuasively reaffirmed that unique and most important gift of his – as a director of actors, with a mesmeric ability to ignite a performer and extract hidden resources from his cast. ("Perhaps the truth is," Bibi Andersson once remarked, "that when Ingmar is creating something, he radiates such hypnotic persuasiveness and intensity that one is intoxicated and overwhelmed.") His capacity for forging an unbreakable ensemble is, of course, directly related to his fabled talent for choosing exactly the right actors – a talent that, in turn, presupposes an intimate familiarity with his players. "We are all closely involved with each other. I know how many parts each carries with him," he told an interviewer shortly after his production of *The Wild Duck*. "Sometimes the actors themselves don't know that they can play [a certain part]. But without actually telling me, they show me the parts they contain."[29] During the great Dramaten years of the early 1970s, even relatively minor roles in a production such as *The Wild Duck* were filled by leading members of the familiar Bergman "company": Anders Ek was available to depict a powerful and commanding Haakon Werle; Harriet Andersson created a stately, gracious Mrs. Sørby devoid of any trace of vulgarity; Holger Löwenadler was Old Ekdal, "a grandiose ruin of someone who was once a human being"; and even Erland Josephson was called upon to impersonate one of the stuffy guests at Werle's dinner party.

At the hub of this superb ensemble was the quartet of characters around whom the action of the play revolves – a quartet carefully selected and finely tuned by Bergman to reveal a subtly shaded lattice of tensions and contrasts, rooted in Ibsen's own character descriptions and articulated by the director in terms of a distinctive rhythm of movements, gestures, facial expressions, and vocal nuances. "The figures reveal themselves in every subtle detail of voice and movement, and they do so with formidable logic until they stand there etched into our consciousness, lit through to the bare skeleton," Tord Baeckström declared in *Göteborgs Handels – och Sjöfartstidning*. With cameralike sharpness, Bergman's direction seemed to cut through the restrictive limits of realism to seek out and lay bare the inner essence of each character. "Driven to its fullest consequence, realism becomes unreal," Baeckström continued, "The X-ray vision suddenly exposes not living and vaguely contradictory human beings, but rather psychological constructs in a laser-sharp, two-dimensional projection."

Hjalmar Ekdal (Ernst-Hugo Järegård) and Hedvig (Lena Nyman) seemed, to many observers, less like father and daughter and much more "like two children of the same age, a loving brother and sister."[30] "Incestuous" was the spurious adjective attached by one or two critics with an inflexibly Freudian cast of mind – but a powerful sense of genuine domestic warmth and tenderness, rather than any suggestion of incest, was the real thematic point at issue here. Their eager embraces and natural displays of affection in the earlier, lighter scenes deepened the sense of Hedvig's naive, almost animalistic dependency on her father. "The warmth in the Ekdal home stems from her hunger for life," commented Leif Zern – and hence the effect of Hjalmar's abrupt rejection of her love, as he tore himself loose from her embrace in the fourth act, acquired added dramatic clarity and poignancy. Järegård's uncomplicated Hjalmar was a totally unsentimentalized, tragicomic figure – a happy egoist in constant need of encouragement from his surroundings, a natural actor "whose family is the most grateful public any performer could wish for," as Zern put it: "even his self-pity is a role he plays, as everyone well realizes." His open cherubic face, his curly hair, and his soft velvet attire all bespoke the charming and much-adored child, who was even assisted in putting on his slippers by a wife and daughter who literally got down on their knees for him. Accordingly, the earthy, maternal Gina of Margaretha Krook played "mother" to both these children, and their simple, helpless dependency on her foretold their defenselessness against the revelations with which Gregors Werle, the outsider, destroys their childish fantasy world forever.

Yet Gregers, the fourth member of the quartet, was in this instance neither the convinced fanatic nor the unsympathetic villain that he can often become in the theater – alone Bergman's choice of Max von Sydow for the role precluded such a result. The character created by von Sydow – "an idealist whose good intentions one cannot doubt for a moment" (*Svenska Dagbladet*) – was in physical terms the diametrical opposite of Hjalmar Ekdal. A very tall man who assumed a stooped, cramped posture, his short nervous laugh and his habit of crossing his arms over his chest to hide his hands under his armpits ("as though he was trying to tie himself into a straitjacket," thought one observer) suggested, to many of the critics, deep inner anxiety and insecurity. "He complains more than he accuses" remarked *Sydsvenska Dagbladet*, and in the two extremely effective scenes with his father – of whom he appeared utterly terrified – "his attacks [were] as shaky and powerless as his gestures and posture; he seems to be ready to run away at any time." Between Gregers and Hjalmar there seemed, despite their physical differences, to be a shared lack of self-knowledge and self-assurance: "they suffer from the same disease, even though the symptoms are different," Leif Zern aruged. "Gregers, too, goes outside himself to find the solution to his problems. Precisely like Hjalmar – and like Peer Gynt, for that matter – he assumes a role that does not express his true self." Critics sought – as critics are wont to seek – sinuous explanations for the behavior of this untraditional Gregers. Thus he was seen variously as being beset by a severe Oedipus complex, conducting a sublimated father-rebellion, or even representing the failed political revolutionary in the class struggle. But, here as elsewhere, Bergman's aim was not to offer an ideological or a psychological comment on Ibsen's play but rather to amplify, in concrete theatrical terms, the matrix of dynamic emotional relationships upon which the play builds. In these terms, the effect of this

Left, Gregers Werle (Max von Sydow) in the third-act scene with his father, played here by Anders Ek. Dramaten, 1972.

new and more complex characterization of Gregers was to
intensify and enrich the dramatic impact of his confrontations
with Haakon Werle, his relationship to Hjalmar, and, above
all, the three crucial conversations he holds with Hedvig on the
subject of the wild duck.

By electing to bring the attic forward and "materialize" it
before the eyes of the audience, Bergman inevitably also
focused more tightly on the process by which Hedvig comes to
take her life, and on Gregers' implication in that process. This
became the prism through which all the other events in the
drama were refracted and assimilated. In their first, oneiric
scene alone, as the plain, shy, snub-nosed little girl told
Gregers about the "different world" of the loft, with its strange
collection of old paintboxes, old picture books, and old clocks
that no longer run, she acquired a radiance "as if sunlight and
soft shadows moved across this childish face, dreaming about
that that will never come to pass" [Zern]. The second of their
scenes together – transferred by Bergman to the shadowy
precincts of the "attic" itself, where the actors could now face
the audience directly – strengthened the sense of mutual
understanding and even comradeship between these two
childlike dreamers. As Gregers implanted the suggestion of
sacrificing the duck to appease Hjalmar, his movements to
draw Hedvig close to him and her response carried implications of a mesmeric, even an erotic seduction of her will. An
incisive cut to eliminate the anticlimax of Gina's return at the
end of this scene allowed the fourth-act curtain to fall on the
line with which Hedvig seemed to signal her compliance: "I'll
do it tomorrow morning" (with the reference to "the wild
duck" deleted).[31] In the third step (in all fairy tales the final and
conclusive one), the process of psychological suasion was
completed, as Gregers – without resorting to the exclamatory
exhortations contained in Ibsen's text and using only one
simple line ("But I still believe in you, Hedvig") – recalled her
to her blunted purpose.

Perhaps the darkest and most fascinating aspect of Bergman's interpretation of *The Wild Duck* was the fact that never
for an instant was the audience in real doubt about the
deliberate and premeditated nature of Hedvig's suicide. On
the one hand, small but telling cuts – in particular the deletion
of the short scene in which Old Ekdal lectures the child about

how to shoot ducks properly – tended to strengthen the impression that the wild duck never *had* actually been intended by Hedvig as the target of her revolver. Moreover, the chance that she might have made a mistake and had killed herself by accident – surely one of the least fortunate of all the ambiguities in Ibsen's drama – now no longer existed as a logical possibility. As Hjalmar, already warming to his new role and calling histrionically for his notes and the draft of his "memoirs", ordered Hedvig from his presence, she slipped out quietly, pistol in hand – only to reappear on the forestage moments later. The projection of the roofbeams rose above her head, while behind her the other characters continued their unwitting discussion in the background. The audience thus experienced these last terrifying minutes through her consciousness, saw them through her eyes. As the dialogue between the overwrought Gregers and the self-centered Hjalmar proceeded, she took aim, hesitated, and fired. "We see her listening to the conversation that makes her shoot herself," observed one reviewer. "And the voluntary sacrifice of her tragic death thereby became, to an even greater degree, a judgment upon the intractable childishness of the adults."[32]

Following the shot, the suspense generated in Ibsen's play by the ensuing confusion over who had actually fired at what deepened into irony, because the audience of this production knew what the characters themselves did not yet realize. Then, as Relling and the parents gathered around the crumpled form on the forestage, Bergman added a startling visual stroke that heightened the oppressive sense of finality and ultimate futility created by Hedvig's suicide. Juxtaposed with the shadowy group in the foreground was the figure of Old Ekdal, seated before the photographer's forest backdrop in his old lieutenants's uniform, intoning his favorite refrain: "The forest takes its revenge. But I'm not afraid." Perhaps Gregers was the only one truly afraid, for he recognized the terrible finality of the judgment that had been passed on them – and as he left the Ekdal home, he held in his hand the revolver that Hedvig had used on herself.

The precisely coordinated, rhythmical orchestration of visual and aural impressions that rendered these closing moments of *The Wild Duck* so moving and poignant reflects perfectly that typically "musical" way in which Bergman goes about translating a play's "score" into the syntax of the theater. Looking back on this experience, Max von Sydow has described this director's practice of providing "a rhythmic outline of the role," a carefully planned scoring of each scene that will serve as a suggestive stimulus to the actor's own creative powers: "not simply a matter of moving someone geographically through space – sitting down here, standing up there, crossing to this or that piece of furniture, sitting down in that chair, and then saying your line – but always also an indication of roughly the tempo and the rhythm with which it should happen." Musical comparisons spring readily to mind, as von Sydow says, because "somewhere or other in the back

The arrangement of Hedvig's suicide on the shadowy forestage, juxtaposed with the image of old Ekdal (Holger Löwenadler) seated in his uniform before the photographer's forest backdrop. Dramaten, 1972.

of your head you hear musical expressions and know approximately how many beats to count on for a move or before introducing an accentuation. If you understand the first direction provided during Ingmar's blocking, then you have grasped the essence of his idea about the role. As a result, as an actor I feel immensely free."[33]

When he at last turned to *A Doll's House* – a challenge he had long contemplated – in 1981, Bergman decided to use the creative presence of the actor in a new and radically different way, as a key part of his design to strip away the surface of photographic details and realistic actions that pervades this work. "You can get lost in all those details," he said at the time. "Suddenly you find the wrong ways. There are always so many *things* lying around everywhere – sofas and chairs and Christmas trees and pianos . . . Just take everything away and then you find out how *fantastic* the shape of this play really is."[34] In his approach, human figure compositions and choreographic patterns, rather than inert scenery, were used to create the world of Ibsen's play.

The undivided focus of Bergman's *Nora*, as his terse, starkly simplified German version was called, was the struggle of the central character to free herself spiritually and emotionally, by breaking out of a narrow, suffocating existence that held her prisoner.[35] This governing image of the play as a drama of destiny and entrapment manifested itself in visual terms in the fact that Nora remained surrounded throughout her ordeal by the silent, dreamlike presences of the figures who populate and define her world. No "entrances" or "exits" as such were needed, for the "offstage" actors never left the audience's sight. "Time has stopped – it doesn't exist any more," Bergman said during rehearsals. "Everyone is there from the outset, surrounding her – and she reacts."

The simultaneous presence of all the participants in the drama placed the action in a profoundly ironic double perspective. Each in turn, the four characters who precipitate Nora's desperate struggle for survival simply stepped forward, as though bidden, to confront her – and then returned again to one of the six simple wooden chairs arranged with severe symmetry along two sides of the playing area. Seated there, they were once again actors, awaiting their cues in a drama in

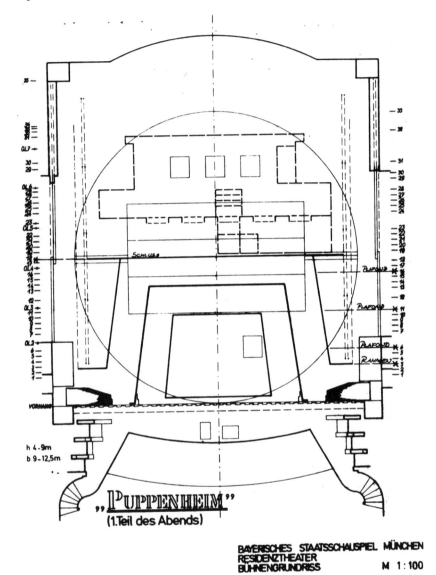

Figure 19 Plan of the stage (Residenztheater) for *Nora* (*A Doll's House*).

which the very concept of masquerade and role-playing is, as Bergman emphasizes, the central metaphor. Yet, at the same time, these watchers were still characters, confined together with Nora in the claustrophobic hell of Ibsen's domestic wasteland. Seated in the subdued, softly diffused light, these four isolated, impassive presences appeared like half-real figures in a dream landscape. Each was dressed in a dark, subdued shade of unrelieved monochrome that ranged from pale gray (Helmer) to spider black (Mrs. Linde). Only Nora's brighter clothing offset the uniform colorlessness of their traditional period costumes – perhaps, as one Munich reviewer suggested, as a sign of her vitality and consequent ability to break out of the unbreakable pattern.

Figure 19, the ground plan for the Residenztheater production (April 30, 1981), provides some idea of the spatial arrangement and proportions of the unusual setting – as well as an indication of how the rear half of the turntable stage was used to accommodate the much more traditional setting for *Miss Julie*, which played for a time in tandem with *Nora* as part of the ambitious triptych known as the Bergman Project.[36] Bergman and his designer, Gunilla Palmstierna-Weiss, employed strongly expressive visual means to communicate his perception of the inner rhythm and tensions of Ibsen's play. The heavy mosaic of realistic details that fill up the "tastefully but not expensively furnished living-room" described in Ibsen's stage directions was condensed into a singularly suggestive theatrical image of oppressiveness and joylessness. The front curtain, a black-and-white depiction of a characterless nineteenth-century house facade, rose to reveal an empty, neutral space cut off from any contact with the world of reality – a void encompassed by a vast non-representational box uniformly lined with dark red velveting. Erected within this closed velvet box was a smaller inner enclosure created by high, dark walls, suggesting the panelled interior of a courtroom or, perhaps, the wainscoting of a polite Victorian parlor. The absence of any doors or windows reinforced the intense feeling of claustrophobia which this arrangement conveyed. "Neither air nor light nor sound from the outside world could penetrate this closed, hermetically sealed realm of fixed social values and convictions," one critic observed.[37]

At the geometrical center of this closed universe stood a low,

"You will, Torvald, won't you?" Nora asks Helmer, as Rank and
Mrs. Linde look on in the Residenztheater production of *Nora*, 1981.

quadrilateral platform, hemmed in by the forbidding wall-
screens and the watchers. This was the acting area proper – the
"magical point of magnetic energy" that Bergman believes
must always be located and defined in every stage space. On
this small platform-stage, a succession of deliberately fragmen-
tary "settings" delineated the broad developmental movements into which *Nora* divided itself. During the first five
scenes, the crowded space was taken up by an old-fashioned
velvet sofa and matching armchair, a decorated Christmas tree,
and heaps of wrapped and unwrapped presents and toys –
including a decorative brass doll-bed and two large dolls with
pale and oddly human porcelain faces. This was the doll's
house of eternal childhood, the Helmer world of games and
make-believe. Then, as the alien forces which shatter this
fragile world came crashing down on it, the playpen was

discarded; the only objects of furniture left in the arena of conflict were a large, round dining-table and four matching straight chairs. For the final bitter and disillusioned settling of accounts between Nora and Helmer, however, the focal object was not, as it is in Ibsen, the dining-table but a large brass bed – an unmistakable replica of the doll-bed seen in the first scene and a reminder of the sexual intimacy that had been the one real bond between them during their eight years of marriage.

When the final confrontation does erupt in *A Doll's House*, it must come as no surprise, Bergman insists. In order to circumvent the entirely unsatisfactory impression that Nora's final repudiation of her shadow-life with Helmer is somehow a transformation or the result of new-found courage, the director and the actress must, he argues, "always start with the last scene – with an understanding of what happens in the last scene. Once you have understood that, then you can go back and begin at the beginning. In that last scene you have the whole solution to the rest of the play."[38] The essence of the firm and organic relationship he established between the beginning of the play and its ending is found in the graphic theatrical metaphor of the waiting, watching characters who surrounded Nora from start to finish. Their very presence signified that a predetermined and ineluctable process was taking its course – a process during the course of which Nora would eventually have to summon and come to terms with each of "her" characters in turn. Alone, in the midst of a setting that was hardly a stage setting at all, she acted out a dream of life from which she was struggling to awake. In this version, the play was no longer governed or even remotely influenced by realistic considerations of time and place. Although the basic plot remained unchanged, its methodically constructed logic of cause and effect – which, in Bergman's view serves only to dissipate its potential imaginative impact on a contemporary audience by "closing doors, leaving no other alternatives" – was displaced by an intuitive logic of feeling, sustained by means of associations and contrasts. The fifteen scenes into which *Nora* was divided were emotional units held together by a virtually cinematic juxtaposition of contrasting moods and emotional states. Characters came and went freely, in neutral space, with no need for parlormaids or ringing doorbells or carefully prepared "motivations" to aid (or impede) them. Fluid, often unexplained transitions from one episode to another created what Strindberg calls "the inconsequent but transparently logical form of a dream." In such a composition the sole unifying factor remains the dreamer – in this case Nora herself.

In Rita Russek's performance, a sense of incipient rage and frustration within the character of Nora was emphasized from the outset, in an emotionally charged mime sequence which prefaced and defined the play. Ibsen's heroine is described as entering in high spirits, humming contentedly to herself as she struggles with an armful of presents for the children. By contrast, Russek was revealed already seated, utterly immobile, in the midst of a wilderness of toys, dolls, and other relics of childhood. Leaned back against the pillows of a plush sofa, she stared out into empty space – virtually the image of a human doll waiting to be taken up and played with. The distant, faintly audible sound of an old-fashioned music-box tune added to the distinctly oneiric mood of nostalgia and suppressed melancholy that was projected by this motionless, oddly dejected figure. Then, as she stood up and quickly pushed off her shoes, the feeling of latent tension and restlessness within her exploded into activity. Impatiently, she tore the wrapping off several of the children's presents and promptly stuffed the paper out of sight under the sofa. A visible and forcible effort to regain control of herself was required before she called out to her husband to come and admire her purchases – and the play proper began.

As Helmer (Robert Atzorn) stepped forward from the chair where, less than fifteen feet away, he waited for her summons, the mood of the scene changed as Nora became the charming, ingratiating doll-wife who takes an essentially naive delight in exploiting her beauty and sexual appeal to gain her own ends. Atzorn's Helmer, too, obligingly took on his prescribed role as the eagerly affectionate but overbearing husband who showers his attractive wife with kisses and attention. As they knelt together on the floor, grasping each other's hands and engaging in laughing, semi-erotic horseplay, they became children playing a treasured and familiar game. Overshadowing this game from the beginning, however, was the clear sense that *both* of them were trapped within the fixed limits of roles that had been assigned to them. The fact that only Nora was consciously, if dimly, aware of the masquerade defined the perceptional gulf between them. The forces of disruption that break loose over the Helmers and shatter their ostensible domestic security were thus, in Bergman's interpretation, more than merely external forces, expressed in plot turns. They arose just as surely from within – from Nora's own growing disillusionment and awareness of isolation, as well as from the sense of resentment and humiliation that seethed within both Krogstad and Mrs. Linde and drew these two emotional cripples together.

This Mrs. Linde bore little resemblance to the innocuous, quietly pathetic friend of Ibsen stage tradition. Throughout the performance, the inert, cramped figure portrayed by Anne-marie Wernicke provided an emphatic contrast to Nora's vivacious mobility and lively, impulsive gestures. She was a woman filled with futility and resentment after her long years of deadening self-sacrifice, corroded in her very being by a bitterness that has consumed her warmth and her humanity and left only the empty shell. "There is poison in her – she's venomous," Bergman observed. "There are those small moments, in the first encounter between Nora and Mrs. Linde, when she bites."[39] In fact, every physical detail about her, from her tightly drawn lips and oddly flat, emotionless manner of speech to her reluctant, angular movements, proclaimed with graphic clarity the spiritual prisonhouse, built of rancor and perceived humiliation, in which she found herself confined. Above all, Wernicke's characterization conveyed the noxious, parasitical quality of a moral fanatic, a self-appointed and vindictive apostle of "truth". She precipitated the conclusive confrontation between Helmer and Nora deliberately, insisting, in a virtual paroxysm of self-righteous evangelical rage, that "this wretched secrecy" must be exposed and "all this lying and concealment must come to an end," in order for judgment to be passed on Nora and punishment meted out. At the chilling moment of Mrs. Linde's outburst and her loveless reunion with Krogstad, moreover, an expressive double perspective ruled the action. Throughout this scene, standing in the shadows beside the low stage-platform, the figure of Nora was seen in full view of the audience. At first she stood, as motionless as a mannequin in the flame-red dancing costume she had worn to the costume ball at the Stenborgs, staring straight ahead into the darkness of the auditorium. Then, drawing her dark shawl around her as if to protect herself from a cold wind, she turned away to await the foregone conclusion of Mrs. Linde's pent-up rancor to be reached.

Hence, Bergman's dark and uncompromising vision of Ibsen's play placed Nora under the oppressive influence of not one but two dangerous opponents – both of whom, he explained, inhabited the same shared hell where "the damned are condemned to torment one another." Both were gripped and deformed by the same sense of entrapment in a hostile social order that conspired to humiliate and annihilate them. As for Krogstad himself, he was neither the simple moral degenerate that Doctor Rank describes nor the deep-dyed theater villain of stage tradition. As acted by Gerd Anthoff, the character of the hole-and-corner lawyer who tries to exploit Nora's forged promissory note became a far more complex and contradictory force in the play – the tormentor who is in turn the sufferer, as it were, infected by the same condition of anguish and dread that he sought to instill in his victim. His hands buried in the pockets of a heavy black overcoat that enveloped him like a straitjacket, this pale, slow-moving figure conveyed the impression of a man who was dangerous and even brutal because he was trapped in a fierce and utterly desperate struggle for survival that involved far more than merely "a modest position in the bank."

In their first confrontation, Nora's reaction to this bitter, melancholy anti-villain was one of cold contempt. In their second and crucial encounter, however, the mood changed and the tension between them became tinged by a curious irony. In this oddly compassionate scene, Krogstad seemed to have come not merely to coerce Nora but also to commiserate with her as a fellow-sufferer – someone locked together with him in a hell (or a nightmare) where everything moves in circles and events are doomed to be repeated over and over again. Condemned to suffer for a crime no different from Nora's, he now watched the fixed pattern repeat itself. In a series of spasmodic, circular moves of approach, he tried awkwardly to reach out to her, in an effort to persuade her of the futility and meaninglessness of the desperate action that "is the first thing most of us think of." But, as Bergman warned, "between oppressor and oppressed there can be no relationship." Nora's

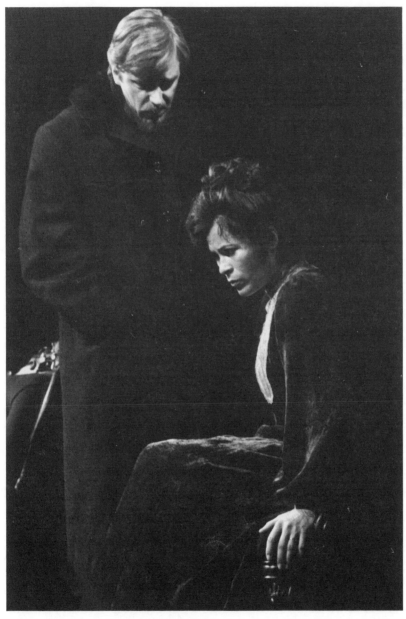

Nora (Rita Russek) with her nemesis Nils Krogstad (Gerd Anthoff) in *Nora*. Residenztheater, 1981.

stubborn resistance rekindled the resentment and sense of humiliation that permeated this shadowy figure's every shaky gesture and every outburst of hollow laughter. At last, after a moment's hesitation, he dropped his letter exposing the lie Nora has been living into a barred, locked mailbox that hung, without any realistic "excuse" for its being there, on the panelled wall beside the watching characters. Once her vain efforts to break the lock with a hairpin had convinced her that the catastrophe was now inevitable, Nora sat quietly on the edge of the table and covered her face with her hands, in a gesture of terror that a child might take.

Krogstad's thwarted, self-contradictory attempt to reach out to Nora was a deformed image of the countless attempts made by all the characters in this production to reach out to one another, without success. The aftermath of the confrontation between Nora and Krogstad – the famous tarantella scene – became the last such effort on Nora's part to reach Helmer, to communicate her anguish to this amiable but hopelessly handicapped emotional illiterate who understood nothing of her pain. In Bergman's staging of this moment, Nora's tarantella was not really a dance at all – at least not the frantic and increasingly more confused and pathetic dance that generations of Noras have performed, to the tuneful accompaniment of Doctor Rank at the upright, in order to distract her husband's attention from the fateful letterbox. Instead, Rita Russek's defiant, whirling tarantella, danced on top of the round table to the rebellious pounding of her tambourine, was not a coy maneuver designed to divert Helmer's attention but a hieroglyph of desperation meant to attract it. This passionate choreographic outburst, watched thoughtfully by Rank and with bewilderment by her husband, was virtually a mute, conscious outcry for help in a situation that Nora herself now knew to be beyond help. The dance was brief; the clattering tambourine she let fall to the floor signified its finality, as the last game in a played-out masquerade.

Only in her scenes with Doctor Rank – who provided the lyrical antithesis to Mrs. Linde's spitefulness – did Nora find brief intervals of rest and sympathetic understanding. The essence of the unusual bond of communication that Bergman forged between these two characters is found in a provocative statement of his that "Rank is Ibsen" in "a play about love"

Nora's tarantella in the Munich production.

that is charged with the spirit of "Ibsen's love for a woman he himself had created."[40] Obviously, such a remark is intended less as a literal statement of fact than as a suggestive, creative metaphor that served, among other things, to inspire the actor who played the role, Horst Sachtleben, to achieve a fresh and extraordinarily moving approach to one of Ibsen's most puzzling physician–observers. Bergman's interpretation made it plain that only Rank's manifest love for Nora held any genuine meaning – although it was only a fleetingly perceived dream-image of love, as wistful and nostalgic as the old music-box melody (*Traümerei*, one of Robert Schumann's Scenes from Childhood) that attached itself to this figure throughout. His deep compassion for Nora was built on his love and his affectionate understanding of her. She, in turn, was the one source of warmth and light that graced his otherwise gloomy and solitary passage into the encroaching darkness.

Particularly in their crucial second-act encounter, nothing was allowed to matter more than this scene's emotional texture – least of all its mechanical function as a plot reversal in which Nora, having made up her mind to ask Rank for money with which to pay off her debt, is prevented from doing so by his unexpected declaration of love. All digressions and interruptions in the text were eliminated, and in the process the "realistic" but emotionally diffused impression of characters talking at cross-purposes disappeared as well. From the very first, kneeling to her in a wryly theatrical gesture of supplication, Rank made the true purpose of his visit perfectly transparent – his need to find a way to leave her some money or some expression of his love that would survive him. And Nora's purpose, as she in turn knelt before his chair and later stood behind him to cradle his head against her bosom, was equally plain – to comfort him by somehow assuaging the anguish and despair that now overcame him in the face of death. Slowly, in an almost hypnotic manner, she helped him to push back the horror of what he knew awaited him. As he began to relax, he leaned his head against her; slowly, she covered his eyes with her hands. Then, with a dreamlike slowness, she drew a silk stocking across his closed lids, as though somehow conjuring up a consoling vision of loveliness for him – a dream of Nora dancing only for him ("and for Torvald, too, of course – that goes without saying"). Thus transformed, this moment became a living icon of compassion asked for and received – the pivotal image in an oneiric scene that shone with warmth and humanity in the midst of the desolate and rapidly darkening world of the play.

Rank's last appearance, in the night scene following the costume ball, emphatically signaled the end of masquerades and "amusing disguises," not only for him but especially for Nora and Torvald. Citing the early modern critic Edvard Brandes, Bergman calls the Helmer marriage "a passion without friendship" – a relationship in which, "without seeing one another, they assign each other roles which they have made up for one another."[41] A crucial irony in this director's interpre-

"Then you must imagine that I'm dancing only for you": Nora (Rita Russek) comforts Doctor Rank (Horst Sachtleben) in the Residenztheater production, 1981.

tation is found in his observation that the play must also be seen as "the tragedy of Helmer," the victim of his own entrapment in the externally imposed role of being the man, the husband: "He tries to play his role as well as he can – because it is the only one he understands." This sincere and boyishly self-centered Helmer perceived nothing of this irony or of the catastrophe that was nearly upon him. Nor did he notice that his Nora had long ago begun to be conscious of the futility of the games they played together.

Nora's wish was for an emotional reckoning, not for an intellectual debate around a table; and any feeling of its "unexpectedness" was confined entirely to Helmer. Naked and asleep in their brass bed, his sexual desire presumably satisfied, he suddenly awakened to find himself face to face with a woman in a black travelling costume, a packed overnight bag in her hand. The utter vulnerability of his nakedness, accentuated by a single, piercing shaft of light that turned his figure and the bedclothes into a blaze of white, was confronted by what Bergman's own script describes as Nora's "complete ruthlessness and brutality." As he listened uncomprehendingly and the other characters watched silently from the shadowy darkness beside his bed, she reviewed the wreckage that he, and her father before him, had made of her life. His uncertain attempt to reassert the ritual of domination ("Oh, you think and talk like a naive child") was met by an assault of vehement physical anger that subsided, at last, into a deep sorrow which overcame her aggressiveness and fury. The anguished conclusion she reaches ("I've got to do it by myself, and that's the reason I'm leaving you") is underscored in the director's script as "absolutely the central line in the whole play" – and his Nora found it the most difficult and painful statement she had to make. But the locked pattern had now been conclusively broken, as in a bad dream from which one finally awakens. No doors slammed. Without a sound, as if by magic, a hidden aperture in the apparently solid "courtroom" wall swung open, and Nora stepped through it to freedom – an escape artist who left the captors of her dream behind.

Seen against the background of Bergman's earlier efforts to disclose and lay bare the inner essence of Ibsen's dramas, the thematic clarity and unencumbered emotional directness of his 1981 Nora came as no real surprise. What was startling to

experience, however, was the changed style of the performance itself, in which the waiting, watching actors became a
fresh and forceful reminder of the theatricality of the theater
and of the participatory bond between actor and spectator that
is the true meaning of theatrical illusion. As such, Nora marked
not a stopping place but a decisive turning point in Bergman's
development, looking ahead as it did to the more overtly
self-reflexive, "metatheatrical" style of his later work.

In terms of A Doll's House, for example, his 1989 revival of
this play at Dramaten transposed it to a plane where the
illusion of reality played, as it were, no part at all, and the
demarcation between past and present vanished along with it.
Leif Zern described his impression of the experience as
"chamber music for five voices," in which "the wide angle of
the camera observes both time present and time gone by."[42]
The basic staging concept had, for the most part, not changed,
but the texture of its surface had been roughened. On one
level, the basic character relationships seemed, in the Swedish
restaging, both coarser and much less perfectly controlled:
Nora (Pernilla Östergren) now hoisted her skirts to dance a
bare-legged tarantella, smothered Rank (Erland Josephson) in
uninhibited hugs and kisses, and virtually copulated with
Helmer (Per Mattsson) as she wheedled money out of him at
the beginning of the play. Paradoxically, however, these and
other moments of explicit, even violent reality were tinged
with a more muted atmosphere of dream and memory. At the
back of the sparsely furnished platform on which Nora played
out (or, more correctly, replayed) her life's struggle, one saw
enlarged projections of old photographs that seemed to recol-
lect and reconsider time past. These faded, monochrome
glimpses of other rooms from another time appeared, in the
words of one critic, like "pictures from a faraway past mat-
erializing from an old album, with subdued color nuances that
are transformed at the end to modern black and white."[43] The
collision in this performance between scenes of almost blatant
reality and a mood of dreamlike detachment produced a
painful sense of dissonance and disjuncture that was, it
seemed, the underlying point of Bergman's new, less conciliatory interpretation of this play.

The one major change, said to have been brought about by
Bergman's dissatisfaction at having cut the children in his

Pernilla Östergren as Nora in *A Doll's House* at Dramaten, 1989. The faded projection of another room from an older period is seen in the background.

Munich version, had in fact nothing at all to do with textual fidelity and everything to do with the feeling of disjuncture which this performance deliberately engendered. In the final scene, Nora's "liberation" from her bondage was rendered much more deeply ambiguous than before, juxtaposed as it was with the silent presence of a small girl, named Hilde in Bergman's script. She was first seen in the opening sequence, listening to a fairy story read by her mother (an apposite tale about a Prince and his Princess "who go off to live in his castle, east of the sun and west of the moon"). Hilde's doll, left on a chair among the watching characters on the sidelines, remained as a reminder of her presence throughout the performance. Then, in its closing moments, the little girl reappeared, standing unnoticed in the background as she watched her mother make her own escape from the time-stopped world of the play – not, as before, through a hidden aperture in the wall but out through the audience, to join the world of actuality.

Bergman's recent productions of *John Gabriel Borkman* and *Peer Gynt* are best discussed in the following chapter, in conjunction with more general trends in his work. In itself, however, the fact that three of his last eight productions have been plays by Ibsen is a telling indication of his deepening preoccupation with this playwright. In a conversation with us more than a decade ago, he made a remark that has often been quoted since: "With Ibsen, you know, you always have the feeling of limits – because Ibsen placed them there himself. He was an architect, and he built. He always built his plays, and he knew exactly: I want this and I want that. He points the audience in the direction he wants it to go, closing doors, leaving no other alternatives." Both before and after he made that statement, Bergman's productions of Ibsen's prose plays have constituted a continuous campaign to probe beneath their surface of photographic accuracy and naturalistic detail in an effort to eliminate the sense of particularity and limitation that this surface imposes when reproduced on a contemporary stage. For, as Bergman puts it, it is only by seeking to look "behind the mask of the weary master architect" that we can hope to see the face of the poet revealed.

6   To begin again

While his highly theatricalized version of *A Doll's House* at the Residenztheater in 1981 clearly marked a turning point in stylistic terms, Ingmar Bergman's production of Ibsen's *John Gabriel Borkman* on the Munich stage four years later signified – and perhaps even precipitated – the end of one phase in his long career and the beginning of a decisively new one. After nine years of self-imposed exile – years, unlike Borkman's, filled with productive activity that included five major films and ten German-language stage productions – he had finally made up his mind to return to Sweden permanently. His longing to regain the precision of directing in his own language had grown too strong to be denied. ("I must have the *mot propre*, the precise word," as he put it: "I must be able to be exact when I talk about a play.") In addition, his direction of *King Lear* in Stockholm in 1984 had, in retrospect, left him with a feeling of dissatisfaction and a determination to change his own working methods. "I'm very dissatisfied with my whole way of making theater. I don't feel happy with it. I feel I need to break down my limitations, find new ways," he said in an interview on the day of the *Borkman* opening (May 31, 1985). "I simply feel a desperate need to begin in a new way."[1]

As this remark suggests, the nine weeks of rehearsal for the *Borkman* production had been a time of creative stimulus and renewal for Bergman. The great demands that Ibsen's late masterpiece places on any director represented a challenge he welcomed and even craved, and in this sense the play joined *Lear* as the first of a series of confrontations with what he calls "impossible" plays, chosen to "shake life into drowsy creativity." "I have a kind of obsession: I want to direct the plays I think I'll never see again," he admitted in our interview. "I'm getting old, you know, and now I only want to direct what's impossible – plays in which it's impossible to find an ultimate solution."[2] In terms of *Borkman* itself, the process of breaking down limitations in search of fresh insights concentrated itself particularly, as one might expect, on the problem

246

of the play's difficult fourth act and its relationship to what has gone before.

By systematically cutting away what he regards – in this play and elsewhere in Ibsen – as *gewollt* (willed, forced) symbolic references and connotations, Bergman sought to anchor his approach firmly in a personal, emotional context, rather than in a vaguely mythic one. By further eliminating the play's much-debated closing lines, with their suggestion of a conciliatory but questionable truce between Gunhild Borkman and Ella Rentheim, her estranged sister, he centered attention and sympathy more surely on the title character and his dilemma. Borkman's final anguished anagnorisis and death on the mountain top thus became the focal moment of knowledge and self-knowledge toward which everything else in this production tended. Bergman did not seek to build a smooth and "believable" transition between the first three acts and the fourth. Rather, he began with that final reckoning as a foregone conclusion, a bleak assumption that coloured every move and every tone in an endgame in which, regardless of the possible moves (stories, visions, evasions) left to the players, the process of ending is irreversible and plain to see.

All three radically dematerialized, monochromatic settings (designed by Gunilla Palmstierna-Weiss, a frequent collaborator of Bergman's in his later productions) purposely altered the audience's perception of an observable place in time – the reality of conventional understanding, as it were – in order to refocus attention on the inner emotional design of Ibsen's play. The raked platform-stage on which the action took place was a dislocated world devoid of stable contours, suggesting a deliberate disjuncture between the three-dimensionality of the actors and the obviously flattened theatrical perspective of the space in which they moved. As a result, the true focus of each composition became not its ground but the figures in it, whose emotional turmoil was literally drawn closer to the audience in this way. This strategy found its boldest expression in the visual treatment of the fourth act, in which the cold winter landscape outside the Rentheim estate was conveyed by a vast, utterly empty expanse of whiteness that covered the full depth of the platform. This bleak, colorless world beyond life was illuminated by searing, remorselessly harsh low-angle projectors whose light emphasized – and compelled – an intense

The opening tableau in the last act of *John Gabriel Borkman*. Residenztheater, 1985.

plastic expressiveness that seemed "chiseled out" with "a spiritual and gestural precision that has been virtually forgotten in today's theater."[3] In the background stood a tall, unearthly tombstone of a house front – "a vision of a blanched ghost-house," thought one observer, "with black cavities for windows."[4] The atmosphere of spiritual and emotional desolation in this final movement of the play – of "death as the extreme of loneliness," as Bergman puts it in *Cries and Whispers* – was instantly evoked by a vivid figure composition. Before the "house" at the very back of the stage stood the inert, strangely distant figure of Borkman, dressed in a heavy black overcoat and hat; at the very front of the platform, a universe away from him, one saw the twin sisters, dark, mournful shapes whose long shadows called to mind the art of Chirico and Munch. Isolated in a loveless world of death-in-life, these three "dreamers and self-deceivers" (as Bergman calls them) remained, throughout the performance, locked within their own separate visions of reality and the past, all blindly groping their way from one emotionally intense, fleeting instant of human contact to the next.

Later in the last act, as Borkman begins his final journey

with Ella to "the clearing high up in the forest," even the eerie house facade in this evocative "setting" vanished. Only the interplay of darkness and light – and the poetry of Ibsen's prose – were left to conjure up the "vast, infinite, inexhaustible kingdom" of his imagination. Borkman (Hans Michael Rehberg) simply walked into the deep, encroaching shadows at the rear of the empty platform, followed closely by Ella (Christa Berndl). Emerging again into the shadowless white light, he cast off hat, cane, gloves, overcoat, and jacket and tore open his collar and cuffs as he came forward to the low, simple bench that had stood at the front of the stage since the play began. Seeming younger and more vigorous now, his figure outlined against the totally bare, contourless white space, Rehberg's Borkman conjured up the dream of his kingdom with an expansive, mantic gesture ("see how the land stretches before us, so spacious and free"). At this moment, virtually Faustian as it was in spirit and scope, his character "acquire[d] a visionary power," remarked *Die Welt* (June 3). "We sense that we hear Faust's last words, 'I'd open room to live for millions,' spoken with so much grandeur, so much pride in the face of death."

As conceived by Bergman and portrayed by Rehberg, Borkman's aspirations and his great emotional vision of his unattainable kingdom with its "bright promise of power and glory" were stretched to embrace, by association, the vision and calling of the creative artists as well. In a characteristically allusive and undogmatic but deeply personal way, Bergman discussed the play with the actors as a "testament" in which "Ibsen is talking about his own poetry, his own life's work – and judging it. Passing a terrible judgment on it."[5] In this sense, the fierce denunciation of Borkman by his wife Gunhild (Christine Buchegger) in the third act and Ella Rentheim's even more savage attack on him at the end were indirect expressions, in their way, of a self-condemnation on the part of what Bergman calls "the imaginative human being" – the artist committed to his vision, suddenly brought to recognize the appalling toll which his single-minded obsession has exacted in terms of human suffering.

So unexpectedly brutal and even vindictive was Ella's final damnation of Borkman, however, that it became, in this performance, a denial of the balm of human compassion and forgiveness that thrust the reality of Borkman's own pain and despair into the foreground, as the focus of the audience's sympathy. By rejecting what he regarded as the imposed reunion of Ella and Gunhild, Bergman further deepened the sense of unresolved and irresolvable ambivalence inherent in the work as a whole. Once her fury and bitterness was spent, Ella rushed forward at the last moment to embrace Borkman, passed her hand slowly over his face, and finally covered his lifeless form with her heavy coat. There was, however, no trace of relief and certainly no hint of a new beginning born of the warring sisters' reconciliation. Instead, summarized in the cold, empty, anaesthetized whiteness of the final tableau, the motionless image of "two shadows and a dead man" bespoke the fractured, incoherent world Bergman saw reflected in Ibsem's bleak "winter's tale."

For all its darkness, meanwhile, possibly the greatest surprise in this production was its subtle blending of tonal contrasts – achieved not (as is so often the case with this play) through a spuriously "comic" approach to the title character but by a symphonic interplay of psychological intensity and bitter, mocking humor. In this regard the figure of Foldal, played by the noted German film actor Heinz Bennent, took on crucial significance as Borkman's comic double. The two Foldal scenes, Bergman remarked, are "so perfect, so precise, so full of black humor" that they seem "like Beckett or Ionesco . . . Or like the dialogue between Lear and Gloucester on the heath." In his long overcoat, black hat, skimpy jacket, and striped trousers, Bennent had Chaplin's eager, whimsical face, his awkwardly dignified walk – and his profound and manifest humanity. No trace of sentimentality was permitted to mar Borkman's relationship with this would-be poet, the one person who has not deserted him during his eight anguished years of self-imposed isolation. Rather, the point in this performance was the seriocomic affinity between these two hopelessly self-deluded dreamers. Borkman's obsessive concern with the power to create a new world was seen reflected in the grotesque mirror of Foldal's own dogged obsession with the poetic "masterpiece" he has been rewriting for most of his life – and from which, in this performance, he was even allowed to read, sonorously declaiming (to the dismay of a few

Heinz Bennent as Foldal, in conversation with his director. The large back-screen, depicting a violent battle scene, dominated the second-act setting for Borkman's study. Residenztheater, 1985.

more conservative critics) the opening lines of Ibsen's first and most bombastic tragedy, *Catiline*.

The dissonant collision of seriousness and absurdity inherent in this relationship reasserted itself even more acutely in the fourth act, where dissonance was the dominant tone at every juncture. Here, the dark pattern of the tragedy was pierced by what Bergman calls the "strange scherzo" of Foldal's return, after he has been knocked down by the speeding sleigh that carries his daughter away with Erhart Borkman and his lively "companion," Fanny Wilton. Here again, however, it was not the potential pathos of the situation but its comic irony that mattered most in this performance. His overcoat now soiled, his umbrella broken, and his hat and glasses lost in the snow, Bennent's Foldal was the awkward and limping but intensely alive refutation of the lifelessness of Borkman himself, who remained virtually motionless through-out their scene. Nearsighted without his glasses and muffled in his scarf to cover his ears from the cold, this comedic casualty of life's heartlessness was figuratively blind and deaf to the personal hardships and sorrows it inflicts, mindful instead only of the fine silver bells on Erhart's sleigh and of the happiness that he hopes will await his "little Frida" in the wide world he himself once dreamed of seeing. In this way, his simple naivety established the counter-theme to Borkman's bitter and disillusioned experience of life; the pain of know-ledge and judgment that awaits the latter was accentuated by the spectacle of the happy ignorance of his double. Ultimately, in this work about the effect of love's denial, the Foldal figure became, for Bergman, "the bearer of love and human life" in metaphorical terms. "Love in the evangelical sense of the word – the deepest and most permanent sense – must inform art and the artist," he explained in our interview with him. "In other words, in this play about the absence of love, it becomes this fool who carries the underlying theme of love – both in a comic and a tragic sense."[6]

Bennent's Foldal and Rehberg's Borkman were only two in a tight cluster of performances that produced what one Swedish critic described as "a mesmeric display of virtuosity." The production exhibited, in this viewer's opinion, "an ensemble playing which no theater in Sweden today could begin to approach, a perfectly balanced musicality that could not be surpassed."⁷ The intense, passionate style of German ensemble acting to which this comment refers was, in fact, the real impetus behind Bergman's determination to adopt new methods of work when he returned to the Royal Dramatic Theatre in Stockholm. "I believe we have a great deal to learn from the best of German theater," he said as he prepared to leave the Munich experience behind. For him, the greatest surprise had been

to see just *how* far the director and the actors, joined in a kind of symbiosis, can expand themselves and one another. *Far* beyond the limits at which I once thought you had to stop, so as not to damage yourself and everyone else. But now the actors here have shown me that their potential is far greater – their psychological strength is much, much greater than I once believed. . . . It's not a question of going home and suddenly standing up and being a dictator. That isn't the point. It's just that we can do more – we can always do more. The actors here teach you that all the time. They're incredibly reckless with themselves, and that's why I find them so enormously fascinating.⁸

The resultant change in outlook and approach has, perhaps, been most clearly demonstrated in the "impossible" plays Bergman has attempted in Stockholm – in the tough, defiant emotionality of his *Hamlet* (1986), in the clockwork precision of the ensemble in his *Long Day's Journey into Night* (1988), in the cool, shimmering formality and exquisite beauty of his *Madame de Sade* (1989), and in the sheer ebullience of his reconstituted *Peer Gynt* (1991). Bibi Andersson, who played Mother Aase in the latter work and Mary Tyrone in the O'Neill production, has offered a revealing insight into the nature of this change, as seen from the actor's point of view. "During rehearsals, he treated me in a way I wouldn't have believed possible," she said in a public discussion of Bergman as a director. "I think he learned a lot in Munich. For me, it was like rediscovering him. Suddenly I understood what people had been saying about him . . . Using intuition and not explaining a lot, I knew exactly what he meant. And that, for me, was creative collaboration such as I have never experienced in my life before."⁹

The freedom of the actor, as a true partner in the intuitive process of creation, is invariably coupled with – and thus upheld by – a rigorous precision on Bergman's part. "Ingmar hates surprises of any kind," observed Erland Josephson

Stina Ekblad as Renée (left) and Anita Björk as her mother, Madame de Montreuil, in *Madame de Sade*. Dramaten, 1989.

(Doctor Rank in *A Doll's House* in 1989) on the same occasion. "He's extremely well prepared at all times, down to every move and detail. That makes him able to change things – because he's very open to the reactions and initiatives and fantasy of the actors . . . [He] is always looking for your personal secrets."[10]

NEW DIRECTIONS AT DRAMATEN

The blend of exactitude and emotional daring for which Bergman has continued to strive found what may be its most perfect expression in the strange and potentially intransigent *Madame de Sade*, by the modern Japanese novelist-dramatist Yukio Mishima. No direct use was made of the Noh tradition with which this drama about the Marquis de Sade "seen through women's eyes" is often associated in Mishima's own country. Rather, the strict grace and musically orchestrated formalism of Bergman's production at Lilla scenen (April 8, 1989) carved out a style that was fully as controlled and tightly disciplined as the highly codified Noh form itself. Beneath a composed facade of elegant feminine gestures and luxurious rococo gowns, a virulent obsession seemed to grip the six women who calmly discuss the infamous exploits of the imprisoned de Sade, who never appears in the play but whose presence is incessantly conjured up by their introspective, solipsistic recollections. "The secret to it, and to directing it, is this absolute restraint," Bergman said in an interview. "What is so important here is that these six women are never permitted to express openly what they think or feel. Their only means of expression is in precisely choreographed movements and gestures."[11]

Musicality and the musical arrangement of words and phrases governed this performance choice from beginning to end. "The phrasing, the pauses, and the controlled crescendos in language and movement patterns transform *Madame de Sade* into an integrated and melodic symphony composition – an autumn sonata for six women," Tove Ellefsen wrote in *Dagens Nyheter*. The multiple paradoxes which de Sade signifies in the eyes of these waiting women – love and betrayal, ugliness that is also beauty, darkness and light, evil that is perhaps created at God's command – comprise the subject of this impossibly disquisitory play. Where other directors of it have failed, however, Bergman succeeded by translating Mishima's verbal rhetoric into a brilliant visual and choreographic rhetoric in which the slightest change in facial expression – a look, a smile, a raised eyebrow – carried significance. Under such tense conditions as these, the mere turn of a head or the snap of a fan that is opened or closed was capable of causing an emotional earthquake.

Bergman has said before that an exploitation of the power of suggestion ("one of the secrets of our business – not to show everything") is the single most important link between his work in film and his work in theater. In this instance, the explicitness of the shocking images of brutality and sexual depravity that engulf Mishima's play was deliberately subdued beneath a ritualized surface of formality and elegance that served to intensify the audience's emotional response to the subtext of implicit violence. "Through this aestheticized filter, emotions are distilled with much greater force and conceptual clarity than if Bergman had chosen a rougher, less polished style of presentation," Ellefsen went on to say.

To strengthen the sense of proximity and actor–audience rapport that Bergman considers essential for this particular play, he and his designer, Charles Koroly, extended the stage of Dramaten's studio theater out over the first five rows of the auditorium.[12] A simple, symmetrical framework of deep red columns and arches defined the open, semi-elliptical playing area. At the back of this fixed, neutral space, projected images established a shifting sequence of purely allusive visual motifs. At first, the delicate outline of a cherry tree was seen against a pastel background. This muted image gave way in the second act to the more disturbing impression of a raging fire. In the final act one saw a black sky filled with storm clouds. The aim here was obviously not to illustrate a concrete action in concrete terms, however, but rather to confront the audience with purely suggestive images of a state of mind – visual corollaries, as it were, to the spiritual process which, to varying degrees, all six of de Sade's women undergo during their eighteen years of waiting for his release. Their wait is a confrontation with the forces of malevolence and anarchy this symbolic figure represents – but, as time passes, it ultimately becomes a struggle against corrosive inner forces that threaten to destroy them. This multifaceted process of disintegration and collapse from within acquired – at least in this particular production – the emotional clarity of music, variations on a theme for six voices, scored in three distinctly phrased movements.

The first of these movements opened on a note of cool composure. In the late summer of 1772, the members of the aristocratic circle of Renée, the Marquise de Sade (Stina Ekblad) gather to discuss the sentence of death passed on her husband, the notorious Marquis. By relying on an extremely economical scheme of sculptural movement that minimized physical contact and emphasized widely spaced figure positionings, Bergman conveyed a graphic impression of characters who are literally and figuratively isolated from one another. Reluctant to establish any contact with others, each of the women seemed locked within a role and a set pattern of convictions – be they moral, social, or religious. No emotion was betrayed, and for long periods even direct eye contact was withheld. Communication took the form of a strictly regulated ceremony – a double game of masks and poses in which they all surreptitiously watched one another (preferably from behind the barrier of a fan), all the while concealing their mutual distrust and opposition beneath a veneer of elaborate formality and courtesy. "With stylized refinement in each pose and gesture, the actors take their places on stage, *en face* or in profile," wrote Ingmar Björkstén in *Svenska Dagbladet*. "They move as if to the measures of an inaudible music – flowing, rhythmical, and pleasantly melodious." This critic was one of several who used the term "psychological filigree" to describe the intricacy of the emotional dynamics underlying Bergman's performance style.

As the action progressed, meanwhile, the earlier sense of statuesque aloofness and reserve began to wear down. Small but telling changes in appearance and tone bore witness to the growing spiritual malaise that threatens to consume each of these women as their waiting game goes on. In the second act, set in the autumn of 1778, the characters wore a somewhat freer and less stately kind of dress, held in strong shades of deep red and black that presented a sharp contrast to the subdued nuances of pale rose and beige dominant in the rococo gowns they wore, like suits of protective armor, in the first act. Even the women's voices now seemed to lose their melodious quality and become progressively harsher and more shrill. The implied metamorphosis was further under-scored by the fact that the faces of Renée and those around her had grown visibly older and more haggard. When de Sade's stubbornly, even irrationally loyal wife at last confronted her tyrannical, manipulative mother, Madame de Montreuil (Anita Björk) at the end of the act, their climactic encounter marked, in Bergman's scoring, the first time in the play that the suppressed forces of violence and aggression within these women were allowed to burst through the taut surface of their composure. Renée's defiant declaration of her absolute identi-fication with the cruel and malignant persona of de Sade marked a decisive stage in her complex inner journey – and it precipitated correspondingly radical changes in the tone and mood of the production.

Its final movement, which takes place on a wintry spring day in 1790, nine months after the outbreak of the French Revolu-tion, was dominated by a much more desolate impression of women inwardly ravaged by a struggle that has destoyed their femininity and warmth and has left them bereft. A new period in history had begun, in which they were – like the scattered pieces of furniture around them – essentially discards. From their ashen faces to the drab gray and black clothing they wore, every detail proclaimed the prisonhouse of the spirit in which they now found themselves confined. Their movements as they stoked a black iron stove to keep warm were accompanied by the remorseless sound of wind. Keeping up appearances – once their sole concern – no longer mattered at all. The fans had literally been laid aside, and now they looked directly into one another's faces – not in a spirit of new understanding, however, but with abject disillusionment. The harsh and chaotic reality of the world around them seemed for the first time to impinge upon their closed universe. Anne (Marie Richardson), Renée's deceitful younger sister and de Sade's sometime lover, cynically exchanges the uncertainties of the Revolution for the decadence of a new life in Venice. For Renée herself, meanwhile, there is no escape from her anguished realization that her loyalty and her efforts to free de Sade have been a meaningless waste of a lifetime – for he alone is free and the regime of evil and cruelty he represents holds her and all humanity in bondage ("the world we now live in is a creation of the Marquis de Sade").

The repulsive "reality" of Alphonse, the Marquis – now a destitute, toothless, obscenely fat old man whom his wife refuses admittance at the end – was juxtaposed by Bergman with a startlingly surreal image that crystallized the doubleness of Mishima's conception of his subject. During her explosive final monologue, Renée appeared (rather like the young witch who is burned alive in *The Seventh Seal*) as if crucified in a blaze of searing white light as she conjured forth her tormented vision of Alphonse as a gleaming crusader of evil loosed upon the world, riding in splendor toward Heaven through the blood of suffering mankind. "And at that moment, the heavens open and a flood tide of light streams through – a beautiful light that strikes all beholders blind. And Alphonse is perhaps the real essence of that light."[13]

The paradox of evil in God's creation – the possibility that a virulent and contagious malice infects human nature – has been, as we know, a thematic concern to which Bergman has returned constantly, both on the screen and in the theater. In his *Madame de Sade*, implications of this theme were explored with all the poetic indirection and suggestiveness of a Bergman film. In his operatic adaptation of *The Bacchae* in 1991, on the other hand, this concern with the irrationality and cruelty of mankind exploded into direct and violent expression, not least in his conception of the threatening figure of an androgynous Dionysus, sung by a woman (Sylvia Lindenstrand) in black biker's jacket and boots. The savage dissonances and colliding contradictions at work in this "orgy of flesh and blood" (as one reviewer called the Euripidean experiment) were, however, already a dominant characteristic of the two much more crucial Shakespearean productions directed by Bergman during the 1980s.

Particularly in his radically antitraditionalist *Hamlet*, first staged in 1986 and subsequently seen on tour by audiences from Moscow to Tokyo, explicit evil and corruption so dominated Hamlet's universe that any attempt to "set it right" was bound to seem a futile and even absurd undertaking. In the scene of Polonius' murder, this antiheroic Hamlet (played by Peter Stormare) even paused to scrawl the word "blood" in red chalk on the black background – a significant act that called attention both to the violence and moral anarchy of the world around him and also to his own corruption at its hands. In its deliberate anachronisms, its jangling clash of styles, and its open defiance of the play's traditions, this rendering of *Hamlet* became a commentary on the Hamlet "myth" itself, akin in this respect both to Bergman's quotation of the myth of Dionysus and to his earlier deconstruction of the Don Juan myth, as seen in his darkly textured 1983 revival of Molière's comedy.

A comparable sense of moral breakup and collapse had also dominated Bergman's production of *King Lear*, staged at Dramaten in 1984 while he was still based in Germany. At the beginning of the play, which he described as "a panorama of our human existence," the director introduced a prologue of wild folk dancing, acrobatics, and other noisy horseplay, overseen by a silent, ominous wall of towering, black-clad

"I am the King himself": Lear (Jarl Kulle) is mocked by the onlookers in the Dramaten production of *King Lear*, 1984. The blinded Gloucester (Per Myrberg) is seen with the disguised Edgar (Mathias Henrikson) at the right of the picture.

warriors. Thus established, the presence of this menacing society grew steadily stronger as the play progressed. Such crucial moments as Lear's humiliation at the hands of Regan and Goneril ("You think I'll weep: No, I'll not weep"), the blinding of Gloucester, and the entrance of mad Lear crowned with wild flowers ("I am the King himself") were watched by groups of snickering, sneering, or mocking onlookers. At the end, after Lear's corpse had been borne out with due ceremony, the waiting crowd again surged forward and, as a vicious sword fight broke out over Lear's crown, the stage world itself came crashing down in ruins around them. Summarized in this final chaotic image was a chilling perception of the decay and fall of our own world.

The collapse of order and the triumph of the forces of anarchy and violence were even more graphically represented in *Hamlet*, however, which began to the ironic accompaniment of *The Merry Widow* but ended in a roar of rock music and blazing machineguns as Fortinbras and his modern-day storm troopers came ("so jump upon this bloody question") crashing through the rear wall to carry on the casual slaughter. Leaving "no room for catharsis," this production's pessimistic conclusion seemed "in principle the same as that reached in *King Lear* – the aggressiveness will never find an end."[14] Horatio's recital of "carnal, bloody, and unnatural acts" found no hearers, as he was summarily dragged outside to be shot. Then, as the bodies of Gertrude and Claudius were roughly dumped into Ophelia's grave, the corpse of Hamlet was placed on a high stage, beneath an inferno of glaring lights, to be photographed and videotaped for posterity. Located in this harsh metatheatrical context, Hamlet's fall thus became, in the words of one commentator, "a death without hope, without consolation, without any mitigating circumstances – a crucifixion devoid of belief and without any resurrection."[15]

This dark vision of the play found its direct emotional expression in the production concept itself – a concept sharply at odds with the basically representational Shakespearean style of Bergman's early years. In *Laterna Magica* he describes his new approach with characteristic precision: "empty stage, possibly two chairs, but not necessarily. Stationary lights, no colored filters, no special atmospherics. A circle, five meters in [diameter], welded into the floor close to the audience. Here

the action takes place."[16] The circular acting area created by
Bergman at the very front of the stage, just touching the curtain
line, was in turn contained within a greater circle, about 48 feet
(14.75 meters) in diameter, which circumscribed virtually the
whole of the main stage at Dramaten. This empty, completely
flexible space, defined by a gray and black cyclorama, was
divided up like some giant cheese wheel into 136 individually
lighted areas.[17] On some occasions, this non-referential black
landscape was splashed with violent movement and color; at
other times, one heard only voices or saw only faces in the
dark. Light alone was used to carve out and connect the figures
and figure compositions in this dense human tapestry. "What
unites them is the scenic space and especially the lighting, this
steady, dream-play light that comes from high above them and
seems pulverized into floating particles of luminous dust by
the time it reaches the bottom of the coal-black shaft," wrote
Leif Zern in *Expressen* (December 21, 1986). "Down below, in a
world without mercy, the human beings crawl about like
animals to reach the light . . ." The setting was thus not a
specific place but an image, an exteriorization of mood and
feeling.

The outright rejection of periodicity in Bergman's *Hamlet*
represented a departure from the stylized suggestions of
historical period incorporated into *King Lear* and his two
earlier productions of *Twelfth Night* in the 1970s. In his *King
Lear*, the crown and the rolled map of Lear's partitioned
kingdom that were left on the forestage throughout the entire
performance were signifiers of a broader referential framework
(history, myth) that did not exist in *Hamlet*. In the latter
production, Bergman sought to bring the inner rhythms and
hidden tensions of the drama closer to the audience by
refusing to allow the spectator to become lost in the details of
an outer reality. From the very outset, this performance called
attention to itself as a performance. At first, waltz music from
The Merry Widow was played on an old piano. Following a
silence, three separate curtains went up in succession – first
Dramaten's ornate, tasseled front curtain, then a painted
replica of this, and finally a simple black screen – as a further
reminder to the audience that it was indeed an audience in a
theater.

Rejected as well, however, was the adoption of any one,

consistent "alternative" style (a "Victorian" *Hamlet*, an "electronic" *Hamlet*, or whatever). Instead, a disharmonious mixture of clashing visual styles bespoke the spiritual and moral disjuncture that the protagonist saw everywhere around him. The shifting, inherently illogical nature of Hamlet's universe stood exposed in the collage of continually shifting, changing costumes, in which the dominant color scheme – black and red – seemed the only constant. Claudius and Gertrude presided over a surrealistic court attired in full wigs and rich scarlet robes that might suggest the Renaissance or perhaps a high court tribunal, while Polonius wore an Edwardian morning-coat and carried a briefcase. Then again, Rosencrantz and Guildenstern were rose-colored operetta dandies with jaunty caps and canes, whereas Horatio was dressed in a subdued gray suit and trustworthy *pince-nez*. The Players were endearing reminders of a bygone age of actors in motley vests and frock-coats. The Gravedigger, sporting a red clown's nose and a black bowler hat, popped up from Ophelia's grave in the company of a pair of masked pierrots armed with trombone and sax. The army of Fortinbras, when first seen, was equipped in World War I gear, only to reappear at the end as hulking, black-clad harbingers of some future Armageddon. Ophelia, set distinctly apart from the forces of violence and bloodshed, was a figure of infinite vulnerability in her simple, light-blue shift.

In his black turtleneck jumper and gray trousers, Peter Stormare's unprincely Prince of Denmark was a manifestly modern man in a bewilderingly anachronistic world. Like many others before them (including Gordon Craig), Bergman and Stormare found a crucial key to the play and the character in Act I, Scene 2. Here, "the trappings and the suits of woe" adopted by Hamlet included, in this instance, a black raincoat and dark glasses ("I am too much in the sun"). As he sat, limp and inert, at the edge of the stage facing the audience, this figure's isolation stood out against the red background of the corrupt court, where sexual and social decay prevailed and Gertrude and Claudius could be seen copulating openly, screaming with laughter to the rhythmic clapping of the watching courtiers. "Bergman's point," noted an English critic when the production visited the National Theatre, "would seem to be that this is a court where everyone is everywhere all

Three faces of Peter Stormare's Hamlet: with Claudius (Börje Ahlstedt) and Gertrude (Gunnel Lindblom) in I.2; with the Players (Per Myrberg and, background, Oscar Ljung) for "To be, or not to be"; with the Gravedigger (Ulf Johanson). Dramaten, 1986.

the time, and where the disaffected, disenfranchised, disengaged central figure can see nothing but unnatural sexuality and corruption of all available flesh."[18] Abruptly, the anger and despair that paralyzed Stormare's Hamlet exploded during his first soliloquy into violent cries of pain and rage ("O that this too too solid flesh would melt") and actual physical convulsions ("Frailty, they name is woman"). The moment manifested not eloquent poetic melancholy but a deep-seated, barely articulate violence and fury to which Hamlet's meeting with the Ghost would soon give welcome purpose and direction.

The remarkable decision to cast the same actor (Per Myrberg) as the Ghost of Hamlet's father and the First Player (renamed the Theater King) and to bring him back, as the Ghost, to witness his son's duel with Laertes was a typical Bergman "suggestion," intended (like the twinning of the Young Lady and the Mummy in *The Ghost Sonata*) to enrich the play's emotional relationships rather than to impose abstract symbolic "meaning" on it.[19]

In the opening scene, played in the dark to the sound of wind, no Ghost appeared; only the words and the spotlighted faces of Horatio, Bernardo, and Marcellus told of his nearness. When Hamlet encountered him, however, he appeared as a strangely real unreality – an ethereal presence in a flowing white robe, humanly and poignantly eager to plead his case. His arms extended toward his son in an almost Christ-like gesture of embrace, this figure struck critics as "a great paradox": "a personification both of a merciless cycle of guilt and revenge, and also of Christian mercy."[20] Finally, as the fading glow-worm warned the Ghost to take his leave, he stumbled and held out his hand for support. As Hamlet clasped his father's hand and crawled forward on the ground to embrace him, a warm image of filial affection was superimposed upon a much colder and darker underlying one – the image of Dom Juan, in almost exactly the same pose, as he grasped the hand of the stone statue in Bergman's final production of Molière in 1983. A pact had been sealed with this ambiguous force, whose shadow stretched the length of the play to the moment when he reappeared at the end as a silent witness to the final devastation, watching impassively as Hamlet perished in the floodtide of violence their pact had unleashed.

Given the significance of Myrberg's double role (triple, if we count Gonzago), the scenes with the Players acquired an importance rarely equalled in other performances of this play (where, more often than not, these scenes are either treated as parody or else trimmed to bare bones). Needless to say, however, the association between the Ghost and the Theater King was purely intuitive and never explicit or forced. The strolling players came, exactly as William Hazlitt once described the coming of English strollers long ago, "like meally-coated butterflies" spreading a welcome before them and shedding "a light upon the day, that does not very soon pass off."[21] Sweeping down the full width of the stage to the music of a fife and drum, their gallant battalion established a breathing space in the oppressive atmosphere. What they had to say bore no trace of bombast or courtly subterfuge. Even the Player's monologue on "the mobled queen," watched intently by Hamlet and acted on the trestle stage they had brought with them, was taken with unaffected seriousness. In general, as one critic observed, the actors seemed to epitomize the sense that "the theater always creates its own reality" – a second reality, as it were, in which Hamlet could breathe and could also make himself understood. In this light, Bergman's much disputed decision to transpose the play's most familiar soliloquy, "To be, or not to be," to Hamlet's second meeting with the Players (III.2) made perfect emotional sense (despite the uproar literary purists might make!). With a blunt dagger in one hand and his other arm around the Theater King's shoulders, this hollow-eyed Hamlet spoke quietly of his heartache and his dread, as the other actors listened attentively. His so-called advice to them about histrionic decorum – a strange anomaly in a world where the mirror of Nature has been shattered and only its splinters remain – was suffused with the bitterest sarcasm. Presented as a direct counterpoint to this set speech, Hamlet's reconstituted soliloquy was a simple, utterly unpoetic appeal for understanding and compassion, directed to the only people capable of comprehending his pain – the people of the theater, the "little world" which, as Oscar Ekdahl reminds us in *Fanny and Alexander*, somtimes "succeeds for a moment in reflecting the big world, so that we understand it better."

The enactment of *The Murder of Gonzago*, the practical test to which the revelatory power of mimesis is put by Hamlet (and his father), opened the second half of Bergman's production. Now wearing a student blazer with a Wittenberg crest (a sure sign that he "means mischief"), Hamlet sat with Ophelia on the forestage as a wild torch dance (rather than the dumb-show) introduced the play-within-the-play. In his little scene, Gonzago (the Ghost impersonating the Player impersonating a theatrical proxy of himself) somehow managed to transform his unpromising role into a profoundly moving and affection-ate parting with his faithless wife. In a state of high excite-ment, Hamlet himself even became an actor, joining the players on their trestle stage as he explicated the design of "The Mousetrap." And when the trap sprang and general confusion erupted ("Lights, lights, lights!"), Hamlet sang his song ("Why, let the strooken deer go weep") in a kind of jubilant frenzy and danced a wild war-dance of his own.

At that moment, Zern observed in *Expressen*, one suddenly noticed Ophelia, sitting at the very front of the stage wrapped in a shawl, "a forsaken, huddled figure with no contact with what is going on around her, a completely still point in the tempest that has passed, like a devastation, over the young girls' body and soul." From that point on, this critic argued, Bergman's *Hamlet* became "primarily the tragedy of Ophelia. Pernilla Östergren is present on stage almost all the time, an Agnes making her final pilgrimage on earth . . . She sees all – and becomes, in the process, everything she sees." Östergren's widely admired performance transformed Ophelia into a dreamlike presence who was, at one and the same time, the suffering victim and the perpetual observer of life's cruelty. Zern's allusion to Agnes, the Daughter of Indra in *A Dream Play*, would come readily to mind, especially as Bergman had revived Strindberg's play only eight months before. An even more direct link exists, however, between the conception of Ophelia as a watching character and the manner in which Cordelia was presented (by Lena Olin) in Bergman's *King Lear*.

Never for a moment in either of these Shakespeare produc-tions was the audience permitted to relinquish its role as an active and aware witness to a tragic action in which the metaphor of theater is recurrent and inescapable. Metatheatri-cal strategies to control and adjust the intensity of the commu-nicative bond between spectator and actor are, as we have by now come to recognize, common to virtually all of Bergman's stage productions. One such strategy is the device of what might be called the "watching" character – a silent specator–actor whose presence is, in itself, an objective critical comment on the action. In *King Lear*, Cordelia was such a figure. Her testing and banishment by her father (Jarl Kulle), played out on a huge map in a circle of light carved out of the darkness of a closed red void, rendered her a prisoner of the play, so to speak, rather than an offstage source of plot development. She, along with most of the other characters, was kept on stage throughout the action, thereby establishing a multiplicity of perspective that reinforced the sense of dramatic irony – the calculated discrepancy between what a character may realize and what the audience realizes – so crucial to this play. Thus, Cordelia could be seen watching impassively as the Fool's wise fooling goaded Lear to his first significant moment of insight: "I did her wrong." She witnessed Kent (Börje Ahl-stedt) placed in the "stocks" (two actors pinning his legs) and waited – as did the audience – for her father's hysterical seizure upon catching sight of this breach of his authority. Then again, in the cold night of fools and madmen, as Lear sat on the bare floor of the "hovel" – the empty stage – conducting his frantic autopsy of her cruel sister, Regan ("Is there any cause in nature that makes these hard hearts?"), Cordelia's presence eloquently counterpointed the disguised Edgar's efforts to comfort the stricken old man. And, even after she had reentered the play in the brief scene with the Physician, she still stood outside it to witness the blinded Gloucester (Per Myrberg) being led to the brink of an imaginary cliff by a counterfeit madman, his own son.

Ophelia's presence in *Hamlet* represented a related but even more complex metatheatrical strategy, designed both to direct and control the audience's perception of the events taking place and also to render transparent, in an intensely palpable manner, the underlying spirit of bleak irony and dis-illusionment that shaped Bergman's interpretation of this play. The embodiment of innocence, Ophelia was gradually deformed and destroyed by the evil and corruption she met all around her as she traversed the landscape of the drama, always watching. "In her face," wrote one reviewer, "the play's movement toward disintegration is seen reflected, as she is transformed from a young girl in love to a bewildered and dispossessed woman." [22] In this performance, Hamlet's sarcastic sexual innuendoes ("Get thee to a nunn'ry") were transmuted into a violent physical assault, a brutal mock rape in which he destroyed Ophelia – who now wore the incongruous red shoes and heavy lipstick of the whore he saw in her and in his (red-wigged) mother. Following their encounter, Hamlet had the Players and Horatio to turn to, while Ophelia – who watched the two friends affectionately conspiring – had no one.

In the subsequent closet scene, played on a blood-red rug, Ophelia also watched as the forces of blind destructiveness that threatened to overwhelm Hamlet were turned against the "wretched, rash, intruding fool," Polonius (Ulf Johanson). His killing was a cruel and quite deliberate act: at first only stabbed in the eye by Hamlet, Polonius emerged from behind the arras and staggered the full width of the stage in mortal agony before his assailant finished him off with his pocket-knife. The violence of this deed, the reappearance of the Ghost, and the furiously emotional recriminations exchanged between mother and son were all thrust into an ironic double perspective by the presence of Ophelia, who circled the action wrapped tightly in her shawl as if to ward off a chill wind. At the end of the scene, after Hamlet had calmly wiped his knife and pocketed it, he dragged the body of Polonius away, taking no notice of the nearby figure of his victim's daughter.

Ophelia's madness was not poetic distraction but a wild, desperate expression of grief and loss. Wearing Hamlet's boots and covered in her shawl, she literally drove the King and Queen around the stage with the scourge of her song of death and sorrow. Small wonder, one might say, that the rosemary for remembrance, the violets for thoughts, and the other flowers and herbs of grace that she distributes to her brother and the court were nothing more than rusty nails. Even after her funeral – simply a small cluster of black umbrellas and a single bouquet of long red roses – she still stood there unnoticed, watching as the Gravedigger closed the stage trap that was her grave. As Hamlet and Horatio rushed forward, they passed by her without a glance.

Ophelia's "ghost" was only one of the many ominous death images that overshadowed Hamlet's return in the somber final

The duel with Laertes, watched by masked courtiers in scarlet robes.

movement of Bergman's production. Here, moreover, the feeling of deep personal identification on the director's part became unmistakable; as Stormare's Hamlet sat joking with Death, in the guise of the clownish Gravedigger, he wore a costume that made clear reference to the Bergman persona: watchcap, seaman's jacket, corduroy trousers, rubber boots. As yet another of the "ghosts," Ulf Johanson brought to the Gravedigger's jocular parables of human mortality a hint of the same chopped logic he had expounded in the role of Polonius. The second station on Hamlet's dark journey was the funeral of Ophelia. At the third and final crossroads, as he listened with impatience to Osric's unctuous delivery of the King's proposal for a fencing match with Laertes, masked courtiers in their scarlet robes and judicial-looking wigs gathered in threatening formation. The moment Hamlet brushed aside Horatio's hesitancy ("the readiness is all"), these masked red figures closed in on them, the Players' trestle stage quickly became the killing ground in the duel, and the chaos and bloodshed erupted that were the foregone conclusion of this black *Hamlet* from the beginning.

"For an idea to stick, it is not enough to state it: it must be burnt into our memories," Peter Brook once observed. "*Hamlet* is such an idea."[23] The Bergman performance of this play was just such an experience, etched into the sensibility and memory of the spectator by allusive, strongly sensual theatrical images and suggestions that sought and found their completion in the activated emotional response of the audience. (For, as Brook also says, "if a play does not make us lose our balance, the evening is unbalanced.") Although no more radical in approach than the Shakespearean experiments of such contemporary directors as Brook or Giorgio Strehler or Peter Stein, however, this "postmodernist" *Hamlet* evidently took some of Bergman's newly readopted Swedish public by surprise. Disapproval of its textual "infidelities" was voiced (the cutting of Reynaldo, Voltemand, and Cornelius was especially noted). Its neglect of proper poetic "diction" was solemnly deplored. Its stubborn refusal to supply a fixed "meaning" or resolve the sense of disjuncture it created was a source of bewildered irritation. And the general unwelcomeness of its deeply pessimistic vision in "our" enlightened social democracy was strongly hinted at.[24] A full-fledged "*Hamlet* war" of divergent opinions broke out in the normally staid Swedish press. In its aftermath, Bergman suffered a nervous collapse and was obliged to cancel a scheduled production of Euripides' *The Bacchae*. Almost a year and a half elapsed before a new production of his was ready for the stage.

In 1988, as part of the centennial celebration of Eugene O'Neill's birth, Bergman returned to Dramaten with *Long Day's Journey into Night* – a rather unexpected choice, given earlier statements by him that this is a play for which no director seems necessary. The basis for his renewed interest was clearly the exceptional strength of the acting ensemble he was able to bring together for this perfectly balanced quartet of family sorrow. Jarl Kulle, who had played Edmund in the world premiere of O'Neill's play at Dramaten thirty-two years previously, was a self-ironic and sympathetic James Tyrone, every inch an actor. Bibi Andersson's portrayal of Mary Tyrone made her the centripetal emotional force in the drama. As Edmund, the younger son and the playwright's alter ego, Peter Stormare depicted a deathly pale spiritual sufferer with burning eyes, a figure whose alienation bore an entirely different cast than that of his fiercely rebellious Hamlet. As the fourth member of the quartet, Thommy Berggren's portrait of the disillusioned elder son Jamie was regarded by some critics as the strongest performance of all, "a grinning but all too clear-sighted boozer on the brink of despair."[25] Eschewing coercion and leaving much to the individual instruments of the actors, Bergman gathered these four distinctive voices and cadences together in a coherently orchestrated chamber symphony of moods, contrasting tones, arias, and silences. Reading the play almost as a conductor reads a musical score, he sought and gained access to the inner Strindbergian landscape that underlies its apparently well-ordered Ibsenian surface. "He really does read a text in a way that's very rare – there is no parallel," Andersson remarked at the time. "And once you agree that his reading corresponds to what you want to do and can do – then he just opens up boxes."[26]

Bergman's tightly focused version of *Long Day's Journey*, which trimmed more than an hour from the play's gruelling running time of four and a half hours, was a distillation calculated to stress what Andersson calls "the electric moments of life that come not when we're talking but in the moments of indirection and in the silences between us."[27] The veritable museum of realistic details that fill up the Tyrone (read: O'Neill) summer house at 325 Pequot Avenue in the stage directions was methodically dismantled, as part of Bergman's total rejection of the conventions of psychological naturalism with which this play is almost invariably associated in performance. This radical dematerialization of the physical setting, accompanied by his familiar emphasis on facial and choreographic expressiveness, served to thrust the action forward, thereby engaging the spectator's active emotional engagement in it in an almost sensual fashion. "The unique occurs, and reality – the very theatrical experience itself – is transcended," wrote *Svenska Dagbladet* (April 17, 1988). "What is projected from the stage touches a rarely activated point of awareness in the audience, which finds itself face to face with the action. This fusion brings about that instantaneous understanding which characterizes all true art, regardless of its complexities."

The naked, unadorned setting (designed by Gunilla Palmstierna-Weiss) was a limbo cut off from the world of familiar reality. On a small, lighted platform furnished with a scattering of significant objects and hemmed in by the encroaching darkness that surrounded it on all sides, the interlocked spiritual and psychological histories of the four Tyrones were enacted – or, perhaps, reenacted, if we see the play as the poet's dream (the facing of his "dead," as the dramatist put it in his dedication to his wife, Carlotta). The furnishings of O'Neill's realistically observed living room were reduced to a dirty brown armchair, a round, covered table surrounded by four mismatched wooden chairs, an incongruous Greek column in one corner that turned out to conceal the obligatory liquor cabinet, and a similar but smaller pedestal in the opposite corner that accommodated both a Madonna with red votive light and the family telephone. In the climactic night scene of shattering confrontations, the perspective was flipped to create a different, emptier space beyond the living room, in which the columns were seen from the rear, the round table of family unity was now absent, and only three widely separated chairs and a small veranda table remained. At this juncture, wrote Sverker Andréason in *Göteborgs–Posten* (April 17), the platform seemed "a raft in a nightmare in which the four main characters try desperately to save themselves from drowning."

Nothing, in other words, was "true to life" here except the inner truth and torment of the human beings themselves. Following the practice adopted for *King Lear*, Bergman and his designer again shrouded the theatre's ornately gilded stucco proscenium in black in order to maintain an unbroken sense of non-referential space, unrelated to place or the passage of time. Projected, obliquely angled images (a house facade, a window, a door, clouds, and, at last, a bare tree of silent promise) appeared and imperceptibly disappeared in the background like fleetingly glimpsed bits of a fugitive reality. (Andréason called these bleached images "a dreamlike accompaniment to the action that seems to say: what is taking place here is an exorcism of demons.") Even the "fog horn" and the "bell" in the harbor were, in fact, dirge-like snatches of atonal music – to which Kulle at one point defiantly hummed La Paloma!

What the audience saw, then, was a performance space for visions, dreams, and memories – above all, the memories of the poet Edmund with his black book, at once the captive and the observer of his life's bitter experiences. In a highly stylized mise-en-scène that revealed and commented on the concurrency of past and present (the essence of Mary's key realization that "the past is the present" and "the future, too"), both Edmund and the others often only turned away from someone else's scene, rather than leaving the stage. The strongest link between the stage world of an enacted past and the real world of the audience was, however, Edmund himself, the playwright's watchful and observant double. From the black notebook which he carried, he *read* his poetic shipboard reminiscences to his father – in a performance from which all other literary recitations from Dowson, Baudelaire, Swinburne, Wilde, and the rest were cut out. At the end of the play, after the others had left the platform and had disappeared slowly into the wings, Edmund remained behind, picked up his notebook thoughtfully, and walked away. As he turned for a last look at the empty stage of his memories, the projection of the spreading, leafless tree, with its suggestion of renewed life, filled the background.

This final visual effect stood in provocative juxtaposition to the equally emphatic tableau with which the performance began. To the menacing accompaniment of the fog-horn music, the four Tyrones emerged from the darkness, grasping one another's hands and putting arms around one another's shoulders. The sons came from one side and the parents from the other, but they quickly joined to form a close-knit unit and paused for a long moment to pose for a family picture of tenderness, togetherness, and good intentions. The tableau soon dissolved, as Jamie and Edmund turned away and the opening dialogue between Mary and James began. Yet this powerful visual image bespoke, more eloquently than any words, the love that binds the stricken family together in this play – written, as O'Neill himself says, "with deep pity and understanding and forgiveness for *all* the four haunted Tyrones." Once established, this strong sense of love remained a ruling force in the production. Throughout it, the family members tried desperately to avoid facing what they clearly knew to be inevitable, clutching like drowning people to each other, embracing and kneeling to one another, stroking each other's hair, hands, and face, or sitting together on the floor (as Edmund and Mary do at one point) like small children. This

Bibi Andersson as Mary Tyrone, with Jamie (Thommy Berggren), in the 1988 production of *Long Day's Journey into Night*.

rhythmic choreographic pattern of groupings and proxemic relationships transcended language in its direct expression of a sense of human understanding and compassion inherent in O'Neill's dramatic memoir.

The visual eloquence of this mise-en-scène reached perhaps its fullest measure of effect in Bibi Andersson's delineation of Mary's hopeless struggle against "the things life has done to us we cannot excuse or explain." At times silently pacing the edge of the platform while the men discussed her or lying prostrate on the floor in an expression of helpless loneliness, her emphatic, stylized actions and pantomime displaced the fili-gree of microrealistic behavior woven into the stage directions. Her long final "leavetaking" at the end of the play was virtually an unbroken monologue-aria in Bergman's version, uninter-rupted by either the poetry recitations or the drinking described in the text. The wedding gown she carried was suddenly dropped absentmindedly ("I'm always dreaming and forgetting"), rather than being taken from her by Tyrone. Her sons, with no words left and Swinburne's borrowed eloquence gone, could only reach out to their mother in mute supplication and grief as she passed. Then, as the men listened in shocked silence to her story of her talk with Mother Elizabeth, she abruptly fell to the floor like a doll (at the moment when she "tosses her head – indignantly" in the text!). At once she was helped into a chair by Edmund – who was now clearly the anguished observer and notetaker of the scene. The poignant closing line of Mary's speech – "I fell in love with James Tyrone and was so happy for a time" – was spoken with the sum total of her life's bitter sorrow invested in that one final phrase: "for a time."

The pantomimic dissolution of the scene (which, of course, does not dissolve in O'Neill's text) was an ironic shattering of the optimistic family tableau that had begun the performance. Lost in her own thoughts and narcotized by the morphine, Mary walked quietly past Tyrone, who stood holding the bridal gown helplessly in his arms. At that critical moment, one reviewer observed, "their silence [made] the sense of hopelessness seem infinite."[28] When Jamie and his father had followed Mary into the darkness, the forgotten wedding dress was left prominently draped over a chair, as a reminder of the inescapable, irrevocable past. Then, as Edmund turned to look

The final tableau in *Long Day's Journey*, with Peter Stormare as Edmund.

back and remember, this potent visual image of a past filled with loss and grief was countered by a contrasting and competing image – the radiant vision of the poet's tree of promise.

PEER'S JOURNEY

"O, endless night, when will you vanish? When will the light reach my eyes?" cries Tamino in profound despondency, as he stands in the dark courtyard of the Temple of Wisdom in *The Magic Flute*. "Soon, youth, soon, or never," answers the shadowy chorus of priests. Encountering this moment of deep despair in Mozart's opera, Bergman has said that he found himself closer at that instant to "the deepest secret of spiritual intuition" than ever before: "He asks his question in darkness and from the darkness he answers himself – or does he get an answer?"[29] Bergman's own question touches the innermost core of his art. In such recent stage works of his as *Dom Juan*, *Hamlet*, *Madame de Sade*, and *Long Day's Journey*, where despair seemed very near and the darkness of eternal night was all around us, the answer the artist seemed to hear was "never." In his luminous film of *The Magic Flute* itself, of course, the darkness is at last dispelled; the images of evil and despair change shape or vanish like dreams; and the finale is an extraordinary theatrical celebration of reconciliation and fruitfulness. Although hardly as unambiguously harmonious and shadowless as that, Bergman's reinterpreted *Peer Gynt* was a buoyant and charmed fairy tale of life fully comparable to his *Magic Flute* and, in particular, to his magnificent farewell gesture as a film maker, *Fanny and Alexander*. Both these films are "theater films," imbued with an essentially Strindbergian perception of a reality that is "more than reality – not dreams, but waking dreams." Precisely this same sense of a sliding, elusive borderline between dream and reality was the ruling characteristic of his new *Peer Gynt* – a play in which, as he said, "we are made to experience the strange reality of the dream and the fairy tale in Ibsen's poetry."[30]

"A poem about life, grand and imposing," is how Lars Ring described this highly acclaimed production in *Svenska Dagbladet* (April 28, 1991): "Bergman has transformed *Peer Gynt* into a dream play about poetry and dreams which – like *A Dream Play* itself – deals with time and death, as a grandfather clock ticks away the days and years . . ." As far from Peter Stein's famous critical quotation of this work as it was from Bergman's earlier, sterner rendering of it in Malmö in 1957, this rich, flamboyant theatrical tapestry of moods and images simply swept aside the shopworn debate between traditionalism and innovation in Ibsen performance. In this grave and somber *Peer Gynt*, humor and even farce were never absent for long; poetry was spoken without affection, irony stressed without the slightest bitterness, deep emotional feeling expressed without a trace of sentimentality or mawkishness. Seated, as it were, within the unchanging confines of Mother Aase's modest cottage, the audience shared and conspired with Peer in a dream of life and passing time and death that seemed to spring from the fecund poetic imagination of this new Everyman ("the artist who at the same time creates poetry and fictionalizes his life," as Ring put it). Yet, when asked about the source of inspiration for this so abundantly original new approach to the play, Bergman replies simply: "It's all right there – all there in the words. It's only a matter of reading Ibsen's words attentively."

Created specifically for Dramaten's intimate 160-seat studio theater, Målarsalen (The Paint Shop), this production utilized a spatial concept and setting (designed by Lennart Mörk) that directly expressed Bergman's interpretation of the play as an inner journey through "a world of Peer's imagination that we see created before us." In essence, neither Peer not the audience ever left the rough wooden cottage that extended well into the auditorium in this little theater. Although its colored windows stuffed with rags and its slightly skewed walls with their faded flowered wallpaper suggested a modest existence, mementos of "the good times" associated with Jon Gynt were still on display in the hut: the spendthrift's crest hanging over the lintel, his faded picture above the narrow bed in the corner, and – most appropriate of all – a smashed pier-glass with a bottle still lodged in it all bespoke the boozer's past glory. Apart from the bed, a dilapidated table and chairs and a ticking clock were the only worldly possessions to be seen in the Gynt homestead. Within the fixed topography of this unchanging setting, however, change took place with the swiftness of a dreamer's thought. A simple, totally flexible rectangular platform capable of being raised or lowered or tilted on edge became, at will, a precipitous cliff or a banquet table, the forbidding wall of a madhouse or the pitching and rolling deck of a ship in a storm. Time and space did not exist as absolutes; anything was possible and likely in the eager, irrepressible, childlike imagination of the Peer Gynt created by the miraculous performance of Börje Ahlstedt. The reality of his long journey – to Haegstad, to the Ronde, to Morocco, to Cairo, and back – was a purely theatrical reality, enacted on the small stage-upon-the-stage that thus became the arena for his monodrama.

Using a superbly coordinated ensemble of thirty-five actors and extras, almost all of whom played at least two and usually three or more roles. Bergman distilled Ibsen's sprawling dramatic poem into three tightly organized movements, with a total running time of just under four hours. Each movement was a miniature play of its own, with a title and a cast of characters; and for each new movement, the flexible platform at the center of the stage changed color, from red to white to somber black. The result was a drama of analogous situations, a system of mirrors that reflected each experience or encounter in continually changing and distorted guises. The configura-

"Out there, under the shining vault of heaven": Johan Rabaeus as
the Troll King, describing the trollish way of life to Peer (Börje
Ahlstedt) in *Peer Gynt*. Dramaten, 1991.

tions of characters met by Peer on his way – the madly stamping red dancers at Haegstad, the livid green trolls in the Ronde, the white-clad madmen in the Cairo asylum, and the dark, androgynous figures who awaited his homecoming – were always drastically different in appearance and yet somehow always the same. In this production, the act of repetition became, as Lisbeth Larsson observed in *Expressen* (April 28), "the very core of Peer Gynt's life. He flees from one fairy tale to the next, but the outcome is always the same . . . Over and over again he is compelled to endure his defeat and to deceive himself."

The first movement, Fairy Tales and Dreams, began with a totally unexpected scene that laid the foundation for all that followed. As the lights came up on the bare cottage interior, an ageless, quick-witted Mother Aase (played by Bibi Andersson) crawled out of bed to begin the day, followed by a middle-aged Peer. It was instantly clear that the point here was not incest, however, but the warmth and companionship that these two inveterate dreamers shared. As she fixed breakfast, he went on with his well-worn, oft-told tale of riding the buck over the Gjendin Edge – related not as an impulsive poetic flight of fancy but as part of an old and cherished game they had long played together to keep the real world of the wind and the rain at bay. In some respects virtually his alter ego, Aase had not only taught Peer the fabulist's *métier* but, as she puffed a morning cigar and ruminated over good and bad times in the bygone days of Jon and Rasmus Gynt, she was also shown to be a willing storyteller herself. Seen in this light, a direct and poignant link was established between the opening episode and Peer's attempt to comfort his dying mother in the scene with which the first movement concluded. Here, as the clock ticked on and Aase lay dying in the same narrow bed, Peer's conjuring up of the sleigh ride to Soria Moria Castle was neither an effort to deceive himself nor (as it so often is) a poetic attempt to distract his mother's attention. Rather, they both sought to push back the horror of death by collaborating on one last fantasy, he by pretending to tell the old bedtime story he had learned from her, she by pretending to listen to it. Wrapped in a red coverlet of sorrows, Ahlstedt sat at the foot of the bed facing the audience, and in the intense close-up of his face all the pain of Peer's anguished awareness and the full depth of his despair were revealed.

"Now our ride is done": Börje Ahlstedt as Peer Gynt, after the death of Aase (Bibi Andersson, background).

The Peer who set out for the wedding at Haegstad (after locking Aase securely in the closet) was a more cheerful, carefree figure, a curious mixture of a wide-eyed child and a randy Silenus in a tattered black coat, baggy trousers, and a bowler hat. As the magic platform carried him on his journey, humiliation and defeat awaited him at every stop as the poetry of his aspirations turned to dust. His cloudy imperial vision of himself riding through the sky at the head of an army was ingloriously terminated by the arrival of Aslak the smith and a rude companion who pulled Peer's pants down around his ankles. As a circle of the riotous wedding guests at Haegstad listened to his tale of the Devil he imprisoned in a worm-eaten nut, he suddenly discovered that his audience had tied a tail of rope to him – an omen of worse ignominies to come in the palace of the Troll King. And as he clung to the precariously tilted platform after a night spent in the mountains with the three risibly vulgar Saeter girls, even the most rapturous of his poetic flights ("Castle rises on castle,/See, what a shining gate") was reduced to the level of a drunken barroom recitation, delivered between slurps from a bottle.

Peer's incorrigible lechery, which stood in such seriocomic contrast to his idealization of Solveig, was the immediate source of his downfall. His farcical, coarsely explicit seduction of the Greenclad One (Gerthi Kulle), the Troll King's lascivious, tail-twitching daughter, brought him (after a short ride with her astride a wild boar with flashing red eyes) face to face with her enraged father and his court of thugs. Though their faces were green and they now had three eyes, these vicious trolls in their little tin helmets were plainly reincarnations of the rabble at the Haegstad wedding. In this scene as elsewhere in the production, comedic absurdity was freely mixed with the monstrous and the grotesque. Thus, pinioned to the same table where Peer struggled to fend off the attempt to give him troll vision ("a little cut so that you'll see awry"), the Greenclad One went into labor and gave birth amidst realistic screams of agony. Her offspring, a hideous child ogre dripping with blood, leaped from between her legs and landed on top of its terrified "father," Peer Gynt. This odious brat's embrace irreparably soiled and deformed Peer, and the ensuing scene with the Great Boyg – here a circle of fifteen identical Peers in the same Chaplin costume, holding up mirrors to him – seemed to indicate that he recognized his own deformity all too clearly.

Although the closely aligned forces of Aase and the gentle, uncorrupted Solveig (Lena Endre) represented Peer's only hope, as his desperation grew it seemed that the trollish powers of negation and hopelessness were all but invincible. When the Greenclad One and her misshapen child returned to his hut in the forest to stake their claim to him, he even put the threat he makes into action by striking her on the head with a hatchet – only to see it remain lodged in her skull while she glibly continued her tirade ("I'm not afraid of blows, Peer Gynt. I'll be back to visit you every day"). In the grotesquerie of this little episode, as in the visually juxtaposed partings from Solveig and Aase that followed it, the powerlessness of the poet–dreamer to dream away the dark, threatening forces of existence stood vividly revealed.

As capitalist, prophet, madman, and Emperor of Self in the turbulent middle movement Bergman called Foreign Lands, Peer seemed more cynical but still no less wide-eyed in his astonishment at the events that befell him. The mighty thunderclap sent by God to annihilate the deceitful hijackers of his yacht and the ostrich that trotted past him in the Moroccan desert were equally emphatic occasions for a childlike delight and wonderment that Ahlstedt slyly shared with his audience. His manifest delight with the cooing, extravagantly voluptuous Anitra quickly turned to humiliation, however, as she and her two thieving accomplices (the three Saeter girls revisited) robbed the selfmade Prophet of all he had, including his clothes. Left with only his bowler hat, a clown's parasol, and a dilapidated red bathrobe, this Beckettian clown of a figure did a jaunty little *chassé* around the platform before turning toward his final destination – the Temple of Wisdom *in buffo* where this absurd pilgrim would at last attain the crown and kingdom he deserved.

In some ways a repetition in chamber-theater format of Bergman's earlier solution to it, the scene of Peer's ordeal in the Cairo madhouse was a harrowing glimpse of the inferno of absurdity and despair into which he was slipping. The moving platform was now a stark white wall. Virtually bursting to tell Peer his secret (the death of Absolute Reason that has made his madmen sane), Begriffenfeldt continually checked his

Peer Gynt in the Cairo madhouse, as the Fellah (played by Maria Ericson) flings the mummy of King Apis at the horrified visitor's feet.

pocket-watch to assure himself of the exact time of the event. Johan Rabaeus brought to his depiction of the madhouse keeper the same dangerously comradely tone and barely controlled lunacy that characterized his portrait of the Troll King. As in the earlier Malmö production, the doubling of these two roles accentuated the impression that these white-clad, humanoid madmen – although indisputably "them-selves" as Napoleon, Van Gogh (a severed ear), Icarus (wings), Beethoven (an ear trumpet), Ophelia (rusty nails), and so forth – belonged to the same fractured, menacing world of "self" as the trolls. The crescendo of shocks and horrors – Peer's reception by the mad folk, the hanging of the Fellah, the blood-spattered sharpening of "The Pen," and the final mock coronation of the egoist as Emperor of the new age of unreason – culminated in the deafening wail of an air-raid siren in the darkness. For Bergman, the effect alluded to the final global annihilation of which this scene was but an image. "I did the same thing in Malmö," he remarked, "without understanding at the time what it meant."

The fairy-tale tone of the first movement and the colorful *lazzi* of the second were displaced in the third section of Bergman's *Peer Gynt* by a much darker and graver mood. This final movement, called Homecoming, was a sharply focused condensation of Ibsen's fifth act that charted an outcast's odyssey through a black wasteland filled with the cries and whispers of his memories and regrets. As the grandfather clock in the cottage ticked on, the storm, the wreck, and Peer's inhumane drowning of the Cook were enacted with perilous intensity on the swaying, tipping platform that now hung suspended in the air. The Peer who survived the shipwreck – if indeed he does survive it – was not visibly older but simply wearier and much more desperate. Of the Chaplin figure of the first movement and the Beckettian clown of the second, only the bowler hat remained. Instead, wearing a long, shabby overcoat and muffler, Peer was now a curiously Strindbergian everyman who wandered through the kingdom of the dead toward an ominous Damascus. It was this final movement in particular that gave one the full opportunity to experience the pure emotional expression, *in nuce*, of the inner drama of Ibsen's complex protagonist.

The remaining stations of Peer's journey were no longer

"actual" places but entirely fantastic dream-states ("perhaps what you dream in the first moments after death," Bergman says). The first of these stations, titled The Auction in the script, was concentrated around a surrealistic rubbish heap composed of cast-off belongings, disembodied human limbs, discarded bits of furniture and travel souvenirs, Aase and her bed, and an enigmatic assortment of distorted presences from Peer's past – some of the men disguised in women's clothing, some of the women in men's. From atop this disordered accumulation of his life's scrap, Peer declaimed the last of his fairy tales: the apt parable of the Devil, his pig, and an unintelligent audience incapable of distinguishing between the truth of reality and the truth of theatrical illusion.

Reduced to a grubber of onions – and watched by Solveig, who sat at one corner of the platform – Peer groped his way toward the realization that, in Bergman's view, is the most crucial and most painful lesson he is made to learn in the play: "The game can never be played again." Ironically, he spoke this line to his vision of Solveig, after having failed to see her when she stood for an instant before him, young and unchanged as she spoke her song of simple, boundless compassion to him.

From the lyrical sequence in which threadballs, leaves, dewdrops, and broken straws address Peer in Ibsen's text, Bergman evolved a remarkably rich image of "a strange funeral procession" that became the next warning Peer had to face. The three women veiled in black who made up this procession, each bearing the small white coffin of a child, were Thoughts Peer should have thought, Songs he never sang, and Tears he failed to shed – but, in this nightmare of relentless recurrence, they were also ghostly reminders of the Saeter girls as well. Mother Aase, standing by her bed in the rubbish heap, had her own recriminations to add to theirs ("A fine driver you are, Peer! The sleigh went in the ditch!"). With the abruptness of a dream, as if in response to the accusations of these witnesses, the Button Moulder burst like a Jack-in-the-box from the same closet where Peer had locked his mother at the start of his circular quest.

A weighty figure in the long winter tunic of a Swedish policeman of some indeterminate period, Jan-Olof Strand-berg's Button Moulder was a helpful, compassionate man who

"Are you sure it says Peer?" The Button Moulder (Jan-Olof Strandberg) shows Peer Gynt the Master's order paper in the 1991 production at Målarsalen.

knew his job and who explained it to Peer with great patience, industriously scouring a huge casting ladle as he did so. Infinitely tolerant of his victim's protests, he let Peer examine the Master's order paper and even thumbed painstakingly through the thick doomsday book he carried in order to show there was no mistake. In a production that eliminated the figure of the Thin Person entirely, the play's abstract metaphysical dimension thus became anchored firmly in Strandberg's thoroughly concrete, alarmingly believable performance.

As a result, the difficult and extremely tentative end scene could be approached with the same direct simplicity and restraint. As the baggage of Peer's wasted life at last lifted into the air and disappeared from view, he found himself once more standing in the bare cottage, where the blind Solveig sat waiting for his return. The redemptiveness of her love and devotion was expressed in a simple image of maternal compassion that seemed to complete the cyclical pattern of recurrences: wrapped in Aase's shawl, the sightless woman sat in the same narrow bed from which the play had emerged, offering solace and repose to her "dearest boy." ("The play, which is a dream, ends where it began," Bergman says, "with Peer returning to the womb.") This fragile moment of tenderness was abruptly shattered by the Button Moulder, however, who pounded on the cottage door and then came bursting through it in search of his quarry. In the bed, meanwhile, Peer Gynt lay completely hidden in Solveig's embrace, protected, as it were, by the secular salvation of her love. The clock, which stood midway between the bed and the retributive figure in the doorway, had stopped ticking; its hands again indicated seven, the exact moment at which the performance had begun.

As we have learned by now, a truly living and organic work of art must, in Bergman's poetics, function solely through its appeal to the imaginative faculty. Be it theatrical or cinematic, it must reach the spectator directly through the medium of the senses, without any intermediary landing in the conscious intellect. The artistic experience is not, he has often argued, a rational phenomenon to be comprehended by logical analysis or circumscribed by a closed framework of prescriptive "meaning." It is, rather, "a matter between the imagination and the feelings." The dynamism of Bergman's directorial method might well be described as a process of arranging images ("suggestions" or "signals," he sometimes likes to call them) in the feelings and minds of the audience, in such a way that the spectator is drawn into the process as it occurs. "One suggestion may contradict the next, but *intentionally*," he writes in *Laterna Magica*, "for then an illusion of simultaneity and depth-effect is created, a stereo effect."[31] In a highly imagistic work like his *Peer Gynt*, the kind of progression Bergman establishes is – to resort to Kenneth Burke's terminology once more – clearly "qualitative" rather than "syllogistic" in nature, in which the arrangement of images, associations, and contrasts is wholly dependent upon a delicate logic of feeling and emotion. As such, this particular production provides a remarkably vivid final illustration of his definition of his art – in the theater as in film – as a language, "the sentences of which are literally spoken by one soul to another and which escapes the control of the intellect in an almost sensual fashion."

7 Bergman's world: a chronology

This annotated chronology is intended to be a guide to Ingmar Bergman's stage productions. (His earlier nonprofessional productions are not included.) Its focus is on Bergman's work in the living theater, and only the more significant of his many radio and television productions have been included. Nor is a complete filmography to be found here, although dates of his major motion pictures have been provided. However, illustrating the breadth of Bergman's repertory during fifty years in the professional theater, this guide bears persuasive witness to his extraordinary productivity and to the astonishing versatility of his art.

1944

With his appointment as artistic director of the Hälsingborg City Theatre, Ingmar Bergman began, at the age of twenty-six, to attract widespread public notice. During the hectic autumn of his first season, which also saw the production of his first screenplay, *Torment*, under the direction of Alf Sjöberg, the young director staged:

Aschebergskan på Widtskövle, a regional folk comedy by Brita von Horn and Elsa Collin, opened on September 21;

Hvem er Jeg? [*Who Am I?*], a Freudian satire by the Danish dramatist Carl Erik Soya (already staged by Bergman as a student production the year before) followed on October 10;

Macbeth, presented as an anti-Nazi drama, opened on November 19.

1945

Kriss-Krass-filibom, a satirical revue subtitled "some things in two acts by Scapin, Pimpel, and Kasper," appeared on New Year's Day (Bergman's interest in Kasper and the *Kasperl* tradition was already established: *Kasper's Death*, one of the earliest of his own plays, had been staged by him as a student show three years earlier);

Sagan [*The Legend*], by Hjalmar Bergman, opened on February 7 as the first of three different productions of this bittersweet fantasy;

Reducera moralen [*Morality Reduced*], a new comedy by Sune Bergström, appeared in April.

The war was over when *Jacobowsky and the Colonel*, Franz Werfel's popular anti-Nazi "comedy of a tragedy" opened the new season on September 12. "Our theater must be a touchstone for our ability to criticize ourselves," the director declared in a program note. The premiere on November 1 of *Rabies* by Olle Hedberg ("much more unpleasant than any of Bernard Shaw's most unpleasant plays") served notice that Bergman meant to keep the implied promise.

The Pelican, Opus IV of Strindberg's Chamber Plays, opened under Bergman's direction, as a guest production, at the Malmö City Theatre's Intimate Stage on November 25. "Great demands are placed on him. But next time he'll do it," remarked Herbert Grevenius in *Stockholms–Tidningen*.

1946

February 26: Bergman's first independent motion picture, *Crisis*, is released by Svensk Filmindustri (SF);

March 6: *Rekviem*, a new Swedish play by Björn-Erik Höijer, is Bergman's ninth and last directing assignment in Hälsingborg;

September 12: He directs one of his own early plays, a "morality" entitled *Rakel och biografvaktmästaren* [*Rachel and the Cinema Doorman*], for the Malmö City Theatre's Intimate Stage;

November 9: *It Rains on Our Love*, his next feature film, is released.

In the autumn, Bergman took up new duties as resident stage director (under the firm hand and watchful eye of manager Torsten Hammarén) at the larger and more demanding Gothenburg City Theatre. The first of his ten productions here, an explosive presentation of Camus' *Caligula*, opened on November 29.

1947

Bergman directed G. K. Chesterton's comic fantasy *Magic* on March 29 and two of his own "moralities," *Dagen slutar tidigt* [*Early Ends the Day*] on January 12 and *Mig till skräck* [*To My Terro*] on October 26 for the Gothenburg City Theatre's experimental studio. He was also deeply involved in film making, both as a screenwriter (*Woman Without a Face*), as a director (*Music in the Dark*), and in his customary double role as writer and director (*A Ship Bound for India*); and he directed the first of numerous radio productions of Strindberg's plays, *Playing with Fire* and *The Dutchman*.

1948

February 8: The premiere of *Dans på bryggan* [*Dance on the Wharf*] by Björn-Erik Höijer opens in the Studio at Gothenberg;

March 12: Bergman's second production of *Macbeth* appears on the main stage;

September 11: He directs Jean Anouilh's "rose" comedy, *Thieves' Carnival*, on the Studio stage;

October 18: *Port of Call*, Bergman's Gothenburg-inspired waterfront film, is released by SF;

November 4: His radio production of Strindberg's short play *Mother Love* continues the Swedish seaside theme.

December 8: *Kamma noll* [*Draw Blank*], the only Bergman stage play *not* first directed by its author, opens in Hälsingborg.

1949

His films, *Prison* (also known as *The Devil's Wanton*) and *Three Strange Loves* (or *Thirst*), were released. In Gothenburg he directed Anouilh's early "black" play, *La Sauvage*, at the Studio on February 11, then concluded his three-season engagement with an impressive production on the main stage (March 1) of Tennessee Williams' *A Streetcar Named Desire*. "With it Ingmar Bergman has created his masterpiece, and with it he leaves Gothenburg," declared *Stockholms–Tidningen*. The remainder of the year was devoted to film work.

1950

Bergman returned to Gothenburg in February with a guest production of Ramón María del Valle-Inclán's savage and erotic "tragicomedy of village life," *Divine Words*.

Two more Bergman pictures, *To Joy* and *This Can't Happen Here*, came out; and the first "summer" film, *Summer Interlude* [or *Illicit Interlude*, as it was titled in the United States], was completed during the spring and summer, but only released more than a year later.

Meanwhile, he was engaged by Lorens Marmstedt to direct at his Intima teatern in Stockholm – but presented only two programs: *The Threepenny Opera*, the sole Brecht work in his career, opened on October 17; and *En skugga* [*A Shadow*], one of Hjalmar Bergman's "marionette plays," and Anouilh's one-act version of Euripides' *Medea* appeared as a double bill on December 28.

"Everything went to hell during this period," Bergman recalls. "There was only one thing that mattered, and that was to make something the public liked."

1951

During the shutdown of the Swedish film industry to protest the heavy entertainment tax, Bergman staged two guest productions:

Det lyser i kåken [*Light in the Hovel*], his third Björn-Erik Höijer drama of life in northern Sweden, opened at Dramaten (Lilla scenen) on April 19; this was the first of many major productions at the Swedish national theater.

The Rose Tattoo, his second Tennessee Williams production, was given a free, imaginative interpretation at the municipal theatre in Norrköping on November 15.

Bergman's experimental radio drama, *Staden* [*The City*], was broadcast on May 9.

1952

Bergman began his richly creative six-year association with the Malmö City Theatre as its artistic director, after a guest production on February 14 of his own controversial drama,

Mordet i Barjärna [*The Murder at Barjärna*], in the 204-seat experimental studio theater (Intiman).

On November 14 he presented a simplified production of Strindberg's folk play *The Crown-Bride* on the main stage. (He also found time to direct five radio productions, including two other Strindberg plays, *Crimes and Crimes* and *Easter*, and Garcia Lorca's *Blood Wedding*.)

As soon as the film embargo was lifted, Bergman also completed two major films in quick succession, *Waiting Women* and *Summer with Monika*.

1953

Gycklornas Afton (renamed *The Naked Night* in the United States and, even more awkwardly, *Sawdust and Tinsel* in Britain) was released on September 14;

The theme of humiliation and the concern with the artist's place in the world link the film to the play with which Bergman elected to begin his first full season as artistic director at Malmö – Pirandello's *Six Characters in Search of an Author* (Intiman, November 21); *The Castle*, adapted from Kafka's novel by Max Brod and presented by Bergman on a virtually bare stage, opened at Intiman four weeks later.

A new radio production of Strindberg's *The Dutchman* was also directed by Bergman on October 9.

1954

The Ghost Sonata, the third and best-known of Strindberg's Chamber Plays, opened on the main stage at Malmö on March 5;

With his sparkling production of Franz Lehár's *The Merry Widow* (October 1), Bergman displayed a command of the musical theater that called forth critical comparisons with Reinhardt's famous staging of *Die Fledermaus*;

Three days later *A Lesson in Love*, a Bergman comedy, was released by SF.

1955

This important year in Bergman's career began with his vigorously ironic rendering of Molière's *Dom Juan* at Intiman

(January 4). John Patrick's commercial success, *Teahouse of the August Moon*, followed on the main stage one month later. In March, he returned to Intiman with *Trämålning* [Painting on Wood], a one-act play that he wrote as an exercise for the acting students at Malmö – and that quickly became the inspiration for one of his most important films, *The Seventh Seal*. His production of the popular Swedish novelist–dramatist Vilhelm Moberg's biblical drama *Lea och Rakel* [*Leah and Rachel*], opened at Intiman on October 27.

On the screen, *Dreams* (British title: *Journey into Autumn*) was released in August, followed at the end of the year by *Smiles of a Summer Night*.

1956

Full international recognition came when *Smiles of a Summer Night* was awarded a Special Prize at the 1956 Cannes Film Festival; during the same year, he completed work on *The Seventh Seal* – in an astonishing thirty-five days! Meanwhile, his absorption in theater work continued unabated. ("It was a theater existence that was totally unneurotic, and it was sheer joy to make theater, a kind of theater vitality.")

The Poor Bride, Alexander Ostrovski's bitter satire of human pettiness and narrowmindedness, opened at Intiman on January 28;

Cat on a Hot Tin Roof, Bergman's third Tennessee Williams production, was seen in his starkly simplified mise-en-scène on October 19;

Erik XIV, Strindberg's demanding historical drama, came to Stora scenen only seven weeks later.

1957

During the year of *So Close to Life* and of the internationally acclaimed *Wild Strawberries*, Bergman still found time to present two of the most important productions of his carrer on the main stage at Malmö: Ibsen's *Peer Gynt* on March 8, Molière's *The Misanthrope* on December 6. Max von Sydow, fresh from his triumph in *The Seventh Seal*, acted both Peer and Alceste.

Bergman also directed his first television production. Hjalmar Bergman's *Herr Sleeman kommer* [*Mr. Sleeman is Coming*]

(April 18) – just over two years after the official inauguration of television transmission in Sweden. "Television cannot demand so much of its audience," he told an interviewer. "My films are constructed much more symphonically, like music, with five or six or more motifs. But that won't work with television – there only one motif is found" (*Kvällsposten*, January 5, 1958).

1958

Bergman directed two more television productions: *The Venetian*, an anonymous sixteenth-century piece, on February 21; a revival of Olle Hedberg's play *Rabies* on November 7.

His last three productions at the Malmö City Theatre displayed three distinct facets of his directorial range:

With *The Legend*, which he now staged for the second time, he reaffirmed his preoccupation with the symbolic fantasies of Hjalmar Bergman (Intiman, April 12);

Goethe's *Ur-Faust* (Stora scenen on October 17) was a daring classical reinterpretation in which Mephistopheles was seen as the diabolical, ever-present mirror image of Faust;

Värmlänningarna [*The People of Värmland*], F. A. Dahlgren's traditional nineteenth-century folk play, was given a scrupulously loyal and uncaricatured revival on December 19, and with it Bergman took leave of his Malmö public.

One week later Bergman's motion picture, *The Face* (called *The Magician* in the United States), was released.

Although he had been engaged by Dramaten in Stockholm as its chief director, he was occupied almost exclusively with film work during the next two years.

1959

Bergman directed nothing new for the theater. He found it necessary to withdraw from a production of Molière's *Amphitryon* planned for the Malmö City Theatre in March (Lars-Levi Læstadius, the theater's managing director, took over the project). The 1958 production of Hjalmar Bergman's *The Legend* was revived at Intiman on March 14, and was later seen at the Théâtre Sarah Bernhardt in Paris. Bergman's production of *Ur-Faust* was also on tour to London during the same Spring.

The principal motion pictures to emerge from this prolonged period of theatrical inactivity (1959–60) were *The Virgin Spring* and *The Devil's Eye*.

1960

Bergman's production of *Storm Weather*, Opus I of Strindberg's Chamber Plays, was telecast throughout Scandinavia on January 22; his production of Strindberg's one-act comedy *First Warning* was also broadcast on August 11.

1961

January 6: A decade after his first directing assignment at Dramaten, Bergman returns with a controversial production of Chekhov's *The Seagull* ("a tired, lax production," he later called it: "I wasn't happy in the theater and felt that everything went wrong");

January 22: His new production of Strindberg's grim one-act comedy, *Playing with Fire*, is broadcast;

April 22: Bergman's brilliant staging of the Stravinsky–Auden opera *The Rake's Progress* at the Royal Opera in Stockholm marks a pivotal highpoint in his directing career;

October 16: *Through a Glass Darkly* ("a theater piece in disguise," Bergman remarks, on which his direction of *The Seagull* "also had its influence") is released by SF.

1962

During the eighteen months that followed *The Rake's Progress* – when the film trilogy of *Through a Glass Darkly*, *Winter Light*, and *The Silence* was completed – Bergman directed nothing for the theater.

1963

On January 14, Bergman was chosen to succeed Karl Ragnar Gierow as head of Sweden's national theater at the end of the season. His first, much-awaited production in this new capacity, an explosive rendering of Edward Albee's commercial success, *Who's Afraid of Virginia Woolf?*, opened on October 4.

Hjalmar Bergman's *The Legend* – revived for the third time in his career – followed at Lilla scenen, Dramaten's 350-seat studio stage, on December 20. During the same year Bergman also directed a television adaptation of Strindberg's *A Dream Play* (May 2).

1964

Tre knivar från Wei [*Three Knives from Wei*], a historical saga of cruelty in seventh-century China by the Swedish poet Harry Martinson, was given its first production by Bergman on June 4. Three days later, Bergman's first color film, the farcical comedy *Now About These Women*, appeared. Neither venture prospered.

Success quickly followed, however, with his radically simplified performance of Ibsen's *Hedda Gabler* (October 17), unquestionably one of the most remarkable stage productions of his career.

1965

February 24: Molière's *Dom Juan*, which Bergman had directed exactly ten years before at Malmö, is revived by him as a school production. (The performance was also broadcast for educational television.)

December 4: Albee's *Tiny Alice*, which Bergman took on when the play's scheduled director fell ill, is seen in a sexually explicit production at Lilla scenen.

1966

Bergman's stark "sonata for two," *Persona* – his first major motion picture since *The Silence* – came to the screen, and he resigned his full-time position at Dramaten. His final production as administrative director was a "theater of fact" presentation of Peter Weiss' documentary "oratorium" *The Investigation*, on February 13.

On November 20 Bergman returned to Dramaten with a controversial production of Molière's *The School for Wives* that a number of the critics found disappointingly "abstract." *The Criticism of the School for Wives* was presented as a provocative prologue to the production, with Erland Josephson, Bergman's successor as the head of Dramaten, cast in the role of Dorante, Molière's spokesman for critical common sense and "the Approbation of the Pit."

This production seemed at the time to represent Bergman's disgruntled retirement from the Swedish theater scene and its vicissitudes.

1967

Much of this year was devoted to film work. The manuscript for *The Shame* was finished by Bergman in the spring, and the production of it began in September. *The Rite*, a highly charged "artist" drama that he wrote and produced independently for television, was completed in July. (It was telecast on March 25, 1969.)

On April 1, however, he again staged Pirandello's *Six Characters in Search of an Author* – this time at Nationaltheatret in Oslo. This production – Bergman's first outside of Sweden – marks a turning point. Although its director seems to have called it a "farewell performance," it has in reality turned out to be the beginning of a continuing series of guest productions that he has staged at theaters throughout Europe.

His earlier production of *Hedda Gabler*, which traveled to Helsingfors in June, opened the new season at Dramaten in September and played to enthusiastic audiences in Berlin the following month.

1968

The Hour of the Wolf and *The Shame* came to the screen, but Bergman directed no new major stage production. However, his *Hedda Gabler* opened for a brief but significant run of guest performances at the Aldwych Theatre in London in June.

1969

Happily, Bergman's "retirement" from Swedish theater was brief. On March 12 his arena-style production of Büchner's *Woyzeck*, for which he had introduced the practice of open, public rehearsals, was given its first official performance at

Dramaten. Three days later he had already begun to work on *Fårö–dokument*, an eighty-minute documentary film about the sheep-raising society on his island retreat in the Baltic. The color film *Passion*, generally regarded as a continuation of *The Shame*, was released by SF and Cinematograph on November 10.

1970

Strindberg's *A Dream Play*, adapted by Bergman as a chamber play, opened at Dramaten's studio stage on March 14;

An English version of his *Hedda Gabler*, performed by members of the National Theatre Company, opened at the Cambridge Theatre in London on June 30;

Reservatet [*Sanctuary*], "a tragicomedy of banality" written by Bergman but directed by Jan Molander, was telecast on Eurovision on October 28.

1971

March 20: *Show*, a new work by the Swedish lyric dramatist Lars Forssell, becomes Bergman's fourteenth production at Dramaten;

April 19: His *Dream Play* opens at the Aldwych Theatre in London as part of the World Theatre Season;

June 6: *The Touch*, Bergman's first film in English, is seen at the Berlin Film Festival.

1972

The Bergman production of Ibsen's *The Wild Duck*, regarded by many as one of his finest achievements in the theater, had its premiere at Dramaten on March 17.

Cries and Whispers, his harrowing film study of the process of death, stems from the same year. (Released March 5, 1973.)

1973

During this important and astonishingly productive year in his career, Bergman directed two very demanding works taken up from his earlier repertory at Malmö. Strindberg's *The Ghost*

Sonata, which had been in rehearsal for two and a half months, opened at Dramaten on January 13. After barely a month's pause, he traveled to Copenhagen to begin rehearsals for a new production of Molière's *The Misanthrope,* which opened at the Danish Royal Theatre on April 6.

Meanwhile, London audiences saw his production of *The Wild Duck* during Peter Daubeny's tenth and final World Theatre Season at the Aldwych. Even New York audiences had a small taste of Bergman, albeit much diluted, when Stephen Sondheim's musical *A Little Night Music,* based on *Smiles of a Summer Night* (and inspired by "a desire to produce a waltz musical"), reached Broadway.

Bergman's popularity touched a high point when his six-part television film, *Scenes from a Marriage,* was seen in weekly episodes on Swedish television (April 11–May 16). (In the United States, the film's subsequent moviehouse distribution was hailed as his "most successful attempt yet at moving a mass audience.")

1974

Bergman's by now customary annual production at Dramaten, an adaptation of Parts I and II of Strindberg's *To Damascus,* opened on February 1. On May 10, a national telecast of the Copenhagen production of *The Misanthrope* was seen on Danish television. The production came to Dramaten for four guest performances later in the same month.

1975

On New Year's Day, Bergman's television production of Mozart's opera *The Magic Flute,* filmed during the preceding spring to commemorate the fiftieth anniversary of the Swedish Broadcasting Company, was seen throughout Scandinavia.

With his production of *Twelfth Night,* which opened at Dramaten on March 7 and ran through the summer, Bergman returned to Shakespeare for the first time since his *Macbeth* productions of the forties.

His preoccupation with the television medium continued with the making of *Face to Face,* a hallucinatory, psycho-analytical television film in four parts that was released the following year.

1976

On January 30, 1976, Swedish police questioned Bergman in connection with alleged tax irregularities. The charges were subsequently disproven and withdrawn, but the incident made a deep impression. On April 25, he announced to *Expressen*, Scandinavia's largest newspaper, that he was leaving Sweden, and shortly afterwards he settled in Germany. In August, he told a Frankfurt audience during his acceptance of the Goethe Prize: "I can no longer live in a land where my honor is publicly and unjustly impugned."

1977

Two very different but equally uneven works emerged as the first products of Bergman's new surroundings. *The Serpent's Egg*, concerned with the violent upheavals in Germany during the chaotic weeks of November 1923, became his thirty-ninth feature film – and the first to be made entirely outside of Sweden. At the Residenztheater in Munich, his new home, he directed *A Dream Play*, which opened on May 19.

1978

During the year that brought *Autumn Sonata* to the screen, Bergman's second German-language production, a provocative reinterpretation of Chekhov's *The Three Sisters*, opened at the Residenztheater in Munich on June 22, following an unusually intensive rehearsal period of nearly fifteen weeks. The production continued to appear in repertory and on tour in Germany during the following season.

Rehearsals for Strindberg's *The Dance of Death*, which had been interrupted by the police in 1976, were resumed at Dramaten in August, but they were once again broken off when Anders Ek, who was to have played the Captain, fell ill.

Nonetheless, when Bergman celebrated his sixtieth birthday on Fårö on July 14, he could look back on an astonishingly productive career: some sixty-five major stage productions and forty films in thirty-four years of professional activity.

1979

Tartuffe, Bergman's sixth production of a Molière comedy, opened at the Residenztheater on January 13 and appeared as part of the Bregenzer Festspiele in July.

A German revival of *Hedda Gabler*, Bergman's third approach to this play, had its premiere at the Residenztheater on April 11.

Twelfth Night was revived at Dramaten during July, the first Bergman production to be seen in Sweden in four years.

1980

Bergman's stark, rigorously stylized rendering of Gombrowicz's tragifarce *Yvonne, Princess of Burgundy* opened in Munich on May 10 to enthusiastic critical accolades in the German press.

Aus dem Leben der Marionetten [*From the Life of the Marionettes*] had its first public screening in July at a small film festival in Oxford. It had its official premiere in Paris on October 8.

Fårö Document '79, an expansion of his earlier study of the island community, was screened in New York on October 30.

Twelfth Night, one of the brightest examples of Bergman's theater art, was summoned to Paris in November to add its lustre to the celebrations marking the tercentenary of the Comédie Française.

1981

Nora und Julie, Bergman's simultaneous production of Ibsen's *A Doll's House* and Strindberg's *Miss Julie*, opened at the Residenztheater on April 30. The third part of the "trilogy," his stage adaptation of *Scenes from a Marriage*, opened on the same evening at the nearby Theater im Marstall.

The making of *Fanny and Alexander*, intended as Bergman's farewell gesture as a film maker, began in September.

1982

Apart from a German touring production of *Miss Julie*, with Christine Buchegger in the title role, all efforts were concentrated on *Fanny and Alexander*. Its long-awaited world premiere took place in Stockholm on December 17.

1983

A new, controversial reinterpretation of Molière's *Dom Juan* opened the Salzburg Festival on July 17 and then moved to the Cuvilliés-Theater in Munich in September.

Molière's *The School for Wives*, redirected by Bergman on the basis of the late Alf Sjöberg's concept, was broadcast on Swedish television on Christmas Day.

The complete, five-hour version of *Fanny and Alexander* was also shown on Scandinavian TV during the Christmas holidays.

1984

During the year in which *Fanny and Alexander* reaped four Academy Awards, Bergman directed two new stage productions. *King Lear*, his first new production at Dramaten since 1975, opened there on March 9. In Munich less than two months later, he staged the historical drama *Aus dem Leben der Regenwürmer* [*From the Life of the Rainworms*], by Swedish writer Per Olov Enquist, at the Residenztheater (May 4).

Following its premiere on Swedish television (April 9), *Efter repetitionen* [*After the Rehearsal*], a chamber film about a director's life in the theater, was released (despite Bergman's objections) for regular movie-house distribution in the U.S.A. It thus became his forty-fourth and final feature film.

1985

King Lear received a triumphant reception on tour in Paris in March. Two months later, following his production of Ibsen's *John Gabriel Borkman* at the Residenztheater (May 31), Bergman ended his nine-year exile and returned permanently to Sweden. His Swedish revival of *Miss Julie* in December marked his official return to Dramaten as a director. *De två saliger* [*The Blessed Ones*], a TV film based on Ulla Isaksson's dark marital drama of love and madness, was also completed during this crowded year.

1986

April 25: Bergman's fourth approach to *A Dream Play* opens for a limited run of thirty-four performances;

September 25: *Laterna Magica*, his autobiography, is completed after a summer of uninterrupted writing on Fårö;

December 20: *Hamlet* opens to a storm of controversy in the Swedish media.

1987

During this troubled year of ill health, Bergman cancelled a scheduled production of Euripides' *The Bacchae* – only to announce plans to rework the play and stage it as an opera, with a new musical score by Swedish composer Daniel Börtz, in 1991.

Both *Hamlet* and *Miss Julie* played at the National Theatre in London in June.

1988

Long Day's Journey into Night, Bergman's eightieth major stage production, opened on April 16 to mark the O'Neill centennial; the play had had its posthumous world premiere at Dramaten in 1956.

While the director himself observed a quiet seventieth birthday on Fårö, his productions of *Hamlet* and *Miss Julie* continued to be carried as far afield as Tokyo and Moscow.

1989

En själslig angelägenhet [*A Spiritual Matter*], written and directed by Bergman, was broadcast on January 14. It was his thirty-eighth radio production since he began working in this medium in 1946.

A planned production of Shakespeare's *The Winter's Tale* was abandoned and, in its place, Yukio Mishima's *Madame de Sade* opened at Lilla scenen on April 8 to rave reviews and packed houses.

In September, Bergman announced that *Best Intentions*, his six-hour television drama about a decade in his parents' troubled marriage, would be filmed by Danish Oscar-winner Bille August, for release on Scandinavian TV at the end of 1991.

Bergman's contribution to the 1989–90 theater season was his restaging of *A Doll's House*, which opened on November 17.

"I'm not afraid of getting old," he told a Copenhagen audience during his acceptance of the distinguished Sonning Prize in October: "You tire more quickly, but you also have a broader vision. Every morning when I wake up, I am still curious."

1990

Work on *Bilder* [*Pictures*], a record of the director's own impressions of his films, was completed in June; the book was published four months later.

1991

Bergman's chamber production of *Peer Gynt* opened at Målar-salen, Dramaten's intimate studio space, on April 27.

In June, a new reworking of *Miss Julie* travelled to New York as part of a Bergman Festival at the Brooklyn Academy of Music, where it was performed together with two other recent Dramaten productions. *Long Day's Journey into Night* and *A Doll's House*.

In November, *The Bacchae* was staged as a music-drama at the Royal Opera in Stockholm. This experiment revealed the same firm command of opera theater that had characterized Bergman's three earlier productions in this medium: *The Magic Flute, The Rake's Progress*, and *The Merry Widow*.

Notes

2 First seasons

1. Nils Beyer, *Teaterkvällar* (Stockholm, 1953), p. 46. Interestingly enough, Beyer's portentous review bore the title "Gycklarnas afton" – the same title Bergman gave to his film masterpiece (*The Naked Night* in English) in 1953. All translations in this book are by the authors, unless otherwise indicated.
2. Interview in *Expressen* (Stockholm), February 18, 1974. The "psychobiographical" school of Bergman criticism, with which the present study is not directly concerned, draws heavily on childhood experiences described in this interview and in Jörn Donner's film interview, "Three Scenes with Ingmar Bergman" (1975). Cf. Martin Drouzy, "Barnet i klædeskabet. Arbejdsnoter til en undersøgelse om Ingmar Bergman og hans film," *Kosmorama*, 13 (Spring 1978), 30–4, and Marianne Höök, *Ingmar Bergman* (Stockholm, 1962).
3. "Dialog med Ingmar Bergman" in Henrik Sjögren, *Ingmar Bergman på teatern* (Stockholm, 1968), p. 295. [Hereafter called "Dialog".]
4. Stig Björkman, Torsten Manns, and Jonas Sima, eds. *Bergman om Bergman* (Stockholm, 1970 & Copenhagen, 1971), p. 13.
5. Sjögren, "Dialog," pp. 302–3.
6. Cf. Henrik Sjögren, "Ingmar Bergman's teater – rörelser i rummet" in *Perspektiv på teater*, eds. Ulf Gran and Ulla-Britta Lagerroth (Stockholm, 1971), p. 122.
7. Cf. Per Bjurström, *Teaterdekoration i Sverige* (Stockholm, 1964), pp. 145–6.
8. Sjögren, "Dialog," p. 299.
9. Quoted in Ann Fridén, "'He shall live a man forbid': Ingmar Bergman's *Macbeth*," *Shakespeare Survey* 36 (1983), 70.
10. Björkman, Manns, and Sima, *Bergman om Bergman*, p. 38.
11. Ibid., p. 59.
12. Ingmar Bergman, *Laterna Magica* (Stockholm, 1987), pp. 179–81.
13. Ibid., p. 231.
14. Sjögren, "Dialog," p. 295.
15. For some discussion in English of Bergman's early plays (which are not a principal concern in this study), *see*, for example, Vernon Young, *Cinema Borealis: Ingmar Bergman and the Swedish Ethos* (New York, 1972), pp. 48–51 et passim.
16. Jean-Paul Sartre, "Forgers of Myths" in *Playwrights on Playwriting*, ed. Toby Cole (New York, 1961), p. 118.
17. Another Swedish production opened in Malmö on the same night (March 1, 1949); Olof Molander's production opened in Stockholm a few weeks later; a very successful Danish production (subtly renamed *Omstigning til Paradis* or *Transfer to Paradise*) opened at the Royal Theatre in Copenhagen on September 1.
18. A. Gunnar Bergman, quoted in Sjögren, *Ingmar Bergmann*, p. 70.

19. The design for the Jo Mielziner backdrop is found in his *Designing for the Theater: A Memoir and a Portfolio* (New York, 1965), p. 144.
20. "Conversation with Bergman" in John Simon, *Ingmar Bergman Directs* (New York, 1972), p. 33.
21. Reprinted in his *Avsidesrepliker: Teaterkritik 1961–1965* (Stockholm, 1966), pp. 146–7.
22. Sjögren, "Dialog," p. 314.
23. Sjögren in *Perspektiv på teater*, p. 124.
24. Höök, *Ingmar Bergman*, pp. 120–1.
25. Carl Cramér in *Ny Tid*, February 4, 1950.
26. Sjögren, "Dialog," p. 307.
27. *Laterna Magica*, p. 207.

3 The Strindberg cycle

1. See Simon's "Conversation with Bergman" (p. 17) and Björkman, Manns, and Sima, *Bergman om Bergman*, p. 26.
2. The comparisons are found, respectively, in Simon, "Conversation with Bergman" (pp. 299–300), Young, *Cinema Borealis* (pp. 276–7), Jörn Donner, *The Films of Ingmar Bergman*, trans. Holger Lundbergh (New York, 1972), p. 153, and Stig Ahlgren, "Riset bakom spegeln," *Vecko-Journalen*, 47 (November 24, 1961).
3. Björkman, Manns, and Sima, *Bergman om Bergman*, p. 124.
4. *The Dance of Death*, which was in preparation when Bergman was arrested on allegations of tax evasion in 1976 and rehearsals for which resumed and were again interrupted in the autumn of 1978 when Anders Ek fell ill, would have been the eighth play.
5. See Fritiof Billquist, *Ingmar Bergman: teatermannen och filmskaparen* (Stockholm, 1960), pp. 18–30.
6. Simon, "Conversation with Bergman," p. 19.
7. Hansingvar Hanson in *Stockholms–Tidningen*, March 6, 1954.
8. *Scenen*, January 1, 1921.
9. Siegfried Jacobsohn, "Vignettes from Reinhardt's Productions" in *Max Reinhardt and His Theatre*, ed. Oliver M. Sayler (New York, 1924), p. 325.
10. *Svenska Dagbladet*, January 21, 1949.
11. August Strindberg, *The Chamber Plays*, ed. Evert Sprinchorn (New York, 1962), p. xxiv.
12. Cf. Gunnar Ollén, *Strindbergs dramatik* (Stockholm 1961), pp. 356–8.
13. Sjögren, *Ingmar Bergman*, p. 128.
14. Discounting its eight-meter (26 ft) removable forestage, the main stage at the Malmö City Theatre measures 24 m (78 ft) both in depth and in height, making it slightly shallower than the Paris Opera (26 m) or the Royal Opera House Covent Garden (27.1 m). But its maximum proscenium width of 22 m (71.2 ft) is more than half again as great as in either of these two theaters, and when – as Bergman did for the final scene of *The Crown-Bride* – the stage is opened to its full width (36 m or 117 ft) it is one-third wider than the Covent Garden stage, and nearly twice the width of the stage of the Aldwych in London.
15. Vagn Børge, *Strindbergs mystiske teater* (Copenhagen, 1942), p. 175.
16. Sjögren "Dialog," pp. 311–12. A film of *The Crown-Bride* had actually been planned with Nordisk Tonefilm, but, given the conclusions about

simplification that Bergman had reached, it is not hard to imagine why he lost interest in this project.

17. Ollén, *Strindbergs dramatik*, p. 322.
18. Quoted in *Directors on Directing*, eds. Toby Cole and Helen K. Chinoy (Indianapolis, 1963), p. 297.
19. Quoted in Billquist, p. 226.
20. Björkman, Manns, and Sima, *Bergman om Bergman*, p. 152.
21. Sprinchorn, *Chamber Plays*, p. 207.
22. Egil Törnqvist, *Bergman och Strindberg* (Stockholm, 1973): The misleading title is clarified by its subtitle, *Spöksonaten – drama och iscensättning, Dramaten 1973*; it is with this one production, rather than with the Bergman–Strindberg relationship in general, that this study deals. It is especially useful for its full transcription of the production script for the 1973 performance (pp. 115–75), which is not included in a short English summary of the book, "Ingmar Bergman directs Strindberg's 'Ghost Sonata,'" *Theatre Quarterly* 3 (July–September 1973), 3–14.
23. Ibid., p. 98.
24. Sjögren, *Ingmar Bergman*, p. 146.
25. Quoted in Törnqvist, *Bergman och Strindberg*, p. 226.
26. Ibid., p. 100.
27. Ibid., p. 157. The actual dialogue here is in Evert Sprinchorn's translation. It is perhaps worth noting that Vernon Young, who has written without great understanding of the Bergman–Strindberg relationship, draws a sarcastic parallel between the dinner party given by Johan Borg's demons in *Hour of the Wolf* (a film Young neither likes nor appears to understand) and the ghost supper in *The Ghost Sonata* – "itself so far over the edge that it can only be viewed without a quaver if you check your risibilities at the cloakroom . . . Naima Wifstrand removing her rubber face [the old woman in the film removes her hat in order to hear the music better, and her face – identity – comes off with it] is only funnier in a desolate way than Strindberg's Mummy who lives in a closet and talks like a parrot." (*Cinema Borealis*, pp. 298–9)
28. Quoted in Törnqvist, *Bergman och Strindberg*, p. 102.
29. Quoted ibid., p. 107.
30. Typed production script, marked *Scenen*, p. 40 (Kungliga dramatiska teatern). This script and the copy of the production stage manager (Arne Hertler) supply all light, sound, and projection cues.
31. Törnqvist, *Bergman och Strindberg*, p. 151.
32. Ollén, *Strindbergs dramatik*, p. 474.
33. Molander's fascinating descriptive argument first appeared in *Göteborgs–Posten*, September 12, 1946. The building itself has unfortunately since been torn down.
34. Hansingvar Hanson suggests these associations in his review in *Stockholms–Tidningen*, March 6, 1954.
35. Henrik Sjögren, *Regi: Ingmar Bergman* (Stockholm, 1969), p. 20. Again, the title of this book makes it sound more general than it actually is; the subtitle, "Dagbok från Dramaten 1969," conveys its true scope.
36. Quoted in Törnqvist, *Bergman och Strindberg*, p. 186.
37. Björkman, Manns, and Sima, *Bergman om Bergman*, p. 47.
38. Quoted in Törnqvist, *Bergman och Strindberg*, p. 192.
39. Quoted ibid., pp. 97–8.

40. Quoted in Törnqvist's "Bergman directs Strindberg's 'Ghost Sonata,'" 8. A curious anecdote in *Laterna Magica* links the idea to Bergman's youthful encounter with the exceedingly odd mother of one of his girl friends: "Within Cecilia's young beauty, shades of her mother's behavior could be glimpsed. Later, this led me to the conclusion that the Mummy and the Young Lady in Strindberg's *Ghost Sonata* ought to be played by the same actress" (p. 164).
41. Törnqvist, *Bergman och Strindberg*, p. 198.
42. Quoted ibid., p. 102.
43. Gunnar Brandell, "Vad har Bergman gjort av Strindberg?" *Dagens Nyheter*, February 19, 1974.
44. In a letter questioning Törnqvist's method and quoted by him in *Bergman och Strindberg*, p. 11.
45. Törnqvist, *Bergman och Strindberg*, p. 167.
46. Quoted ibid., p. 192.
47. Quoted ibid., p. 108.
48. Cf. Frederick J. Marker and Lise-Lone Marker, *Ingmar Bergman: A Project for the Theatre* (New York, 1983), which contains the script for *Julie*.
49. Fifty-six rehearsals in all were held, including four public previews.
50. Michael Meyer's translation of the Bergman text, *Strindberg, A Dream Play, Adapted by Ingmar Bergman* (New York, 1973), follows the typed production script exactly. However, the stage directions contained in this translation are not Bergman's and are, in many cases, quite misleading. We have taken floor plans and other details about the staging from the production script, marked *Scenen* (76 pp., Kungliga dramatiska teatern). Other relevant items in the Dramaten library include a ring binder containing some of the director's rehearsal notes.
51. Quoted in Sjögren, *Regi: Ingmar Bergman*, p. 19.
52. A special production script for Daniel Bell contains a list of music cues. In general, the character of Bergman's musical selections for *A Dream Play* – a simple barrel organ melody, piano or cello music, occasional harp tones, and the like – affords an interesting contrast to the more grandiose, "operatic" style of musical accompaniment usually adopted by Olof Molander. For instance, the script for Molander's 1940 production of the play in Copenhagen describes an extremely complex pattern of musical cues. Most of the prologue in heaven was spoken to music from Ravel's ballet *Daphnis et Chloé*, while during the remainder of the play an orchestral potpourri composed of a Beethoven quartet, Chopin's Funeral March, Ravel's ballet, and his orchestral suite *Rapsodie espagnole*, Bach's *Toccata con Fuga* No. 10 (Strindberg's choice), a little Mozart, and much else provided an almost continual symphonic accompaniment. (The Molander script is in the Royal Theatre Library, Copenhagen.)
53. Although these two attributes of the Stage-Door Keeper – *stjärntäcket* and *schalen* – are quite distinct, they are for some reason translated with the same word ("shawl") in the Meyer edition (p. 11).
54. *Laterna Magica*, p. 46. It must be said that the director's depressed account of this production's reception does not correspond to the generally favorable tone of the reviews.
55. Ibid., p. 49.
56. Typescript, with copious handwriten notations, marked *Regiexemplar* (118 pp., Kungliga dramatiska teatern). Other sources include the script

of the director's assistant, Kari Sylwan, and the separate scripts for sound, lighting, and projection cues.

57. Letter dated May 24, 1898.
58. *Svenska Dagbladet*, January 21, 1899.
59. Henrik Sjögren in *Arbetet* (Malmö), February 2, 1974.
60. In a letter to Gustaf af Geijerstam, dated October 17, 1898.
61. Carl Hammarén in *Nerikes Allehanda* (Örebro), February 2, 1974.
62. Jarl W. Donnér in *Sydsvenska Dagbladet* (Malmö), February 2, 1974.
63. *Regiexemplar*, p. 70. Translation by the authors.
64. Ibid., p. 85. The passage is also a good example of Bergman's skillful cutting.
65. Leif Zern seemed unaccountably puzzled by the deliberately ironic mode of the production. In an American interview, he objected to the choice of Jan-Olof Strandberg for the part of the Unknown because he is not "a psychological actor. He presents a role instead of playing a character . . . He is an actor with a great sensitivity for the theatrical and comical, with a feeling for space; a physical actor." Though these would appear to be the very qualities Bergman was seeking, Zern evidently intended the comment as a negative one: "As a result, his Stranger became a rather comic figure; it gave the production an ironic tone, and I wasn't sure that was intended." In the light of the evidence, the conclusion to which this critic is led seems little short of astounding: "One might almost think Bergman didn't take the play seriously, or at any rate did not take the character of the [Unknown] really seriously." *Scandinavian Review*, 3 (1976), 22–3.
66. *Regiexemplar*, pp. 117–18.
67. Sjögren, "Dialog," p. 293.

4 A theater for Molière

1. Interview in *Helsingborgs Dagblad*, February 2, 1973.
2. *Laterna Magica*, pp. 191–2.
3. *Theater Rundschau*, 25 (March 1979), 8.
4. "Bergmans Sünden wider Molières Geist," *Süddeutsche Zeitung*, January 15, 1979.
5. *Meyerhold on Theatre*, ed. and trans. Edward Braun (New York, 1961), p. 133.
6. *Süddeutsche Zeitung*, September 20, 1983.
7. From the authors' unpublished rehearsal diary.
8. "Das Spiel der Verlierer," Residenztheater program.
9. Quoted in Sjögren, *Regi: Ingmar Bergman*, p. 14.
10. Ibid., p. 132.
11. Törnqvist, *Bergman och Strindberg*, p. 111.
12. Sjögren, *Regi: Ingmar Bergman*, pp. 104–5.
13. *Journal 27 maj 1971–27 okt. 1976* (ms. volume, Royal Theatre Library).
14. *Aktuelt*, February 13, 1973.
15. Sjögren, "Dialog," p. 300.
16. Sjögren, "Ingmar Bergmans teater – rörelser i rummet," *Perspektiv på teater*, p. 121.
17. Hans Ruin in *Sydsvenska Dagbladet Snällposten*, December 7, 1957.

18. Alceste's time-honored attire as "the gentleman with green braids" was deliberately altered by Bergman to unrelieved black. The line was changed to match the alteration.
19. Ulf Ekman in *Information*, December 7, 1957.
20. Sjögren, *Ingmar Bergman*, p. 196.
21. Sjögren, "Dialog," p. 308.
22. The actual text used by Bergman was the rhymed and splendidly playable Danish translation of the play by P. Hansen. The translation quoted here and other lines quoted in this chapter are taken from Richard Wilbur's version of *The Misanthrope* (1955).
23. This point is emphasized in Jytte Wiingaard's *Teatersemiologi* (Copenhagen, 1976), a book which uses Bergman's *Misanthrope* as a clinical example in the author's discussion of the "language" of signs and gestures in the theater.
24. Jarl W. Donnér, "Herre mot strömmen," *Svenska Dagbladet*, December 7, 1957.
25. Documentation for specific details of placement, movement, and line interpretations in this production have been drawn not only from the director's own script but also from the very meticulous record of the performance compiled by his assistant, Ulla Elmquist. In addition, videotapes made available through the courtesy of Danmarks Radio have been immensely useful in substantiating personal recollection.
26. Bibi Andersson, "Ingmar Bergman," in the Royal Theatre program for the production (unpaginated, n.d.).
27. *Sydsvenska Dagbladet Snällposten*, December 7, 1957.
28. Wügaard, *Teatersemiologi*, p. 95.
29. *Berlingske Tidende*, December 26, 1972.

5 The essence of Ibsen

1. *Laterna Magica*, p. 226.
2. Carsten Nielsen in *Berlingske Tidende* (Copenhagen), March 10, 1957, and Tord Baeckström in *Göteborgs Handels – och Sjöfartstidning*, March 9, 1957.
3. On this production, see Frederick J. Marker and Lise-Lone Marker, *Ibsen's Lively Art: A Performance Study of the Major Plays* (Cambridge, 1989), pp. 25–6.
4. Baeckström in *GHT*.
5. Billquist, *Ingmar Bergman*, p. 229.
6. Sjögren, *Ingmar Bergman*, p. 190.
7. Ebbe Linde in *Dagens Nyheter*, October 18, 1958.
8. Per Erik Wahlund in *Svenska Dagbladet*, March 9, 1957.
9. Nils Beyer in *Morgon–Tidningen*, March 9, 1957.
10. Sjögren, "Dialog," p. 310.
11. Quoted in Billquist, *Ingmar Bergman*, p. 232.
12. Siegfried Melchinger in *Theater heute* 10 (1967), 8.
13. Jeremy Kingston in *Punch*, 77 (July–September 1970) and Ronald Bryden in *The Observer*, July 5, 1970.
14. Quoted in Randolph Goodman, *From Script to Stage: Eight Modern Plays* (New York, 1971), p. 67.
15. Tord Baeckström in *Göteborgs Handels – och Sjöfartstidning*, October 18, 1964.

16. The device of the half-raised curtain, which conveyed its own strong suggestion of oppressiveness, caused its share of difficulties when this popular production toured through Sweden, Finland, and Germany. The tale is told that in the small town of Växjo, in southern Sweden, the local theater manager was beseiged at intermission by complaints that part of the audience could not see the stage at all because of the curtain. Entreaties to raise it to alleviate the situation were rebuffed by the director, however, and complainers were told that those wishing their money returned could take it and leave.

17. Sjögren, "Dialog," p. 312.

18. Lennart Josephson in *Sydsvenska Dagbladet* (Malmö), October 18, 1964.

19. Quoted in Vilgot Sjöman, *L. 136: Diary with Ingmar Bergman*, trans. Alan Blair (Ann Arbor, 1978), p. 212.

20. Detailed information about this scene and about Bergman's instructions to the Residenztheater cast is derived from the script of *regieassistent* Johannes Kaetzler, whose generous help is gratefully acknowledged.

21. Francis Fergusson, *The Idea of a Theater* (Princeton, 1949), p. 93.

22. *Four Stories by Ingmar Bergman*, trans. Alan Blair (Garden City, N.Y., 1977), pp. 86, 87.

23. Cuts based on the stage manager's script, marked *Scenen* (247 pp., Kungliga dramatiska teatern), and on the director's own script. The translation is by Michael Meyer (published Garden City, N.Y., 1961); Meyer supplied the text for Bergman's London production.

24. From Heiner Gimmler's excellent German translation, mimeographed typescript (178 pp., Residenztheater), pp. 149–50.

25. Quoted in *Kvällsposten* (Malmö), October 18, 1964.

26. Björn Samuelsson in *Folket* (Eskilstuna), March 24, 1972.

27. Quoted from Michael Meyer's translation of *The Wild Duck* (Garden City, N.Y., 1961), p. 180.

28. Jens Kistrup in *Berlingske Tidende* (Copenhagen), April 27, 1973.

29. Charles Thomas Samuels, "Ingmar Bergman: An Interview," in *Ingmar Bergman: Essays in Criticism*, ed. Stuart M. Kaminsky (Oxford, 1975), p. 106.

30. Kistrup in *Berlingske Tidende*, April 27, 1973.

31. All information about cuts is taken from the prompter's copy, marked *Sufflörexemplar* (161 pp. Kungliga dramatiska teatern).

32. Kistrup in *Berlingske Tidende*, March 18, 1972.

33. Quoted in Henrik Lundgren, "Bergman og skuespillerne," *Kosmorama*, 13 (Spring 1978), 43.

34. From Lise-Lone Marker and Frederick J. Marker, "Of Winners and Losers: A Conversation with Ingmar Bergman," *Theater*, 13 (Summer/Fall, 1982), 47.

35. Cf. Marker and Marker, *Ingmar Bergman: A Project for the Theatre*, which contains the script for *Nora*.

36. The third part of the Project was Bergman's stage adaptation of his filmscript, *Scenes from a Marriage*, which opened on the same evening at the adjacent Theater im Marstall.

37. *Rheinischer Merkur*, May 8, 1981.

38. Marker and Marker, "Of Winners and Losers," 49.

39. Ibid., 48.

40. Ibid., 49.

41. *Berlingske Tidende* (Copenhagen), November 16, 1989.
42. *Expressen* (Stockholm), November 8, 1989.
43. Tove Ellefsen in *Dagens Nyheter*, November 18, 1989.

6 To begin again

1. Lise-Lone Marker and Frederick J. Marker, "Bergman's *Borkman*: An Interview," *Theater*, 17 (Spring, 1986), 54.
2. Ibid., 50.
3. Gerhard Pörtl in *Südwestpresse* June 3, 1985. It is worth noting that, as in many of his other productions, Bergman designed his own light plot for *Borkman* and also led the lighting rehearsals.
4. Hansris Jacobi in *Neue Zürcher Zeitung*, June 6, 1985.
5. From the authors' unpublished rehearsal diary.
6. Marker and Marker, "Bergman's *Borkman*," 50–1.
7. Björn Nilsson in *Expressen*, June 2, 1985.
8. Marker and Marker, "Bergman's *Borkman*," 55.
9. Frederick J. Marker and Lise-Lone Marker, "Bergman and the Actors: An Interview," *Theater*, 21 (Spring, 1990), 75–6.
10. Ibid., 78.
11. Unpublished interview with the authors, April 25, 1991.
12. When this production played on tour, the sacrifice of this necessary intimacy was, Bergman says, "a disaster."
13. Yukio Mishima, *Markisinnan de Sade* (Stockholm: Schultz, 1989), p. 131.
14. Carlhåkan Larsen in *Sydsvenska Dagbladet*, December 21, 1986.
15. Jens Kistrup in *Berlingske Tidende*, December 21, 1986.
16. *Laterna Magica*, p. 60. Bergman himself mistakenly writes "radius" when he means "diameter," in reference to the five-meter circle. See following note.
17. This information is taken from the official blueprints for the production, signed by the designer, Göran Wassberg.
18. Sheridan Morley in *International Herald Tribune*, July 17, 1987.
19. Not realizing what his friend had in mind, Erland Josephson made the staggering blunder of turning Bergman down when he asked him to play "the Ghost in *Hamlet*."
20. Kistrup in *Berlingske Tidende*.
21. *London Magazine*, No. III, March 1820.
22. Tove Ellefsen in *Dagens Nyheter*, December 21, 1986.
23. Peter Brook, *The Shifting Point* (New York, 1987), p. 54.
24. More or less clearly defined, these prejudices underlie the inadequately supported criticism of the *Hamlet* production put forward in Jacqueline Martin's "The Role of Language in Ingmar Bergman's Shakespeare Productions," *Nordic Theatre Studies* (Special International Issue, 1990), 112–20. This rather biased account was also printed in *Shakespeare Bulletin*, 7 (July/August, 1989). By contrast, a balanced critical commentary on both the *Hamlet* production and the controversy is found in Lars Gyllensten's (unfortunately untranslated) article, "Vem är Hamlet?" ["Who Is Hamlet?"] in *Kungliga Dramatiska Teatern, 1788–1988*, eds. Erik Näslund and Elisabeth Sörenson (Stockholm, 1988), pp. 263–7.
25. Lars Linder in *Dagens Nyheter*, April 17, 1988.
26. Marker and Marker, "Bergman and the Actors: An Interview," 76.

27. Ibid., 78.
28. Jarl W. Donner in *Sydsvenska Dagbladet*, April 17, 1988.
29. Peter Cowie, *Ingmar Bergman: A Critical Biography* (London, 1982), p. 299.
30. This and other comments by Bergman about *Peer Gynt* are from an unpublished interview with the authors, April 25, 1991.
31. *Laterna Magica*, p. 180.

Select bibliography

Andersson, Elis. *Tjugofem säsonger, 1926–51*. Gothenburg, 1957.
Bark, Richard, *Strindbergs drömspelsteknik – i drama och teater*. Lund, 1981.
Bergman, Ingmar. *Autumn Sonata*, trans. Alan Blair. New York, 1978.
    Bilder. Stockholm, 1990.
    "Each Film is My Last," *Drama Review* T–33, vol. 11 (Fall 1966), 94–101.
    Face to Face, trans. Alan Blair. New York, 1976.
    Fanny and Alexander, trans. Alan Blair. New York, 1982.
    Filmberättelser, 3 vols. Stockholm, 1973.
    Four Screenplays, trans. Lars Malmström and David Kushner. New York and London, 1960.
    Four Stories, trans. Alan Blair. Garden City, 1977.
    From the Life of the Marionettes, trans. Alan Blair. New York, 1980.
    Jack hos skådespelarna. Stockholm, 1946.
    Laterna Magica. Stockholm, 1987. English version: *The Magic Lantern*, trans. Joan Tate. London, 1988.
    Moraliteter: Tre pjäser. Stockholm, 1948.
    Persona and Shame, trans. Keith Bradfield. London, 1972.
    The Serpent's Egg, trans. Alan Blair. New York, 1977.
    Scenes from a Marriage, trans. Alan Blair. New York, 1974.
    Three Films by Ingmar Bergman, trans. P. B. Austin. London, 1967.
    Trämålning: En moralitet. Stockholm, 1956.
Bergman om Bergman, eds. Stig Björkman, Torsten Manns, and Jonas Sima. Stockholm, 1970; Copenhagen, 1971. English version: *Bergman om Bergman*, trans. Paul Britten Austin. New York, 1973.
Bergom-Larsson, Maria. *Ingmar Bergman and Society*, trans. Barrie Selman. London and South Brunswick, N.J., 1978.
Bergström, Beata. *Teater: ögonblickets konst, fångad i bilder*. Stockholm, 1976.
Beyer, Nils. *Teaterkvällar, 1940–53*. Stockholm, 1953.
Billquist, Fritiof. *Ingmar Bergman: Teatermannen och filmskaparen*. Stockholm, 1960.
Brunius, Niklas, Göran O. Eriksson, and Rolf Rembe. *Swedish Theatre*. Stockholm, n.d.
Børge, Vagn. *Strindbergs mystiske teater*. Copenhagen, 1942.
Cowie, Peter, *Ingmar Bergman: A Critical Biography*. London, 1982.
Donner, Jörn. *The Films of Ingmar Bergman* (earlier title: *The Personal Vision of Ingmar Bergman*). New York, 1972.
Dyfverman, Henrik, ed. *TV-teatern i tio år, 1954–1964*. Stockholm, 1964.
Fergusson, Francis. *The Idea of a Theater*. Princeton, 1949; rept. Garden City, N.Y., 1953.
Goodman, Randolph. *From Script to Stage: Eight Modern Plays*. New York, 1971.
Gran, Ulf and Ulla-Britta Lagerroth, eds. *Perspektiv på teater*. Stockholm, 1971.

Grevenius, Herbert. *Offentliga nöjen.* Stockholm, 1946.
    Dagen efter. Stockholm, 1961.
Höök, Marianne. *Ingmar Bergman.* Stockholm, 1962.
Kaminsky, Stuart M., ed. *Ingmar Bergman: Essays in Criticism.* Oxford, 1975.
Kungliga Dramatiska Teatern, 1788–1988, eds. Erik Näslund and Elisabeth
    Sörenson. Stockholm, 1988.
Lagerroth, Ulla-Britta. *Regi i möte med drama och samhälle.* Stockholm, 1978.
Marker, Frederick J. and Lise-Lone Marker. *Ibsen's Lively Art: A Performance
    Study of the Major Plays.* Cambridge, 1989.
    Ingmar Bergman: A Project for the Theatre. New York, 1983.
    The Scandinavian Theatre: A Short History. Oxford, 1975.
Marker, Lise-Lone and Frederick J. Marker. *Ingmar Bergman: Four Decades in
    the Theater.* Cambridge and New York, 1982.
Meyer, Michael. *Not Prince Hamlet.* London, 1990.
Meyer, Michael, ed. and trans. *Strindberg: A Dream Play,* adapted by Ingmar
    Bergman. New York, 1973.
Ollén, Gunnar. *Strindbergs dramatik,* rev. ed. Stockholm, 1982.
Rydeberg, Georg. *Ridån går alltid ned.* Stockholm, 1970.
Simon, John. *Ingmar Bergman Directs.* New York, 1972.
Sjögren, Henrik. *Ingmar Bergman på teatern.* Stockholm, 1968.
    Regi: Ingmar Bergman. Dagbok från Dramaten 1969. Stockholm, 1969.
    Stage and Society in Sweden, trans. P. B. Austin, Stockholm, 1979.
Sjöman, Vilgot. *L 136: Diary with Ingmar Bergman,* trans. Alan Blair. Ann
    Arbor, 1978.
Sprinchorn, Evert, ed. and trans. *August Strindberg: The Chamber Plays.* New
    York, 1962.
Steene, Birgitta. *Ingmar Bergman: A Guide to References and Resources.* Boston,
    1987.
Strømberg, Ulla and Jytte Wiingaard, eds. *Den levende Ibsen.* Copenhagen,
    1978.
Teater i Göteborg 1910–1975. 3 vols. Stockholm, 1978.
Thalia 25 – et kvartsekel med Malmö Stadsteater, ed. Ragnar Gustafson.
    Sydsvenska Dagbladets Årsbok, 1970.
Törnqvist, Egil. *Bergman och Strindberg: Spöksonaten – drama och
    iscensättning, Dramaten 1973.* Stockholm, 1973.
Törnqvist, Egil and Barry Jacobs. *Strindberg's Miss Julie: A Play and Its
    Transpositions.* Norwich, 1988.
Wahlund, Per Erik. *Avsidesrepliker: Teaterkritik 1961–1965.* Stockholm, 1966.
    Scenväxling: Teaterkritik 1951–1960. Stockholm, 1962.
Wiingaard, Jytte. *Teatersemiologi.* Copenhagen, 1976.
Wood, Robin, *Ingmar Bergman.* New York, 1969.
Young, Vernon. *Cinema Borealis: Ingmar Bergman and the Swedish Ethos.* New
    York, 1972.

Index